A CENTURY OF CONSERVATION

SAVING WILDLIFE

A CENTURY OF CONSERVATION

WILDLIFE
CONSERVATION
SOCIETY

GENERAL EDITOR
DONALD GODDARD

RESEARCH EDITOR
SAM SWOPE

FOREWORD BY
PETER MATTHIESSEN

EPILOGUE BY
WILLIAM CONWAY

HARRY N. ABRAMS, INC.,

IN ASSOCIATION WITH

THE WILDLIFE

CONSERVATION SOCIETY

Editor: Sharon AvRutick
Designer: Carol A. Robson
Photo Editor: John K. Crowley

PAGE 1: *Grevy's zebra.*
PAGES 2–3: *Silvered leaf monkeys in the lowland rain forest in JungleWorld.*

Library of Congress Cataloging-in-Publication Data

Saving wildlife: a century of conservation/general editor, Donald Goddard.

    p.   cm.

    Includes articles, essays, and letters originally published or written 1887–1993.

    Includes index.

    ISBN 0–8109–3674–7

    1. Wildlife conservation. 2. Endangered species. 3. Nature conservation. I. Goddard, Donald Letcher.

QL82.S28 1995

333.95′16 — dc20   94–22874

Published in 1995 by Harry N. Abrams, Incorporated, New York

A Times Mirror Company

Printed and bound in Hong Kong

Guam rail chick.

*Lowland
gorilla baby.*

CONTENTS

(continued)

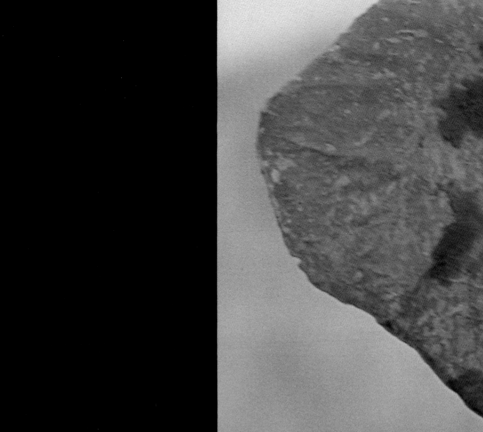

White-cheeked gibbon mother and young;
African elephants.

Polar bear mother and cub;
white-naped cranes.

Snow leopard.

Blesbok calving.

John Iaderosa feeding sable antelope calf.

Opposite: Parson's chameleon;
Lake Titicaca frogs mating.

Green tree boa in Brazil.

I am grateful for the happy days throughout my life that association with the Wildlife Conservation Society has provided. Safaris uptown to the "Bronx Zoo," as I first knew this wonderful institution, were a part of my life even in early boyhood, and I don't doubt that a lifelong interest in wild creatures, shared with my brother, Carey, had its inception in those lordly Victorian halls of the old zoo, where lions and elephants kept solitary counsel. We were scarcely in our teens when we—and Carey especially—developed a passion for snakes. On our family property in the country, at least seven or eight species were quite common, and our ardor quickened after a rock-ledge wooded hillside overlooking a pond was cleared off by our father, who inadvertently brought into being one of the most prosperous copperhead dens in southwestern Connecticut. To our mother's distress, we soon became expert at catching and handling copperheads—at one point we had seven, each in its own sliding-glass-doored wooden cage—to which we would feed white mice and frogs for the awestruck edification of neighborhood children.

My parents were friends of Marjorie and Society President Fairfield Osborn (whose epochal *Our Plundered Planet* is the focus of Chapter Three of the present volume), and one summer in the early 1940s a meeting at the zoo was arranged for my brother with his hero, the Society's great herpetologist Dr. Raymond L. Ditmars, who presented him with a magnificent indigo snake, in those days a mere food item for the zoo's cobras but a glorious addition to our rather drab local collection. The indigo snake is now a threatened species.

From snakes, Carey moved on to marine life—he is a marine biologist to this day—while I became obsessed with birds, my only topic of conversation for the next decade, or until my girlfriend, fed up with the whitening experience of being dragged all day through a night heron rookery, pushed me off a dock into a harbor. Though an English major at college, I took courses in biology, zoology, and ornithology (and later botany), all of which have proved most useful in world travels.

In 1957, I set off on an extended journey to almost every wildlife refuge and national park in the United States, doing research for a book (*Wildlife in America*) about the rare and vanishing wildlife of North America. Henry Fairfield Osborn, a founder and longtime president of the Society, is prominently quoted in that text, and so is his bristling zoo director, William T. Hornaday, whose timely if sometimes intemperate tirades against the destroyers of wildlife are also featured in this anthology. The concluding chapter of my book is entitled "Another Heaven and Another Earth," drawn from the celebrated passage composed by William Beebe, the Society's longtime curator of birds and director of its Department of Tropical Research:

> The beauty and genius of a work of art may be reconceived, though its first material expression be destroyed; a vanished harmony may yet again inspire the composer; but when the last individual of a race of living things breathes no more, another heaven and another earth must pass before such a one can be again.

In the 1960s and '70s came a long series of expeditions to wilderness regions all around the world. In 1961, on the way to an expedition to New Guinea (sponsored and accompanied by Laurance Rockefeller's nephew, Michael, who was to die there), I made my first trip to East Africa, hitchhiking south from Khartoum to Nairobi. From Nairobi, I made my way south to Arusha, in what was still the British protectorate of Tanganyika, where I presented a letter of introduction from President Fairfield Osborn to John Owen, the director of the Tanganyika National Parks. Not long before, just when Dr. Owen was endeavoring to raise financial support for the protection of Tanganyika's wildlife, Osborn had celebrated in print the astonishing wildebeest and zebra migrations and the other abounding wildlife he had beheld on a recent trip to the Serengeti. I caught Owen at a moment when he was scarcely speaking to his friend Fair, and in consequence he scarcely spoke to me.

In 1965, I was kindly invited by Laurance Rockefeller to become a trustee of the Society, joining my friend the late diver and filmmaker Peter Gimbel. One day back in the 1950s, Peter had chartered the deep-sea fishing boat that I was operating out of Montauk Point, Long Island; his friends showed up but Peter didn't, for the excellent reason that he was making his historic dive down to the *Andrea Doria*, which had sunk on the Nantucket shoals the night before. Gimbel had already become fascinated by the toothy head of a stuffed great white shark protruding from the wall in the Montauk Bar, and in the next years, I would join him on the white shark expedition in the Indian Ocean and around Australia that resulted in his astonishing film *Blue Water, White Death*.

Meanwhile, John Owen, doubtless forgetting our first rather brisk and brusque encounter, had invited me to return to Africa as a guest of the Serengeti Research Institute, which was sponsored in part by the Society, and I lived in the Serengeti most of that winter of 1969. Much of my time there was spent very profitably with George Schaller, who was working on his fine Society-backed study of the Serengeti, and sometimes I stayed at Manyara with Iain Douglas-Hamilton, who was doing exciting pioneer work on the elephant, also sponsored by the Society. The following year, I became acquainted with David Western, known as Jonah, who had recently established his base at Amboseli and would later become the Society's international conservation coordinator and a major force in the entire savanna area. He was kind enough (together with Schaller, Douglas-Hamilton, and others) to review the manuscript of my first book on East Africa, *The Tree Where Man Was Born*. That book would be nominated for the National Book Award, which it was to lose to *The Serengeti Lion*, by George Schaller.

In the fall of 1973, I accompanied George on a 250-mile trek across the Himalayas to the Crystal Mountain, in the old Tibetan kingdom of Dolpo, which turned out to be one of the great journeys of a lifetime. George established what he had in fact already postulated, that the bharal, or blue sheep, was closer to the goats, and the journey laid the ground for the eventual establishment of a huge new sanctuary for high-altitude wildlife, including the wolf and the snow leopard.

In 1976, with wildlife photographer Hugo von Lawick, I did a second Africa book located in remote regions of the great Selous Game Reserve in

Blue-and-yellow macaw.

Tanzania. Ten years later, in 1986, I accompanied Jonah Western on a survey of the forest elephant populations in Central African Republic, Gabon, and Zaire, a round-trip journey across the green seas of the Heart of Africa that turned out to be a great deal more exciting than we bargained for. On the first part of that trip, which was sponsored by the Society, we worked with the young elephant biologist Richard Barnes and on the second part with John and Terese Hart, all of whom would subsequently join the Society's distinguished African staff. Jonah's and Richard's pan-African documentation of the degraded habitat and poaching pressure on the rapidly diminishing forest race of the African elephant would become a critical factor in establishing the worldwide ban on ivory trading declared at Geneva in 1989.

In 1978, having resigned as a trustee, I joined the advisory board of the Society, whose meetings provide a welcome chance to visit with old friends among the field scientists, and with the charming and wonderfully knowledgeable Bill Conway, who for more than twenty-five years has been consistently generous with time and assistance on various wildlife and environmental projects in which I have been involved. Because of the high quality of the Society's work (including the unselfish dedication of its trustees and administrations), the meetings are always very stimulating, and I am happy for this opportunity to thank all the people mentioned here, not only for carrying on so capably the great conservation traditions established by Hornaday, Beebe, and two generations of Osborns, but for enlarging upon those traditions in the work of Dr. Schaller and many others in which, occasionally, I have been fortunate enough to share. In this era when enlightened attitudes toward land and life are more sorely needed than at any time in human history, the Wildlife Conservation Society is bound to make a significant and lasting contribution.

Peter Matthiessen
Sagaponack, New York

*Wild species and their habitats,
where the Wildlife Conservation
Society works: African elephant and
Ngorongoro Crater, Tanzania;
mountain gorillas and Mt. Sabinyo
on the border of Rwanda, Uganda,
and Zaire (pages 30–31); Palm
Island, Belize, and researcher Jacque
Carter diving (pages 32–33);
yellow-rumped cacique at its nest
and sapucaia tree in Brazil's flooded forest (pages 34–35); white-lipped
deer of Mongolia and antelope on the
Tibetan Plateau (pages 36–37).*

During the last two years of its first hundred, the New York Zoological Society became, inexorably and fittingly, the Wildlife Conservation Society. The change of name reflects the Society's evolution.

The New York Zoological Society was founded in 1895 primarily to create a great zoo in New York City. Its first field study (in Alaska) was launched in 1897, the Bronx Zoo was opened to the public in 1899, and the New York Aquarium, in Battery Park, was absorbed by the Society in 1902. Underlying its role as a popular purveyor of natural wonders were the serious goals of preserving wildlife and instructing the public.

As wildlife has disappeared, these goals have pushed to the forefront. In 1995, the Society operates five public wildlife sanctuaries in New York City, an endangered species facility in Georgia, more than 225 conservation projects in forty-six nations, an environmental education program that reaches teachers and students in forty-three states and several countries, and a scientific program that conducts groundbreaking work in conservation biology, wildlife ecology, animal management, nutrition, pathology, and genetics.

Thus the change from the New York Zoological Society to the Wildlife Conservation Society.

The Society was founded as a nonprofit membership organization by leaders of science, commerce, government, and the arts. Support was based on a partnership between enterprising citizens and the city of New York. Private donors helped build the Bronx Zoo, administer the Society, and conduct programs of conservation, field study, education, and science. The city owned the land and paid for basic infrastructure, construction, and maintenance at the zoo and the aquarium, as it continues to do to this day. Over the years, public revenues from zoo and aquarium visitors have become increasingly important, as has support from foundations, corporations, New York State, and federal agencies.

The five men at the heart of this book—William Hornaday, William Beebe, Fairfield Osborn, George Schaller, and William Conway—and many other scientists and conservationists celebrated here achieved what they did with the support first of the founders and then of successive generations of volunteer trustees and friends who continued the tradition of Society leadership.

During the last twenty years, perhaps the period of greatest change, this effort has been led by Howard Phipps, Jr., serving as president of the Society, then chairman of the board of trustees. Continuing his unique association, Laurance S. Rockefeller served as honorary chairman of the board for much of that time. As trustee officers and heads of committees—executive, conservation, development, aquarium, education, Wildlife Crisis Campaign, and others—major leadership roles have been played by Robert Goelet, Charles W. Nichols, Jr., Frank Y. Larkin, John Pierrepont, David T. Schiff, Henry Clay Frick II, George F. Baker, Jr., C. Sims Farr, Mrs. William Ward Foshay, Mrs. Gordon B. Pattee, John Elliott, Jr., John N. Irwin II, Landon K. Thorne, Jr., Nixon Griffis, Augustus G. Paine, Frederick A. Melhado, Eben W. Pyne, Mrs. Judith C. Symonds, Anthony

D. Marshall, Robert Wood Johnson IV, and Richard A. Voell.

Remarkable supporters will always be associated with certain landmark projects or programs: Lila Acheson Wallace with the World of Birds and the Central Park Wildlife Center; Mrs. Brooke Astor with the World of Darkness, Wild Asia, and the renovation of Astor Court; Mr. and Mrs. Frank Y. Larkin with the Wildlife Survival Center in Georgia; Enid A. Haupt with JungleWorld; Mr. and Mrs. James Walter Carter with the Carter Giraffe Building and important scientific chairs; Mr. and Mrs. William Ward Foshay and Sue Erpf Van de Bovenkamp with wildlife conservation chair endowments; Nixon Griffis with scientific expeditions around the world; John R. Hearst, Jr., with Sea Cliffs; Liz Claiborne and Art Ortenberg with conservation projects in Congo, Papua New Guinea, East Africa, Argentina, and elsewhere; Mrs. Shirley Katzenbach and Mr. and Mrs. Joseph A. Thomas with the Wildlife Health Center; Robert Wood Johnson IV with international conservation and Zoo Center; and Anne Pattee and Mr. and Mrs. Gordon B. Pattee with the Elephant Protection Plan.

Other crucial contributors include Mr. and Mrs. Rand V. Araskog, George F. Baker III, the Irwin Family, Betty Wold Johnson and Douglas Bushnell, John W. Livermore, Lucy G. Moses, Mr. and Mrs. George Eustis Paine, Carroll and Milton Petrie, Mr. and Mrs. Howard Phipps, Jr., Mary and Laurance S. Rockefeller, the Schiff Family, and Mrs. Joan Tweedy. Their commitment and that of tens of thousands of other members and donors stand behind the Society's achievements in international conservation, wildlife exhibition and care, environmental education, and the biological sciences.

This volume owes its existence to a concatenation of centennial epiphanies, encouraged by Society President and General Director William Conway. Research Editor Sam Swope prospected and read voraciously in the Society's archives of texts and photographs, contributing much to the book's character and shape. Archivist Steve Johnson was a tireless source and guide in this process, as were Curator of Photographic Services William Meng and Associate Photographer Dennis DeMello, whose pictures appear throughout the book. Julie Larsen Maher, art director of the Society's *Wildlife Conservation* magazine, was full of helpful suggestions and encouragement about pictures. And the recording of text and its final reduction to one small disk was done with much appreciated zeal by Mary Anne O'Boyle. My thanks to all of them.

"A GREAT CAMPAIGN OF CONSERVATION"

By the mid-1840s, when Henry David Thoreau was spending his two years in the woods at Walden Pond, more than half of Massachusetts' dense forest cover had been cleared for farms and towns. A decade earlier, the artist George Catlin had set about recording the lives of Indian tribes, recognizing their impending sacrifice to Western civilization's advance. "Nothing short of the loss of my life," he said, "shall prevent me from visiting their country, and becoming their historian."

Primeval America, so revered by the young nation's explorers, poets, naturalists, philosophers, and painters, was rapidly disappearing. The Industrial Revolution, in tandem with westward expansion, was taking its toll. In Europe, the land was reshaped and reduced over centuries. In the New World, it took just decades. Disappearing with the forests, coastal wetlands, and tallgrass prairies were the animals and people living there.

In the land of progress, the paradox of development and conservation was established early. Development flourished, but, with the exception of a few stray voices like those of Thoreau and naturalist George Emerson, support for conservation did not take hold until the later nineteenth century. Yellowstone National Park was established in 1872 as the country's first recreational refuge, based on the findings of a public-spirited federal commission. George Bird Grinnell, editor of *Forest and Stream*, founded the first Audubon Society in 1886 to protect the birds of America through legislation and public pressure. John Muir came howling out of the California woods to found, in 1890, the Sierra Club, which soon mobilized support to make the Yosemite area a national park.

In 1887, Grinnell, along with Theodore Roosevelt and other hunter-sportsmen, was also in on the creation of the Boone and Crockett Club, which focused on saving the great game animals, many of which, including the buffalo, had already been practically exterminated. Roosevelt, as president of the club, appointed a committee in 1894 to explore the idea of creating a zoological park in New York City. The idea was inspired by a young lawyer named Madison Grant, who joined with several prominent citizens, including Columbia University paleontologist Henry Fairfield Osborn, to push a bill through the New York State legislature chartering the New York Zoological Society and the great zoo it would operate. Thus was born, in 1895, the nation's fourth major private conservation organization and the first comprehensive effort to save wildlife and its habitat.

From the very beginning, conservation was the main point. The zoo itself was conceived as a wildlife preserve, according to the Society's *First Annual Report* in 1897, "in which the living creatures can be kept under conditions most closely approximating those with which nature usually surrounds them." The park would be a place of study and inspiration, as well as recreation, where the Society could "serve a good purpose in this community by extending and cultivating in every possible manner the knowledge and love of nature." Education was a necessary function of the zoo in promoting the cause.

Preceding page: The Society's first emblem, with a bighorn sheep, introduced in 1898.

In this first statement of purpose lurks the Society's principal source of energy—powerfully if somehow tentatively stated: "No civilized nation should allow its wild animals to be exterminated without at least making an attempt to preserve living representatives of all species that can be kept alive in confinement."

It is likely that this trenchant section of the Society's plans and purposes was written by William T. Hornaday, who, more than anyone, defined the mission and course of the Society during his tenure as director of the New York Zoological Park (1896–1926). Grant and Osborn, in various positions from secretary to president, were central to the formation and development of the Society and the zoo, and they remained on the front lines of conservation. For instance, from 1917 on both were involved in saving California's redwoods.

But it was Hornaday, former taxidermist and founding director of the National Zoological Park in Washington, D.C., who was the driving force. He stomped through the "perfect combination of ridge and hollow, glade and meadow, rock, river, lake and virgin forest" that was south Bronx Park, then devised, with Grant, Osborn, and architect C. Grant La Farge, an extraordinary plan of natural settings and magnificent beaux-arts buildings for the zoological park. He supervised the construction of much of this vision—from its beginning on August 1, 1898, to the zoo's opening on November 8, 1899—and presided over its completion and elaboration over the next twenty-seven years. It was immediately the largest zoo in the world and, during its first few years, became the most comprehensive.

From the beginning, the Society relied on a partnership of public and private support. In the first five years, New York City provided more than

Theodore Roosevelt (center), who encouraged the Society's founding, visited veterinarian William Reid Blair (second from left) at the zoo's Administration Building in about 1912.

The Society's founders were led by paleontology professor Henry Fairfield Osborn (below) of Columbia University and the American Museum of Natural History, and lawyer Madison Grant (opposite center left), who introduced the idea of a great New York zoo. Osborn served as executive committee chairman, then president from 1909 until 1925, and Grant was secretary, then president from 1925 until 1937. Levi P. Morton (opposite center right), former governor of New York and vice president of the United States, was president of the Society from 1897 to 1909.

$425,000 to improve the Bronx Park site and build the zoo. The Society's share of $250,000 from private donors, called the Park Improvement Fund, was raised by January 1, 1902. Most of the money came from members of the founding families and other leaders in commerce and industry contributing $5,000 or more. Among them were Andrew Carnegie, Jacob H. Schiff, Percy R. Pyne, Levi P. Morton, Henry A. C. Taylor, William C. Whitney, William K. Vanderbilt, Oswald Ottendorfer, John L. Cadwalader, William E. Dodge, Robert Goelet, J. Pierpont Morgan, William D. Sloane, C. P. Huntington, George J. Gould, Cornelius Vanderbilt, Samuel Thorne, John S. Barnes, Charles T. Barney, George F. Baker, and John D. Rockefeller. Nearly one thousand Society members were signed up at $10 for each year. Special funds were soon established for a variety of purposes, including wildlife protection. Caroline Phelps Stokes, for instance, created the Stokes' Bird Fund to protect bird life. And in 1910 another endowment fund was started with major contributions by many of the earlier donors and by such new enthusiasts as Cleveland H. Dodge and Ogden Mills.

For Hornaday, the zoo was always a reflection of the larger world of nature, the destruction and contraction of which he lamented and fought against with all his strength. Every action he promoted, in Congress, state legislatures, and private groups, and every word he wrote, in books, pamphlets, and articles, had a purpose: to change the world and to bring the slaughter of wildlife under control.

Even as he supervised the continuing construction of the zoo, and as the New York Aquarium came under Society management (1902), Hornaday joined and then led the battle to preserve remnants of the once-ubiquitous American bison. As the Smithsonian Institution's chief taxidermist, he had already closely studied the issue and published a scientific paper, in 1886, called "The Extermination of the American Bison." In 1905, he proposed the first of several transactions that would place Bronx Zoo bison stock on government lands in the West. Subsequently, the Society supplied animals for the Wichita Mountain Preserve in Oklahoma (1907), the Montana National Bison Range (1908), and the Wind Cave Bison Range in South Dakota and Fort Niobarra Bison Range in Nebraska (both 1913).

Starting in 1905, Hornaday took on at least one conservation issue per year. In 1905, the Society helped defeat the repeal of a New York State law prohibiting duck shooting in the spring. In 1908, Hornaday joined the battle to save the breeding colony of fur seals on the Pribilof Islands in the Bering Sea from hunters for the fur trade. The result was an international fur seal treaty signed by Canada, Japan, Russia, and the United States that outlawed open-ocean sealing for the first time. From 1909 to 1911, Hornaday worked on ending the sale of wild game, achieving success with the passing of the Bayne-Blauvelt Bill in New York State. From 1912 on, he led the fight to protect migratory birds and end the sale of game birds and bird plumage. The results were a federal ban on the importation of bird feathers and skins for commercial use and the Weeks-McLean Migratory Bird

Charles T. Barney was a founding manager and chairman of the executive committee during the first efforts to save the American bison.

William White Niles, a New York State assemblyman from the Bronx, pushed the bill creating the Society through the legislature in 1895.

Act (both 1913), as well as an international migratory bird treaty with Canada, England (1918), and later Mexico. Hornaday's most effective book, *Our Vanishing Wild Life*, was published by the Society in 1913 and distributed to every member of Congress and influential legislators throughout the United States. It was in support of Senator George McLean's bill that the book was said to have "put a fourteen-inch hole through the hull of the enemy from side to side."

In the 1920s, Hornaday involved the Society in Africa for the first time, working on a program to help save the white rhinoceros, responding, in part, to the wholesale slaughter of wildlife backed by South Africa's Natal Provincial Government in 1921. In 1929, three years after his retirement, he was rewarded for his ten years of work on the U.S. Migratory Bird Conservation Act, which ultimately established fourteen inviolate migratory

John L. Cadwalader (above left), John S. Barnes (above center), and C. Grant La Farge (above right) were three of the seven men, including Grant and himself, whom Osborn considered "the real founders of the Society." Lawyer Cadwalader, counsel for the board of managers, drafted the contract with the city for the Bronx Zoo land. Barnes was in on early negotiations with the city and later designed the Society's bookmark. La Farge teamed with Grant and Hornaday in the early planning. His firm, Heins & La Farge, designed the Zoo's early buildings.

bird sanctuaries from California to New York. And he battled on from his home in Stamford, Connecticut, until his death in 1937.

There was hardly a conservation issue during his time in which Hornaday was not involved. No one accomplished more, or compromised less. But he could be difficult to work with and could be as hard on allies in the cause as he was on enemies. Hornaday's wrath was felt even by a close Society colleague, Charles Haskins Townsend, who directed the New York Aquarium from 1902 until his retirement in 1937. Their differences arose over Townsend's recommendation, as a member of the federal government's Fur Seal Service, that populations of fur seals on the Pribilof Islands would not be depleted by, and in fact might benefit from, the hunting of unattached males on land. Hornaday was adamantly opposed and waged and won a campaign for a five-year ban on such hunting, though Townsend's position was not unreasonable and was based on his years of experience in the islands. The two men remained bitter enemies thereafter.

In his own quieter way, though, Townsend exerted an important influence on conservation. Under his direction, the aquarium, then on the Battery at the southern tip of Manhattan, became New York's most popular attraction. He drew attention to the plight of seals and sea lions and to the pollution of streams. He reported the rediscovery of the northern elephant seal and won protection for the species on Guadalupe Island in the Gulf of California. Perhaps most influential was his exhaustive study, published in 1930 and 1935, of the distribution of whales in the world's oceans.

While building the world's greatest zoo, which was then complemented by a great aquarium, the Society landed itself in the forefront of the conservation movement. As Henry Fairfield Osborn wrote in the *Zoological Society Bulletin* of June 1909, "In spreading the love of animals we have already made thousands, perhaps millions, of new friends for wild life. We now propose to unite them all in a great campaign of conservation."

He seemed to me then, ay, and he did later on, the grandest quadruped I ever beheld, lions, tigers, and elephants not excepted. His huge bulk loomed up like a colossus, and the height of his great shaggy hump, and the steepness of its slope down to his loins, seemed positively incredible. Like Bartholdi's statue of liberty, he was built on a grand scale. His massive head was crowned by a thick mass of blackish-brown hair lying in a tumble of great curly tufts, *sixteen inches* long, piled up on each other, crowding back upon his horns, almost hiding them, and quite onto his shoulders. Back of that, his hump and shoulders were covered with a luxuriant growth of coarse, straw-colored hair that stood out in tufts six inches long, and opened in great dark furrows up and down whenever the bull moved his head from me. The upper half of each fore leg was lost in a huge bunch of long, coarse black hair, in which scores of cockleburs had caught and hopelessly tangled. The body itself and the loin quarters were covered with a surprisingly thick coat of long, fine, mouse-colored hair, without the slightest flaw or blemish. From head to heel the animal seemed to possess everything the finest buffalo in the world should have, and although by that time no stranger to his kind, I sat gazing upon him so completely absorbed by wonder and admiration that had he made a sudden charge he might easily have bowled me over.

It was an opportunity of a lifetime, such as falls to the lot of few men whose business it is to reproduce animal forms. I studied his lines with absorbing interest, and took one mental photograph of him after another as he stood there with lowered head and angry eyes, watching me intently. Several times his head sank very low, and he viciously pawed the wet snow with his wounded fore leg. But these intervals of anger would pass away, his eyes would lose some of their fire, and he would content himself with simply regarding me.

With the greatest reluctance I ever felt about taking the life of an animal, I shot the great beast through the lungs, and he fell down and died.

At last the game butchers of the great West have stopped killing buffalo. The buffalo are all dead! The time has now arrived for the Territories to enact stringent laws against the killing of these animals, and I am pleased to see that the Montana Legislature has just rushed through a bill to that effect—only ten years behind its time! Next year, when the last buffalo of the eighty head still alive in the Panhandle of Texas is hunted down and killed, it will be time for the Lone Star State to frame a bill for his protection; but its final passage can hardly be expected until about 1897.

While the Territories are passing laws against the killing of buffalo, they ought also, by all means, to make the killing of mastodons between August 15th and December 1st punishable by a fine or imprisonment. They should also pass laws against the shipping of mastodon carcasses out of their respective territorial limits; for there is such a world of difference between

WILLIAM T. HORNADAY

from "Our Last Buffalo Hunt—Part II"
A WILD ANIMAL ROUND-UP, 1925

In this passage from a book of recollections about his long career, Hornaday describes an American bison he killed during a trip to the eastern plains of Montana for the Smithsonian Institution in December 1886. The animal became part of a diorama of six bison at the National Museum of Natural History in Washington, D.C.

WILLIAM T. HORNADAY

from "The Passing of the Buffalo—I"
THE COSMOPOLITAN, OCTOBER 1887

Hornaday's biting and self-serving argument in THE COSMOPOLITAN *magazine marks an early stage in his evolution as a conservationist; he would blossom in this role after he became director of the Bronx Zoo in 1896. It also reflects the part played by hunters and outdoorsmen in the early conservation movement.*

American bull bison.

the killing of twenty-six head of game for an Eastern market and the slaughter of that number in one season by one hunter (on Sunday Creek, for instance) to eat, to feed to his dogs, and to let lie in a heap until half of it spoiled.

I am really ashamed to confess it, but we have been guilty of killing buffalo in the year of our Lord 1886. Under different circumstances, nothing could have induced me to engage in such a mean, cruel and utterly heartless enterprise as the hunting down of the last representatives of a vanishing race. But there was no alternative. The Philistines were upon them, and between leaving them to be killed by the care-for-naught cowboys, who would leave them to decay, body and soul, where they fell, and killing them ourselves for the purpose of preserving their remains, there was really no choice. Perhaps you think a wild animal has no soul; but let me tell you it has. Its skin is its soul, and when mounted by skillful hands, it becomes comparatively immortal.

Now a days it is such an honor to kill a buffalo that whenever a cowboy sees one he chases it, in order to be able to say that he has "chased buffalo;" and if he possibly can, he shoots it to death, in order that he may carry back to his camp five pounds of lean buffalo hump, and have his name go thundering down the ages. It would be an interesting psychological study to determine the exact workings of the mind of a man who is capable of deliberately slaying a noble animal, in the full knowledge that he can make no earthly use of it, but must leave its magnificent skin, its beautiful head, and several hundred pounds of fine flesh to the miserable coyotes and the destroying elements. If such an act is not deliberate murder, in heaven's name, what is it? And yet, there are hundreds of intelligent men who can do such things, and others who can even kill half a dozen tuskless elephants in one forenoon, and call it "sport."

Foreseeing that the great American bison is absolutely certain to be exterminated in a few years, the distinguished Secretary of the Smithson-

ian Institution determined last year to step in ahead of the cowboys and hunters before it became too late, and secure a large series of specimens of all ages and both sexes for the National Museum. It was also determined to lay in store specimens for other museums that will want them just as

soon as it becomes too late to collect any. Inasmuch as the specimens of bison then in the National Museum were few in number, and far below the standard in quality, it was vitally necessary that we should secure, at all hazards, a series that should be the finest extant.

Dear Sir:

We have the honor to inform you that the New York Zoological Society is desirous of taking steps toward the establishment of a herd of American bison which shall have for its sole object the perpetuation of the species from total extinction. It is our belief that the preservation of the species can most surely be secured by the establishment of at least four herds, either wholly or partly owned by the United States Government, and which therefore never could be broken up and dispersed amongst private individuals. . . .

The Zoological Society hereby offers to place in the Wichita Forest Reserve, as soon as it is fenced by the Government, a herd of eighteen pure-blood buffaloes, all carefully selected with reference to the creation of a great herd. The Society offers to convey to the United States Government a proprietary half interest in this herd, or greater if necessary,—to take effect as soon as the animals have been liberated on the reserve.

Regarding its own proprietary interest, the Zoological Society would agree to ask nothing beyond the privilege of drawing stock for its exhibition herd in the New York Zoological Park, provided this should ever become necessary. It is the belief of the Society, however, that very few animals ever would be withdrawn under that privilege, for the reason that the bison herd in the Zoological Park is already quite large for such an institution located in a great city and is now virtually self-perpetuating. I beg to assure you that the Zoological Society does not seek to gain any profit by the arrangement proposed, and practically its sole object is to establish a buffalo herd, under favorable conditions, which can be maintained without

Having witnessed the last days of the American bison, Hornaday became one of the leaders in restoring the species to protected sanctuaries in the Western plains. It is estimated that before the Civil War some fifty million bison populated the Western territories. By 1880, most of them were gone, killed during the seventies at the rate of up to five million a year to deprive the native American tribes of their livelihood and feed the railroaders, ranchers, farmers, and others involved in the westward expansion. Fewer than one thousand bison survived, mostly in small private herds, when Hornaday wrote to Secretary of Agriculture James Wilson in 1905 to propose that a government herd be established at Wichita Forest Reserve in Oklahoma based on stock from the New York Zoological Park. Fifteen head were shipped in 1907, and the Society's photographer-editor Elwin R. Sanborn went along to record the eighteen-hundred-mile train journey. Hornaday continued to lobby for protected herds, and the zoo supplied animals until 1913. Today, the bison population in North American reserves has grown to some 100,000 animals.

Opposite: With William Hornaday (left) and reserve superintendent Frank Rush (holding stick) in attendance, fifteen bison were rounded up at the Bronx Zoo in 1907 for shipment to the Wichita Forest Reserve in Oklahoma.

Left: Two forty-four-foot Arms Palace Horse Cars carried the bison west, with Rush, Sanborn, and others finding berths on bales of hay.

expense either to the Society or to the Government, but which in time will increase to grand proportions.

If the outline of this proposal seems to you commendable, and acceptable to the United States Government, the Zoological Society will be very glad to discuss details, with a view to making an arrangement that will be mutually satisfactory.

Respectfully submitted,
Wm. Hornaday—Special Committee

After a lapse of many months, the National Bison Herd has become an accomplished fact, and the energy and perseverance of the Director at last realized in the establishment in the Wichita Preserve of fifteen of the Zoological Park's finest bison.

In 1905, an agent of the Society visited the Wichita National Forest and Game Preserve to select a suitable location for a range. The conditions proved to be all that could be desired, and Mr. Loring's enthusiastic description of the wonderful possibility was a powerful incentive to the consummation of the plan. . . .

The work of rounding-up the herd was commenced in October, upon the arrival of Mr. Frank Rush, the Government agent, who was to accompany the bison on their long journey, and the work of separating the selected stock from the main herd proceeded with precision and dispatch under Keeper McEnroe. A chute, fifty feet in length, had been erected between the two main corrals fronting the Buffalo House, communicating with both and terminating with a very ingenious sliding iron gate. Against this gate the crates were placed. The herd of fifteen was driven into the north corral, and the animals, one at a time, liberated into the chute. . . .

These arrangements having been quickly and satisfactorily arranged, the cars were stored with hay and water for the animals, provisions and blankets for the attendants. On Friday night they were attached to train No. 37,

ELWIN R. SANBORN

from "The National Bison Herd—An Account of the Transportation of the Bison from the Zoological Park to the Wichita Range"

NEW YORK ZOOLOGICAL SOCIETY BULLETIN, JANUARY 1908

The Society initiated four of the ten major public
bison herds in North America.

of the Central's fast passenger service, in charge of Chief Clerk Mitchell, and the long journey began.

We signed our lives away to the Express Company and secured accident policies at the Grand Central Station, for four days' duration, to balance the account.

It was a bit awe inspiring, a train of thought superinduced no doubt by our reckless barter, to realize that in the midst of this vast station with its multitudes of people, its coughing, booming trains, in the center of the greatest city of the new world, were fifteen helpless animals, whose ancestors had been all but exterminated by the very civilization which was now handing back to the prairies this helpless band, a tiny remnant born and raised 2,000 miles from their native land. Surely the course of Empire westward takes its way. . . .

We rolled into Buffalo late in the forenoon and gladly leaped out of our airy quarters to attend the needs of the animals in the rear car. Here we encountered the first obstruction to our journey, which afterwards occurred so frequently that it became a habit. The inspectors blankly reported to us that the steam-hose had been pulled off in the night and the bolts in one of the brake-beams had loosened, almost dropping it to the level of the rails. The cars must be run into the cripple track and jacked up, and with the customary yards of railroad red-tape surrounding such events, Mr. Mitchell could readily understand what a delay this would mean. . . .

The steam connections had to be repaired again at Indianapolis, and this, together with delayed trains, held us there until nearly ten o'clock Sunday night. The temperature still remained low, and when the train crossed Ead's Bridge into St. Louis, the structure glittered with frost. . . .

The cars were thoroughly taken care of and the stock watered and fed. We found every one of the bison in as good condition as we expected. All the animals had become thoroughly accustomed to the unusual situation, and behaved exactly as if peacefully grazing in the Zoological Park. . . .

As nearly all of the western papers had described the bison transfer, our arrival at the various towns south of St. Louis was awaited with considerable interest, and in some places it approached enthusiasm. As the side doors would be opened throngs of men, women and children rushed up to get a glimpse of the famous animals, and if the stop was long enough, they climbed in, and inspected the bison through the openings of the crates. In some places the car was packed to suffocation, and the people only departed when they were forced out by the speed of the train. . . .

The air became milder hourly, and it was possible to open the side doors, and view a country at once both interesting and strange. Gradually the hills gave way to low swells and the wooded portions were confined to the streams, whose course could be marked for miles by the narrow ribbons of green which finally lost themselves in the distant blue of the horizon. Fields of corn, some standing, others stacked, with an occasional field of cotton, lay on every side basking in the mellow light of the early fall. . . .

The station at Oklahoma City was thronged with interested people who crowded the cars on both sides; and in fact these visits developed into ovations, the farther toward the promised land we progressed. At Lawton, we were surrounded by citizens who pined to see the bison, and as our hunger had by this time superseded all other considerations, we left the car in charge of a strong man who had kindly volunteered his services, so that we might satisfy the cravings of healthy appetites. After a ride of seventeen miles from Lawton, it was a relief to arrive at Cache at last, and know that our railroad trip was at an end, just seven days from the leaving time at New York.

Mr. Rush and Mr. Matton, the Acting Forest Supervisor, met us here upon the arrival of the train at 7:30 P.M. We commenced early in the morning to transfer the crates to the wagons provided, and by ten o'clock Friday all were safely loaded. The entire population of Cache turned out, together with a band of Comanche Indians, resplendent in their gayest clothes. At eleven o'clock we started for the Reserve. . . .

We rode three miles over a flat, sandy road, bordered with prosperous farms, and through prairie land, studded with mesquite, and all along the streams with oaks, elms and various hard woods. The line of the Reserve is just within the borders of the Wichita Mountains. Once inside, the road was more uneven, and except for short distances became fairly rough, making the progress of the wagons rather slow. The direction was almost due north for a matter of six miles as far as Pattersons, and from that point is extended toward the northwest. At Pattersons the trail winds through a forest of oaks; white, post, black jack and Texas red oak, which become scattered as Winter Valley is approached. Not a single evergreen of any kind can be seen in the low land, but a variety of cedar, scrubby and gnarled, grows on the mountain sides. The leaves of the oaks were a rich, glossy green, showing not the least sign that it was autumn. The country is certainly one of the fairest the sun ever shone upon. All one has read and all that imagination could conjure would be inadequate to picture this vision of loveliness, of nature scarcely touched by the hand of man, which spread before my astonished eyes when once we were fairly in the valley. . . .

Below: After the seven-day journey from New York, a caravan of horse-drawn carts took the bison fourteen miles from the railway head at Cache, Oklahoma, to the reserve.

The eastern boundary of the Bison Range crosses the end of the valley and five miles beyond are the corrals, where the bison arrived about twelve o'clock. The wagons were driven in and the rear wheels dropped into depressions dug in the ground. . . . Aside from a very slight lameness, [the buffalo] were in perfect condition, greedily eating their allotment of hay. The corrals, three in number, each about 200 feet square, are placed just inside the southern boundary of the line fence, separated from it by a passage of 15 feet in width. . . .

The bison will be kept in the corrals until spring, when Mr. Rush expects to liberate them into a range of some 200 acres. This pasture will be fenced in the winter and the grass burned. A number of cattle graze through the valley, and as it is quite well known that they carry the tick which causes Texas fever, the spraying with oil and burning of the grass have been thought expedient to prevent the bison from becoming infected. Mr. Rush is thoroughly familiar with all methods of prevention, and has adopted the most stringent measures to carry the animals through the dangerous season. Once they become acclimated, the danger line will be passed. . . .

The people of Oklahoma are enthusiastic over the Reserve, and are duly grateful to the New York Zoological Society for having thus established, in the finest portion of the great southern bison range, a herd which will soon increase to grand proportions, and play its part in the permanent preservation of the great American bison.

The Rainey Memorial Gate by Paul Manship was erected in 1934, a gift of Grace Rainey Rogers in honor of Paul Rainey, who had provided many of the zoo's important animals.

Early Years at the Bronx Zoo

In his opening day remarks at the Bronx Zoo on November 8, 1899, Henry Fairfield Osborn called the park "another step in the progress toward the great New York of the future."

"After twenty years of unnecessary waiting," reported the News Bulletin of the New York Zoological Society in May 1900, "New York at last possesses an institution for the exhibition of live animals, founded on a scale commensurate with the dignity of a city of the first rank." In 1899, following just sixteen months of construction, the New York Zoological Park (Director Hornaday forbade the use of "Bronx Zoo," but it stuck anyway) opened to the public with a core collection of animals in twenty-two buildings and enclosures. By 1912, the last of the major animal buildings in the original plan were completed, annual zoo attendance was approaching two million, and there were nearly five thousand animals, ranking the Bronx first among the world's zoos.

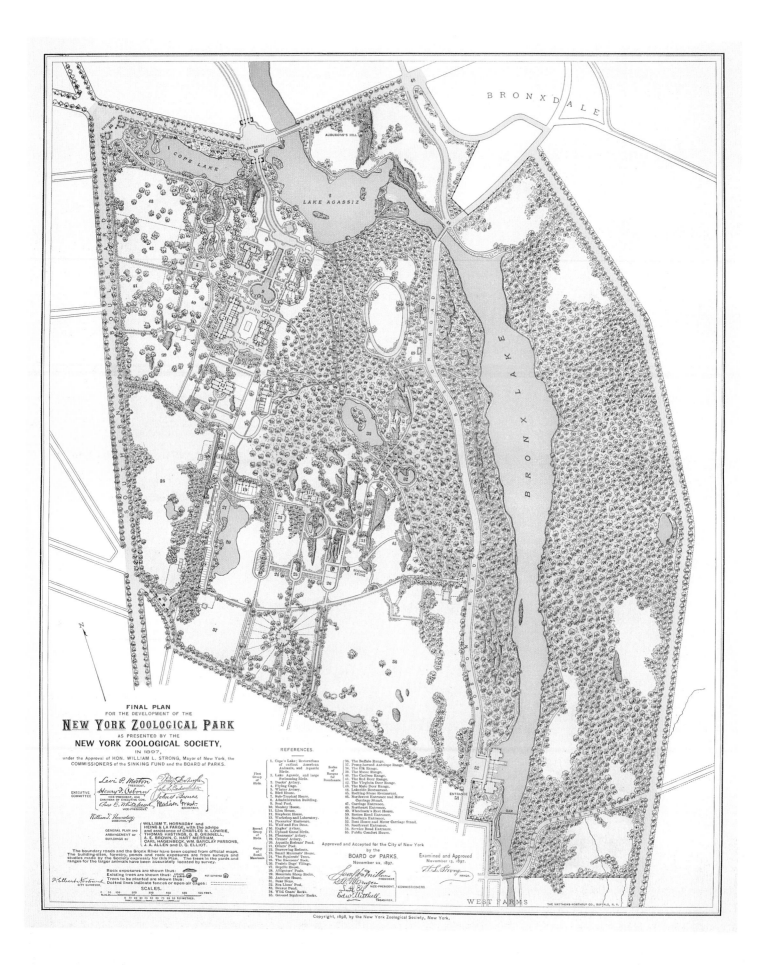

FINAL PLAN
FOR THE DEVELOPMENT OF THE
NEW YORK ZOOLOGICAL PARK
AS PRESENTED BY THE
NEW YORK ZOOLOGICAL SOCIETY,
IN 1897,
under the Approval of HON. WILLIAM L. STRONG, Mayor of New York, the
COMMISSIONERS of the SINKING FUND and the BOARD OF PARKS.

EXECUTIVE
COMMITTEE

Levi P. Morton
PRESIDENT

Henry F. Osborn
VICE-PRESIDENT, AND
CHAIRMAN OF EXECUTIVE COM.

Chas. E. Whitehead
VICE-PRESIDENT.

John L. Cadwalader

John S. Barnes

Madison Grant
SECRETARY.

William T. Hornaday,
DIRECTOR.

GENERAL PLAN and
ARRANGEMENT OF
BUILDINGS BY

WILLIAM T. HORNADAY and
HEINS & LA FARGE, with the advice
and assistance of CHARLES N. LOWRIE,
THOMAS HASTINGS, G. B. GRINNELL,
A. E. BROWN, C. HART MERRIAM,
CARL HAGENBECK, WM. BARCLAY PARSONS,
J. A. ALLEN and D. G. ELLIOT.

The boundary roads and the Bronx River have been copied from official maps.
The building-sites, forestry, ponds and rock exposures are from surveys and
studies made by the Society expressly for this Plan. The trees in the yards and
ranges for the larger animals have been accurately located by survey.

Rock exposures are shown thus:
Existing trees are shown thus:
Trees to be planted are shown thus:
Dotted lines indicate fences or open-air cages.

NOT SURVEYED

P. Gilbert Nostrand,
CITY SURVEYOR.

SCALES.
0 50 100   300   500   600 FEET.
0 10 20 30 40 50 60 70 80 90 100 METRES.

REFERENCES.

First
Group
of
Birds.

1. Cope's Lake: Restorations
   of extinct American
   Animals, and Aquatic
   Birds.
2. Lake Agassiz, and large
   Swimming Birds.
3. Ducks' Aviary.
4. Flying Cage.
5. Winter Aviary.
6. Bird House.
7. Sub-Tropical House.
8. Administration Building.
9. Seal Pool.
10. Monkey House.
11. Lion House.
12. Elephant House.
13. Workshop and Laboratory.
14. Poncarine Enclosure.
15. Wolf and Fox Dens.

Second
Group
of
Birds.

16. Eagles' Aviary.
17. Upland Game Birds.
18. Pheasants' Aviary.
19. Cranes' Aviary.
20. Aquatic Rodents' Pond.
21. Otters' Pool.

Group
of
Small
Mammals.

22. Burrowing Rodents.
23. Small Mammals' House.
24. The Squirrels' Trees.
25. The Raccoons' Rock.
26. Prairie Dogs' Village.
27. Reptile House.
28. Alligator Pools.
29. Mountain Sheep Rocks.
30. Antelope House.
31. Bear Dens.
32. Sea Lions' Pool.
33. Beaver Pond.
34. Wild Goats' Rocks.
35. Ground Squirrels' Rocks.

Series
of
Ranges
for
Ruminants.

36. The Buffalo Range.
37. Prong-horned Antelope Range.
38. The Elk Range.
39. The Moose Range.
40. The Caribou Range.
41. The Red Deer Range.
42. The Virginia Deer Range.
43. The Mule Deer Range.
44. Lakeside Restaurant.
45. Northwest Restaurant.
46. Rocking-Stone Restaurant.
47. Northwest Entrance and Motor
    Carriage Stand.
47. Carriage Stand.
48. Carriage Entrance.
49. Northeast Entrance.
50. Wheelmen's Rest House.
51. Boston Road Entrance.
52. Southern Entrance.
53. Boat House and Motor Carriage Stand.
54. Southwest Entrance.
55. Service Road Entrance.
56. Public Comfort House.

Approved and Accepted for the City of New York
by the
BOARD OF PARKS.
November 22, 1897.

Geo. McAneny
PRESIDENT.

E. A. Bruges
VICE-PRESIDENT,

Smith Ely
COMMISSIONERS.

Edw. Mitchell
TREASURER.

Examined and Approved
November 13, 1897.

H. L. Strong
MAYOR.

THE MATTHEWS-NORTHRUP CO., BUFFALO, N. Y.

Opposite: The Final Plan of the Bronx Zoo was devised by William Hornaday, with help from C. Grant La Farge, and signed by Mayor William Strong in November 1898. The Zoo opened a year later.

Above: All the buildings and exhibits in the original plan had been completed when William Adickes made this 1913 panorama of the Bronx Zoo.

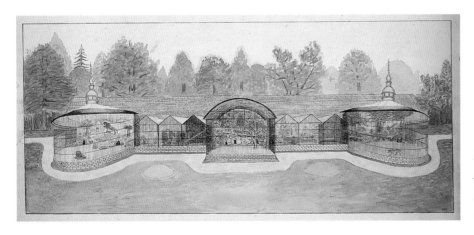

In watercolor drawings of 1897, Hornaday sketched several zoo buildings, including the Lion House (left). He considered the actual building, opened in 1903 (below), excessively elaborate in its sculptural decor.

Right: Visitors were still enthralled by the snow leopard from Central Asia in 1906, three years after the first specimen, bought by Mrs. Emma Auchincloss, arrived at the new Lion House.

Below: A fleet of 120 rowboats and the electric launch Albatross *began their seasonal service at the boathouse on the Bronx River in 1907.*

Opposite above: By 1910, the Italian seventeenth-century fountain donated to the Society by William Rockefeller had become the centerpiece of the parking circle at the foot of Blair (now Astor) Court.

Opposite below: The Flying Cage, fifty-five feet high at its peak, was considered the zoo's most magnificent structure when it opened in 1900. It has been rebuilt twice and was rededicated as the DeJur Aviary for Colonial Seabirds in 1982.

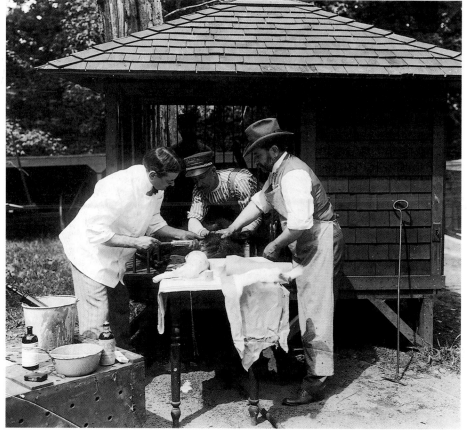

Above: Educational wildlife films made by zoo staff were seen by thousands of children under a big tent throughout the 1920s.

Left: Open-air veterinary practice was common before the animal hospital opened in 1916. Here Dr. William Reid Blair operates on a Mexican grizzly bear in 1904, assisted by Director Hornaday.

Opposite above: Artists like A. Phimister Proctor, here at the bear dens in 1906, were encouraged to work directly from animals in the zoo. The Society even provided an art studio in the Lion House.

Opposite below: School tours, like this one at a chimp party in 1936, often had direct contact with animals, though in a human setting.

Above: The zoo's kitchen in 1909. Rudolph Bell, hired as cook in 1899, fed the zoo's animals for more than thirty-five years.

Opposite: Among the twenty big cats bought for the new Lion House in 1902 was the Barbary lion Sultan (above), donated by Nelson Robinson. Andrew Carnegie also gave a lion, named Hannibal. A Bengal tiger in the Lion House (1935, below).

Opposite: Seventeen rungs, spaced one foot apart, measured the giraffe's height (1926).

Of Helen Keller's visit to the Bronx Zoo in 1923, Elwin Sanborn wrote, "She seemed to know the bears, monkeys, lions, deer—in fact anything with which she came in contact—as we know them; they did not seem strange, unsolved forms."

In the zoo's first decade, Baldy was known in the newspapers as "the chimpanzee that knows everything," with some subtle promotion by Curator Raymond Ditmars. Thousands of visitors came to see him.

CHARLES H. TOWNSEND

from "Pollution of Streams—an Appeal to Anglers"

THE ANNUAL REPORT OF THE NEW YORK
ZOOLOGICAL SOCIETY, 1907

The pollution of streams and rivers still persists, although the problem was addressed in the United States by the Clean Water Act of 1972. The New York Aquarium, under Charles Townsend, helped in efforts to measure sewage in New York Harbor for years and reduced fatalities in its own collections by 50 percent by establishing its own ocean-water reservoir. Townsend tackled the national problem in the March 1919 Zoological Society Bulletin, *writing, "In spite of the existence of statutes broad enough to meet most of the conditions, little headway is being made. It is not our national habit to begin reforms when serious results are threatened, but rather after trouble has actually arrived." About New York Harbor he wrote, "It is possible that with increasing pollution, fish life will not exist in the water of the Harbor at all, and that the lower forms of marine life, which assist in the disposal of waste matter, will themselves be dispersed." It has not been until recent years that cleanup efforts have allowed life in the river and harbor to revive to a degree. Unfortunately, though, this work involved dumping the sludge that once covered the bottom of the harbor out to sea. This practice was ended by federal law in 1992.*

All our fish commissioners of experience, both National and State, are agreed that the decrease in the supply of food fishes is traceable more to the pollution of waters than to any other cause, and stream pollution is going on at a rate proportionate to the increase in population and the development of manufacturing industries.

The effects of pollution are most serious in the more densely populated States. It begins almost at the sources of streams and extends to the very mouths of the largest rivers.

The conditions would probably not be so serious in their effect upon the supply of fresh-water fishes had not the flow of streams been lessened by deforestation. With the cutting away of forests and the cultivation of the land, the summer temperature of streams has become higher and the breeding grounds of game and food fishes covered by silt washed down by floods.

Happily the movement for reforestation is gaining ground. It is most important, and all anglers should be active supporters of the efforts now being made for forest preservation.

The pollution of streams not only affects fishing for sport and commercial fishing, but the all-important matter of public health.

The agencies at work are almost too varied for enumeration. In general the pollution of waters is caused by sawmills, pulp and paper mills, tanneries, starch, cheese and sugar factories, gas, wood-alcohol, chemical, glass and dye works, oil refineries, distilleries and breweries, logging, smelting and mining, and by factories of all sorts. To this catalogue might be added the item of dead animals, which in the aggregate is an important one.

There is also the depositing in the waters of cinders, garbage and trash by the vast fleet of fresh-water steamers everywhere. In addition to these sources of pollution there is practically all the city and town sewage of the country.

With such facts confronting us there is no need of inquiring why we do not get better results from our admirable National and State fish cultural work. It is not merely the class of anglers who are concerned—the people everywhere are becoming alive to the danger of the situation.

The streams of western Pennsylvania, for instance, are already ruined by coal mining. I have recently visited some of the streams in which I fished as a boy. They are to-day little more than sulphur-yellow drains of coal mines, disfiguring the fair face of nature, in many cases throughout their entire courses and for distances sometimes as great as the width of two or three countries. They contain no living thing—neither fish, frog, cray-fish, nor any form of animal or plant life.

The coal and coke industries which have brought about these conditions may possibly be regulated at some future time. At present their vast importance and the state of public opinion do not give us any hope for stream purification in coal mining regions.

The well-known conditions of pollution extending throughout the Hudson River and its tributaries may be found in all rivers of the country where the population is great and the manufacturing industries well developed.

Boards of health throughout the country are considering the conditions, but little is accomplished except where local conditions here and there become intolerable. Officers are usually unable to enforce existing laws and juries will not convict.

The Herculean labor involved in setting things right will require the consent of the population and a liberal use of the money and effort of the present generation, while the next generation will need to be vigilant in sustaining whatever protection may be secured. . . .

Without further cataloguing of the injurious wastes liberated into streams from factories of all kinds, we may truthfully assert, with the support of numerous National and State fishery documents, that the maintenance of fish life is becoming impossible.

Our whole national system of disposing of wastes is an immoral one; the town and the mill can be kept clean, but the condition of the stream itself has been utterly disregarded.

In spite of the fact that there are laws in all States which prohibit the drainage of dangerous matter into public waters, there exist in factories without numbers secret waste pipes which are opened during the night, the outpourings of which are so deadly to fish life that the practice of operating them can only be named as dastardly.

We have lived under these conditions so long that we are used to them. It is the old case of each for himself, with no thought of the health, wealth or happiness of those farther down stream.

In many beautiful streams, where fishing is still possible, fishes have become uneatable through tainting of the water. This is true in a greater degree of shad and other sea fishes which succeed in passing through the unspeakable waters of New York Harbor. . . .

Charles Haskins Townsend, director of the New York Aquarium from 1902 to 1937.

Coal mines, such as this one in Kentucky at the end of the nineteenth century, produced, in Townsend's words, "sulphur-yellow drains. . . . They contain no living thing—neither fish, frog, crayfish, not any form of animal or plant life."

It has taken a quarter of a century to get pure food laws through Congress, and it will take longer to clean up the streams of the country, but it seems possible by concerted action of the anglers of America that our mountain streams can be cleared up, and in a very few years—soon enough for most of us to derive benefit from our labors. The results desired can only be secured by united effort. . . .

Anglers should be able to secure help from commercial fishermen everywhere, since market fishing, even when excessive, is not as bad as wholesale stream pollution, and they should also be able to secure the support of all communities desiring clean water for town use. As organized bodies they could exert a most wholesome influence on the work of fishery boards in all the States.

The interests engaged in polluting our higher waters are not yet sufficiently powerful to claim everything for their side of the question. A reasonable amount of discussion ought to make it clear that the waters of our higher lakes and streams are vastly more valuable as sources of municipal water supply, for fisheries, and for summer homes, than they can possibly be to a minority of small manufacturers. It is to be expected that all industries concerned will protest vigorously, but they are still greatly in the minority, and therefore the prospects are hopeful.

FUR SEALS: ENLISTING THE PRESIDENT

WILLIAM T. HORNADAY

from a letter to Henry W. Elliot
Lakewood, Ohio

MARCH 4, 1908

Charles Haskins Townsend photographed fur seal rookeries in the Pribilof Islands off Alaska in 1896 during one of his yearly inspection tours for the U.S. government. By 1904, male fur seals were reduced by hunting at sea to precarious populations.

Dear Henry:—

I have read very carefully your letter and the clipping of February 29th.

Now let me give you some sound advice. Take the matter up directly with the President [Roosevelt]. If you can make an impression upon him, the thing is done out of hand. Do not say too much; but treat the matter calmly and dispassionately, as an independent American citizen who on the one hand deplores the pending extinction of the fur-seal herd, and on the other would be glad to render some assistance to the Government. If you make the whole matter short enough that the President will take time to read it, you may win out easier than you think. The President is interested in all animal life; he is a thorough naturalist, and if you can convince him that Canada is now right to join in an agreement to prevent the extinction of the fur-seal herd, he may simply direct that the necessary action be taken.

I have before now appealed to the President three different times on matters which were utterly hedged in elsewhere. In each case, he took a friendly interest, and the thing that I desired was done. If I had not already asked him for so much, and bothered him so often, I would try my hand at the fur-seal matter myself; but as it is, I do not dare. I must not have him feel that I am a nuisance, and that the more I get, the more I want. It would not be a bad plan for you to draft a letter and send it to me to read over before you put it into final form. You might even go so far, if you choose, to suggest that he refer the matter to some naturalist of standing, who is familiar with the history of the fur-seal controversy; but who thus far has never been called upon to take any active part in it either way.

I had the honor of lunching with the President yesterday, we discussed a number of important matters. He seemed keenly alive to every movement calculated to benefit the wild animal life of the United States. You can do far more with him than with his successor,—no matter who his successor may be. . . .

Yours very sincerely,
W. Hornaday

Hornaday, of course, did get involved in the fur-seal matter and was largely responsible, along with Henry Elliot, a naturalist and former associate of the Smithsonian Institution, for having fur-seal harvesting in the seas around the Pribilof Islands banned in 1911. His conflict with Charles Townsend, who was active in this effort long before Hornaday, is described in the introduction to this chapter.

THE LAST OF ITS KIND

John James Audubon. Passenger Pigeon. *Drawing. 1824.*

WILLIAM T. HORNADAY

*Letter to Mr. S. A. Stephen, Superintendent
Cincinnati Zoological Gardens
Cincinnati, Ohio*

JUNE 1, 1907

In 1810, the nature artist Alexander Wilson had claimed to have seen more than two billion passenger pigeons in one flock in the Indiana Territory, and in 1813 John James Audubon witnessed a migration of the species that filled the sky in Kentucky for three days.

Dear Mr. Stephen:

We are anxious to procure one or two specimens of the Passenger Pigeon. I hear that there are four in your gardens. If that information is true, I would like to ask, with all due deference, whether you would be willing to sell one or two of the birds to us. We have a fine collection of pigeons; but thus far have never had an opportunity to obtain any of the old Passenger species.

Yours very truly,
Director

The species, indeed, was totally extinct by 1914,
with the death of that last specimen.

Dear Sir:

In all the world, there is only one living specimen of the Passenger Pigeon, and that is in the [Cincinnati] Zoological Gardens,—where it has been for eighteen years. When that bird dies, the species will be totally extinct. We would willingly give $500 for one specimen of a genuine Passenger Pigeon; but the only specimen in existence is not for sale.

Yours very truly,
Director

PROTECTING WILD GAME:
"EXTREME MEASURES ARE NECESSARY"

One of the most notable achievements of this session of the Legislature has been the passage of the Bayne-Blauvelt Bill for the prohibiting of the sale of wild game. This measure marks the most important step in the movement for the protection and conservation of wild life on this continent. Game laws are never popular, and it is a source of constant wonder to those who realize the fierce independence of the average American citizen, to realize how he has, more or less quietly, acquiesced in certain restrictive measures. Each step in the campaign has been marked by protests and sometimes by set-backs, but it will be a surprise to all lovers of nature to realize that the destruction of the wild life has now gone so far, that the prohibition of public sale has become imperative.

In the past, the citizen was at liberty to enter into state forests and cut such timber as he liked for sale or for his own use; so up to this date it has been one of the privileges of the hunter and trapper to kill and catch as many birds and fur bearing animals as he could, and to sell them for his own profit. This could be permitted so long as the hunters were few and the game abundant. That time passed away in the middle of the last century.

First, skin hunting for deer was prohibited; next, close seasons were provided; then followed limitation of the bag and shorter open seasons; then the entire prohibition of the killing of certain kinds of game threatened with extinction; then came limitations on the mode of killing, such as hounding, water hunting, jacking, the use of snares and swivel guns and the like. All these measures, excellent as they were, checked the slaughter, but the game continued to decrease. . . .

The Director of the Zoological Park, Dr. Hornaday, was one of the first to realize that a new principle of game protection must be inaugurated in this state, and with the assistance of a number of very energetic workers, and the endorsement of practically every organization in the state interested in the subject of the protection of wild life, he caused to be prepared and introduced the bill now known as the Bayne-Blauvelt Bill. This bill passed through a long and tedious struggle, being attacked with special bitterness by the game dealers. . . .

The bill passed the Senate by a vote of 38 to 1, and in the Assembly the vote was unanimous. The New York Zoological Society entered actively into the campaign. It subscribed $500 to the expenses, and sent the Chairman of the Executive Committee to Albany to appear on behalf of the Society, along with the representatives of other organizations, in support of the bill.

The new law provides for the repeal of all provisions of the existing law authorizing the sale of native wild game, mammals and birds, taken either within or without the state of New York. The only exception relates to hares and rabbits, which have grown so numerous as to constitute a pest in certain sections. It amply provides for licensed game preserves, and the breeding therein of certain species of mammals and birds for the market. . . .

If this measure proves to be insufficient to protect some of the species now threatened with extermination, the next step in the protection of game will be the total prohibition of killing of such birds or animals for at least a long period of time. Extreme measures are necessary unless we wish our woods, meadows and the fields to be entirely devoid of wild life.

Dan Beard. "The Regular Army of Destruction, Waiting for the First of October. Each Year 2,642,274 Well-Armed Men Take the Field Against the Remnant of Wild Birds and Mammals in the United States" (*from* Our Vanishing Wild Life, *1912*).

WILLIAM T. HORNADAY

from "The Former Abundance of Wildlife"

OUR VANISHING WILDLIFE, 1912

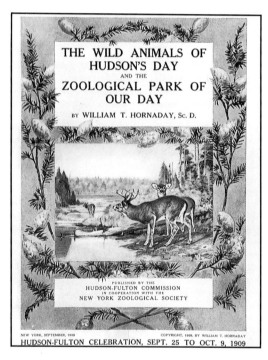

A special issue of the Zoological Society Bulletin, *with a cover by Carl Rungius, was published in connection with the Hudson-Fulton Celebration in 1909, marking the three hundredth anniversary of Henry Hudson's exploration of the area.*

Any man who reads the books which best tell the story of the development of the American colonies of 1712 into the American nation of 1912, and takes due note of the wild-life features of the tale, will say without hesitation that when the American people received this land from the bountiful hand of Nature, it was endowed with a magnificent and all-pervading supply of valuable wild creatures. The pioneers and the early settlers were too busy even to take due note of that fact, or to comment upon it, save in very fragmentary ways.

Nevertheless, the wild-life abundance of early American days survived down to so late a period that it touched the lives of millions of people now living. Any man 55 years of age who when a boy had a taste for "hunting,"—for at that time there were no "sportsmen" in America,—will remember the flocks and herds of wild creatures that he saw and which made upon his mind many indelible impressions.

"Abundance" is the word with which to describe the original animal life that stocked our country, and all North America, only a short half-century ago. Throughout every state, on every shore-line, in all the millions of fresh water lakes, ponds and rivers, on every mountain range, in every forest, *and even on every desert*, the wild flocks and herds held sway. It was impossible to go beyond the settled haunts of civilized man and escape them.

It was a full century after the complete settlement of New England and the Virginia colonies that the wonderful big-game fauna of the great plains and Rocky Mountains was really discovered; but the bison millions, the antelope millions, the mule deer, the mountain sheep and mountain goat were there, all the time. In the early days, the millions of pinnated grouse and quail of the central states attracted no serious attention from the American people-at-large; but they lived and flourished just the same, far down in the seventies, when the greedy market gunners systematically slaughtered them, and barreled them up for "the market," while the foolish farmers calmly permitted them to do it. . . .

To me the most striking fact that stands forth in the story of American wild life one hundred years ago is the wide extent and thoroughness of its distribution. Wide as our country is, and marvelous as it is in the diversity of its climates, its soils, its topography, its flora, its riches and its poverty, Nature gave to each square mile and to each acre a generous quota of wild creatures, according to its ability to maintain living things. No pioneer ever pushed so far, or into regions so difficult or so remote, that he did not find awaiting him a host of birds and beasts. . . .

In the early days, shotguns were few, and shot was scarce and dear. The wild turkey and goose were the smallest birds on which a rifleman could afford to expend a bullet and a whole charge of powder. It was for this reason that the deer, bear, bison, and elk disappeared from the eastern United States while the game birds yet remained abundant. With the disappearance of the big game came the fat steer, hog and hominy, the wheat-field, fruit orchard and poultry galore.

The game birds of America, as a class and a mass, have not been swept away to ward off starvation or to rescue the perishing. Even back in the sixties and seventies, very, very few men of the North thought of killing prairie chickens, ducks and quail, snipe and woodcock, in order to keep the hunger wolf from the door. The process was too slow and uncertain; and besides, the really-poor man rarely had the gun and ammunition. Instead of attempting to live on birds, he hustled for the staple food products that the soil of his own farm could produce.

First, last and nearly all the time, the game birds of the United States as a whole, have been sacrificed on the altar of Rank Luxury, to tempt appetites that were tired of fried chicken and other farm delicacies. Today, even the average poor man hunts birds for the joy of the outing, and the pampered epicures of the hotels and restaurants buy game birds, and eat small portions of them, solely to tempt jaded appetites. If there is such a thing as "class" legislation, it is that which permits a few sordid market-shooters to slaughter the birds of the whole people in order to sell them to a few epicures.

The game of a state belongs to the whole people of the state. The Supreme Court of the United States has so decided (Geer vs. Connecticut). If it is abundant, it is a valuable asset. The great value of the game birds of America lies not in their meat pounds as they lie upon the table, but in the temptation they annually put before millions of field-weary farmers and desk-weary clerks and merchants to get into their beloved hunting togs, stalk out into the lap of Nature, and say "Begone, dull Care!"

And the man who has had a fine day in the painted woods, on the bright waters of a duck-haunted bay, or in the golden stubble of September, can fill his day and his soul with six good birds just as well as with sixty. The idea that in order to enjoy a fine day in the open a man must kill a wheel-barrow load of birds, is a mistaken idea; and if obstinately adhered to, it becomes vicious! The Outing in the Open is the thing,—not the blood-stained feathers, nasty viscera and Death in the game-bag. One quail on a fence is worth more to the world than ten in a bag.

※

In working with large bodies of bird-shooting sportsmen I have steadily —and also painfully—been impressed by their intentness on killing, and by the fact that *they seek to preserve game only to kill it*! Who ever saw a bird-shooter rise in a convention and advocate the preservation of any species of game bird on account of its beauty or its aesthetic interest *alive*? I never did; and I have sat in many conventions of sportsmen. All the talk is of open seasons, bag limits and killing rights. The man who has the hardi-hood to stand up and propose a five-year close season has "a hard row to hoe." Men rise and say: "It's all nonsense! There's plenty of quail shooting on Long Island yet."

Throughout the length and breadth of America, the ruling passion is to kill as long as anything killable remains. The man who will openly advo-cate the stopping of quail-shooting because the quails are of such great value to the farmers, or because they are so *beautiful* and companionable to man, receives no sympathy from ninety per cent of the bird killing sports-men. The remaining ten per cent think seriously about the matter, and favor long close seasons. It is my impression that of the men who shoot, it is only among the big-game hunters that we find much genuine admiration

WILLIAM T. HORNADAY

from "The Savage View-Point of the Gunner"

OUR VANISHING WILDLIFE, 1912

for game animals, or any feeling remotely resembling regard for it.

The moment that a majority of American gunners concede the fact that game birds are worth preserving for their beauty, and their value as living neighbors to man, from that moment there is hope for the saving of the Remnant. That will indeed be the beginning of a new era, of a millennium in fact, in the preservation of wild life. It will then be easy to enact laws for ten-year close seasons on whole groups of species. Think what it would mean for such a close season to be enacted for all the grouse of the United States, all the shore-birds of the United States, or the wild turkey wherever found!

To-day, the great—indeed, the *only*—opponents of long close seasons on game birds are the gunners. Whenever and wherever you introduce a bill to provide such a season, you will find that this is true. The gun clubs and the Downtrodden Hunters' and Anglers' Protective Associations will be quick to go after their representatives, and oppose the bill. And state senators and assemblymen will think very hard and with strong courage before they deliberately resolve to do their duty regardless of the opposition of "a large body of sportsmen,"—men who have votes, and who know how to take revenge on lawmakers who deprive them of their "right" to kill. The greatest speech ever made in the Mexican Congress was uttered by the member who solemnly said: "I rise to sacrifice ambition to honor!". . .

Really, it is to me very strange that gunners never care to save game birds on account of their beauty. One living bob white on a fence is better than a score in a bloody game-bag. A live squirrel in a tree is poetry in motion; but on the table a squirrel is a rodent that tastes as a rat smells. Beside the ocean a flock of sandpipers is needed to complete the beautiful picture; but on the table a sandpiper is beneath contempt. A live deer trotting over a green meadow, waving a triangular white flag, is a sight to thrill any human ganglion; but a deer lying dead,—unless it has an exceptionally fine head,—is only so much butcher's meat. . . .

It is time for the people who don't shoot to call a halt on those who do; "and if this be treason, then let my enemies make the most of it!"

Manhattan's Aquarium

On May 31, 1934, during the Navy visit to New York, 50,640 people went to the aquarium.

The main hall of the aquarium in Battery Park in 1905.

In 1896, the New York Aquarium was established in a fortress at the southern tip of Manhattan that had been built in 1807–11 to protect New York Harbor; it had subsequently become a celebrated theater and reception hall (1823–55) and the federal government's Emigrant Landing Station (1855–90) before Ellis Island. The gloomy, poorly run, but immensely popular fish palace had a rather shady reputation as a Tammany Hall patronage scheme, and in 1902 the city contracted the Society to take on its management. Director Charles Haskins Townsend brightened up the place and introduced high standards of exhibition and research, but it was not until 1921 that major renovations, including the addition of a third floor, were carried out. The building was permanently closed on September 21, 1941, by which time 84,336,316 people had visited the old aquarium, an average of 2,162,469 a year.

Some of the aquarium's fish collections were obtained by seining Lake Agassiz at the Bronx Zoo (1906).

New rockwork was created for many exhibits in 1923–25, including the display of blue and black angelfish.

In 1938, sea lions occupied the aquarium's center pool.

WILLIAM T. HORNADAY

Letter to Henry Ford

MARCH 14, 1913

Henry Ford took up the cause with a vengeance. He directed his advertising men in Chicago to "Go to Washington and don't return until that bird bill has been passed." According to the May 1913 Zoological Society Bulletin, "A thousand newspapers have been supplied with articles, of at least twenty different kinds, intended to awaken the sleeping American people. Thousands of telegrams have been sent in all directions, demanding attention for the bill and help in placing the needs of the birds before the people. For the first time, 'big business' has been called upon for help, by a voice strong enough to compel attention." And the bill did pass, helped in part by the following night letter Hornaday circulated to hundreds, if not thousands, of concerned citizens.

My Dear Sir:

There is at this moment a great opportunity for the friends of the birds of the world to strike a tremendous blow at the abuse involved in the use of wild birds' plumage for millinery purposes. If you can spare time to refer to Chapter XIII in my book—"*Our Vanishing Wild Life,*" you will quickly be able to judge the extent of the slaughter and extermination of beautiful species for millinery purposes that now is going on throughout the world. The feather trade is unspeakably cruel and inexorable.

A new Tariff Bill is now being framed by the Committee on Ways and Means. The Zoological Society, and the National Association of Audubon Societies, have joined in asking Congress, through that Committee, to prohibit by a clause in the new Tariff Bill the importation of the plumage of wild birds for millinery purposes. The Audubon people limit their demand to the plumage of American birds, but the Zoological Society demands an exclusion that will benefit *all the birds of the world.*

The Committee is considering the matter in a most friendly spirit and I am sure that we are going to get *something*! If the American people can be sufficiently aroused within the next four weeks to make their wishes known in this matter, there will be a demand for the total exclusion of wild birds' plumage so overwhelming that Congress will respond to our appeal. It may be years before another Tariff Bill is framed, and before another opportunity of this kind comes before us. It is truly a golden moment, and we are going to do our utmost to arouse the country on this subject. Our Society is just about to issue a circular letter,—of which the enclosed manuscript is a copy. In this campaign we shall expect the American women to come forward and do their duty, and we will also expect the men to join them.

This campaign greatly needs your help. You are in a position to put the matter quickly before millions of people. From the chapter in my book, Mr. Buck could easily prepare a series of articles that would strongly appeal to the public. You can reach millions of people to whom I have no access through the press! We beg you to join in this campaign.

Yours very truly,
W. Hornaday

WILLIAM T. HORNADAY

Night letter

JUNE 18, 1913

The feather milliner's lobby has captured the majority members of Senate Committee on Finance, which has adopted an amendment that will kill half the force of our clause if it prevails. The amendment would admit the feathers of all birds killed as food, or game, also all eagles, hawks, owls, kites, and many insectivorous birds. Shall two dozen importing millinery houses who are out for money be permitted to dictate to ninety millions of American people who demand that the cruel and shameless traffic in wild birds' feathers shall cease? It would be an outrage. Protest vigorously to all Senators.

J. N. Ding. "What News Travels Fastest in the World?" (1919).

The cause of wild life protection by the Zoological Society has been placed in the front rank of importance among the objects of the Society. The serious conditions that now surround the wild birds and mammals of our country, and the world at large, actually relegate to third place some of the zoological causes that twenty years ago were of paramount importance. Strange as it may seem, ours is the only Zoological Society in existence that regards the saving of wild species from extinction as a duty decidedly paramount to the comfortable and unruffled study of the anatomy and habits of those species.

The year 1913 has been marked by great activity on the part of the Zoological Society in the promotion of measures calculated to be of far-reaching benefit to the wild life of our continent and the world at large. The Society's campaign book, "Our Vanishing Wild Life," was designed to stir up the laggard states of our country as they have not before been aroused, and spur them to action. To the printing and circulating of that volume the Society devoted the largest sum of money that ever has been expended by any protective organization in a single campaign effort. The volume reached Congress and 48 State legislatures while they were in session, and giving consideration to wild life measures. The struggle for the McLean-Weeks migratory bird law was fairly at its crisis when the volume was

WILLIAM T. HORNADAY

from "Wild Life Protection"

EIGHTEENTH ANNUAL REPORT OF THE NEW YORK ZOOLOGICAL SOCIETY, 1913

placed in the hands of all members of Congress, and the expressions which it elicited were entirely satisfactory.

In support of the federal migratory bird bill, the Society labored long and arduously, especially directing its efforts to arousing the newspaper and agricultural press of the nation and the granges, both state and national. Articles furnished by the Society were published in about 1,250 newspapers and magazines, and called forth hundreds of editorials in support of the general cause.

Before the McLean-Weeks measure was fairly out of the way, the Society assumed before Congress the risk of proposing a clause in the new tariff bill to provide for the protection of the birds of the world against the agents of the millinery trade. The campaign that ensued placed upon the Director of the Park an extra burden of work which continued without a break from January 30 to October 4, when the tariff bill was signed, containing the feather millinery clause identically as originally drawn by the Society. . . .

In view of the needs of the future for a regular annual income of at least $5,000 which can be wholly devoted to the protection of wild life, with the unofficial approval of two officers of the Society, the Director of the Park has undertaken to raise by methods of his own, and chiefly among his own friends, a fund of $100,000 which he has named the Permanent Wild Life Protection Fund. This effort has the sympathy and best wishes of the Society, and the results that already have been achieved point to complete success in the reasonably-near future.

Two things are absolutely certain:

(1.) The struggle for the preservation of wild life must be kept up continuously, to the end of Time.

(2.) It is not possible to meet and combat the organized and well-financed forces of destruction without permanent campaign funds with which to support the army of the defense. This Society must have for this purpose at least $5,000 per year, and more if it can be provided.

With the McLean-Weeks federal migratory bird bill "fairly out of the way" in 1913, the Migratory Bird Treaty was passed in 1918 by act of Congress, protecting 1,022 species of North American birds from the Mexican border to the North Pole. The Permanent Wild Life Protection Fund, which Hornaday had established in 1911, reached $104,750 by 1915. Hornaday administered the fund largely to battle the hunting establishment, mostly through publications, until his death in 1937, when the Society took it over. In the late 1950s, the fund was still providing money for Society programs, this time for new African initiatives.

A NATIONAL TASK

WILLIAM T. HORNADAY

from "Duty and Power of the Citizen"
WILDLIFE CONSERVATION, 1914

The trouble is that very, *very* few men and women, even among the fabulously rich, are willing to give anything substantial to the wild-life cause. As a result, our cause is financially on a half-starvation basis, and seems likely to remain so. . . .

The saving of the wild life and forests of the world is a *duty* that by no means is confined to a small group of persons who work for nothing and subsist on their own enthusiasm. The saving of the fauna of a nation is a national task. It is literally everybody's business. It rests upon the shoulders of the educated and the intelligent, and the motives that prompt it are not found in the breasts of the sordid and the ignorant. . . .

We have a right to demand services for this great cause from the educators, the scientists, the zoologists in particular; from lawyers and doctors and merchants; and above all, from editors. Intelligent people who ignore this cause fall short of their duty to humanity and to themselves. The universities and colleges, the high schools and the normal schools, all have it in their power to exert an enormous influence in this cause. Think what it would mean if 30 per cent of the annual graduates of all American institutions of learning should go forth well informed on the details of this work, and fully resolved to spread the doctrine of conservation, far and near! And think, also, what it would mean if even one-half the men and women who earn their daily bread in the field of zoology and nature-study should elect to make this cause their own! And yet, I tell you that in spite of an appeal for help, dating as far back as 1898, fully 90 per cent of the zoologists of America stick closely to their desk-work, soaring after the infinite and diving after the unfathomable, but never spending a dollar or lifting an active finger on the firing-line in defense of wild life. I have talked to these men until I am tired; and the most of them seem to be hopelessly sodden and apathetic. . . .

The people of America who have money to give away to causes for the betterment of humanity should consider the campaigns that are being made, and that should be made, to save the remainder of our wild life for the benefit of mankind at large. This cause is entitled to a share of betterment funds, and it should *not* be compelled to live on the husks and crumbs that fall from the million-dollar tables of other causes. The sight of scores of causes and institutions struggling with undigested wealth, while the wild life of the world is being swept away, and its defenders are working on a starvation basis, is fairly maddening. . . .

The greatest of all obstacles in the way of the conservator of wild life and forests is the deadly American spirit of restless and heedless wastefulness. The American continent has been developed by men who, time and time, settled down, robbed the soil of its fertility, then moved on westward to new lands. The American national spirit is for quick, wasteful *conquest*, not calm and patient conservation. It is our way to cut down, slash up, kill, lay waste, get rich quick,—and a fig for posterity! Our rich men strive to leave great fortunes in cash to their children, but they rarely reforest or restore wild life. That is too slow for them.

The forest champions of America now are making a Herculean effort to instill into the American mind the idea of the systematic replanting of denuded forest lands: but it is like rolling a huge stone up a steep hill. Quite recently I journeyed through several hundred miles of southern pine forests, always watching for signs of systematic reforestation, but not once did I see a pine, young or old, that clearly appeared to have been planted by the hand of man. In the denuded forest areas of Florida, Georgia, the Carolinas and Virginia, nature was bravely struggling to restore what man had greedily destroyed, but not once did I see a single acre on which nature was being assisted by man. . . .

The preservation and increase of the forests is a very different matter from the salvage of the birds and beasts. Man and nature, jointly or severally, can replant a denuded forest, and the lapse of time will bring the renaissance. With forests, there is a modicum of time available in which to act. With wild life, it is a case of now or never. *A fauna once destroyed can not be brought back!* The destroyers of wild life are so omnipresent, persistent and relentless that the defenders and preservers must act at once, or very soon it will be hopelessly too late. . . .

Mrs. Margaret Olivia Sage, "Benefactor of Science, Art, Literature, Education and the Cause of Human Welfare."

Extinction has been described more poetically by others, but Hornaday was as relentless in stating the case as he was in asking for money to support it. However, it was actually Chairman of the Executive Committee Madison Grant, with the help of a picture show put together by Reptile Curator Raymond Ditmars, who in 1914 solicited the $100,000 Pension Fund from Andrew Carnegie. (Carnegie's earlier major contributions had included funds for the purchase of a lion in 1902.) The World War I years were lean, but in 1918 the estate of Margaret Olivia Sage established a fund that would reach more than $600,000, and the 1920s were prosperous, with large endowments being given to the Society by John D. Rockefeller, Jr., Edward S. Harkness, George F. Baker, Anna M. Harkness, and Mrs. Frederick Ferris Thompson.

THE NATURALIST TRADITION

William Beebe cut a romantic figure—brilliant scientist, fearless explorer, and philosopher-poet. From an early age, he attracted attention: As an undergraduate at Columbia College he so impressed one of his professors, Henry Fairfield Osborn, that Osborn convinced William Hornaday to hire the twenty-two-year-old and make him head of the zoological park's bird department. Osborn's protégé reported for work on October 16, 1899, beginning an epochal association for the New York Zoological Society, which was to find in William Beebe a defining genius, and an epochal tie for William Beebe, who was to find in the Society a lifelong champion and home.

The blessings of that day were more mixed for the director of the zoological park. Beebe's independent spirit and freewheeling style irked the regimentarian in Hornaday, yet the new curator's energy and talent were undeniable. Beebe assembled an impressive collection of birds, conducted important research on their keeping, and designed an interior plan for the new Bird House so radical in size and scope that many aviculturists predicted disaster. From its opening in 1906, however, the Bird House worked brilliantly, bringing together an unparalleled variety of avian species in an immensely popular exhibit.

Following this resounding success, Beebe spent less and less time in the Bronx. His spirit was too large, and his interests too wide-ranging for the confines of even the grandest zoo. Beebe's expeditions—to Nova Scotia, Florida, Mexico, and South America—grew longer and more frequent, much to the director's chagrin. (Hornaday wanted his curator at the zoological park, attending to his birds.)

However, Osborn, the Society's president, encouraged these excursions, and in 1909 Beebe was persuaded by the first of his many patrons, Anthony Kuser, to undertake an expedition through Asia for the purpose of studying and cataloguing pheasants from the Himalayas to the Malay jungles. Kuser, a wealthy businessman and pheasant enthusiast from Bernardsville, New Jersey, backed both the trip and the publication of *A Monograph of Pheasants*, the definitive, lavishly illustrated four-volume study that resulted. This episode, during which Beebe was away from the zoo for seventeen months, seems to have proved that Beebe was best suited to the task of fulfilling the Society's corollary objective of promoting zoology through research, exploration, and publication. In 1916, Beebe was named director of the Society's newly formed Department of Tropical Research, and from then on he was only loosely associated with the operations of the zoological park.

In spite of Beebe's absence, the zoo thrived. Lee Crandall, who had joined Beebe's staff in 1908, was put in charge of birds. Crandall proved to be exceptionally gifted and eventually, in 1943, was made general curator. By the time he retired in 1952, Crandall was recognized as a leading international expert in animal exhibition and care. (His book *The Management of Wild Mammals in Captivity*, published in 1964, became known as "the zoo man's bible.")

The park's reptiles and mammals were cared for by Raymond Ditmars.

Possessed of enormous enthusiasm and a flair for drama, Ditmars lectured widely, and his seventeen books, many of which are peppered with behind-the-scenes anecdotes too topical to stand the test of time, enjoyed a large audience in their day and greatly increased the public's understanding of and sympathy for many animals, especially snakes, creatures with which Ditmars was forever linked in the popular mind.

Both Ditmars and Crandall went on expeditions that, for the most part, served the important purpose of collecting specimens, but their studies of animals in the zoo revealed basic information that could rarely or never be attained in the wild. Countless contributions from their work form the foundation of what we know about the physical development, behavior, longevity, courtship, gestation, and maternal care of many species.

In 1916, William Beebe (far head of table) and his staff received Mr. and Mrs. Theodore Roosevelt, the first visitors to their field headquarters at Kalacoon, Venezuela. Roosevelt wrote about his experiences at the station in the January 1917 issue of Scribner's Magazine.

The expeditions of William Beebe, of course, had a different goal: to fathom wildlife in the wild. In 1916, the first field stations of the Department of Tropical Research were started in the jungles of British Guiana (now Guyana), and Beebe spent much of the next eight years there with a small but growing staff. From the beginning, the department's work was based on the idea that greater knowledge would come from the observation of life in its native habitat than from the cold study of specimens in a laboratory. Seeking a fuller understanding of living environments as a whole, Beebe took the unconventional step of focusing the department's activities on a limited area that would be returned to and studied year after year. Beebe thus established new principles for zoological field research and at the same time helped refine the idea of biodiversity central to ecological thought today.

Some of Beebe's greatest prose came out of his jungle experiences. Possessed of unusual powers of observation and an uncommon gift with words, Beebe wrote twenty-four books, many of which achieved popular success

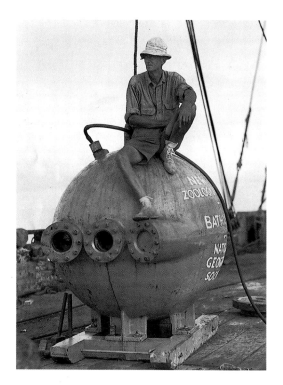

Beebe on top of the bathysphere a day after dive number thirty to 2,510 feet, on August 12, 1934, three days before the record dive to 3,028 feet.

internationally. His elegant prose is everywhere infused with an empathy with animals and a cosmic sense of the interconnectedness of life. Beebe saw the universe in a grain of sand, and with a naked curiosity and never-failing reverence he probed the bodies and pondered the minds and souls of birds, mammals, reptiles, amphibians, fish, and invertebrates, looking for connections.

In the 1920s and '30s, Beebe turned his attention from the jungle to the world beneath the sea. This was completely unexplored territory. A succession of patrons provided Beebe with boats that he turned into floating laboratories. Harrison Williams backed the Galápagos expedition in 1923 and the great *Arcturus* adventure of 1925, which explored underwater life from the Sargasso Sea to the Galápagos, using silk nets and other devices to gather up a vast variety of deep-sea creatures, from microorganisms to giant sharks and many forms unknown to science.

In 1929, Beebe established the Society's marine research station at Nonsuch Island, Bermuda, where his staff included several longtime associates: Gloria Hollister; Jocelyn Crane, who would one day assume Beebe's duties at the Department of Tropical Research; and John Tee Van, who, after twenty-five years in the field with Beebe, would become the Society's executive secretary in 1942, Bronx Zoo director in 1952, and general director of the zoo and aquarium in 1957.

By the early 1930s, Beebe's literary output had already made him something of a celebrity, but that decade's bathysphere dives made him a star. The deepest anyone had ever been beneath the ocean surface was a mere 525 feet, and when in 1934 Beebe and the craft's designer, Otis Barton, daringly descended 3,028 feet crammed into a steel ball just 4½ feet in diameter, the whole nation waited for news. In 1932, thanks to a cable and a telephone hookup, Beebe's observations had been transmitted to radios everywhere by the National Broadcasting Company. It was that era's version of a media event, and millions listened, eager for news of a world that had never before been visited by a human being. The publicity generated by the dive was important, but Beebe was well aware that its scientific value was limited (as was the value of dredging fishes wholesale from the deep). Ultimately, he found it more instructive and more satisfying to don a diving helmet and settle down in shallower waters where he could closely observe the live workings of marine environments.

World War II forced the abandonment of the Bermuda station, and Beebe's department moved to Venezuela, where his attention returned to the jungle. Beebe purchased 228 acres of paradise at Simla, in the Arima Valley of Trinidad, and the department moved to that remote region with its rich and varied fauna in 1950. Beebe deeded this property to the Society, and upon his retirement in 1952 he remained at Simla as director emeritus, continuing to study the workings of nature until his death ten years later.

As a scientist, Beebe was demanding and rigorous. He wrote some eight hundred meticulously detailed technical articles, making important contributions to numerous fields, including ornithology, icthyology, mammalogy, entomology, and oceanography. Along with other firsts, he merits the title of "world's first neotropical ecologist." He conducted more than sixty expeditions and discovered hundreds of previously unknown species of animals, scores of which now bear his name. But in the popular imagination

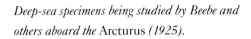

Deep-sea specimens being studied by Beebe and others aboard the Arcturus *(1925).*

he was a romantic hero. In his pith helmet or diving gear, Beebe seemed dashing, living a life full of adventure. Because of him, generations of children have dreamed of becoming naturalists. In the course of his long career, Beebe worked with every director of the Society, serving as mentor to some, including the present director, William Conway, whose early career included expeditionary work with Beebe at Simla. No one has had a more profound—or more colorful—effect on the direction and fortunes of the Wildlife Conservation Society.

A Masterpiece of Evolution

Earth has few secrets from the birds. With wings and legs there is hardly a spot to which they cannot and indeed have not penetrated. Some find food and contentment in the desolate wastes of the far North; others spend almost all of their life on or above the sea far from land; thousands revel in the luxuriance of reeking tropical jungles; a lesser number are as perfectly suited to the blazing dust of the desert; and there are birds which burrow deep into the very earth itself. Day and night; heat and cold; water, earth, and air, have all been conquered by the thirteen or fourteen thousand species of birds which share the earth with us at the present day.

These brethren of ours, whose clans have so bravely conquered the dangers of millions of years, and at last have gained a foremost rank in the scale of living creatures, now find themselves face to face with the culminating effort of Nature,—Mankind. They cannot escape from us, though the least among them laughs to scorn our efforts at following through the air. Yet all

WILLIAM BEEBE

from "Ancestors"

THE BIRD, 1906

Scarlet macaws.

Keel-billed toucan.

must return sooner or later to earth for rest and food, and thus all are at our mercy.

Let us beware of needlessly destroying even one of the lives—so sublimely crowning the ages upon ages of evolving; and let us put forth all our efforts to save a threatened species from extinction; to give hearty aid to the last few individuals pitifully struggling to avoid absolute annihilation.

The beauty and genius of a work of art may be reconceived, though its first material expression be destroyed; a vanished harmony may yet again inspire the composer; but when the last individual of a race of living beings breathes no more, another heaven and another earth must pass before such a one can be again.

MIGRATION NIGHT—1904

WILLIAM BEEBE

from "Migration Night—1904"

ANIMAL KINGDOM, BULLETIN OF THE
NEW YORK ZOOLOGICAL SOCIETY,
APRIL 1954

William Beebe was ever alive to nature, even in the stony jungle of New York, and his fascination with birds led him in 1904 to the top of the Statue of Liberty, where he observed their night migration. Recent springs have offered but a ghost of the great migrations of Beebe's day. Warblers, in particular, have declined, with some species perhaps doomed to disappear forever by Migration Night—2004.

To write honestly and with conviction anything about the migration of birds, one should oneself have migrated. Somehow or other we should dehumanize ourselves, feel the feel of feathers on our body and wind in our wings, and finally know what it is to leave abundance and safety and daylight and yield to a compelling instinct, age-old, seeming at the time quite devoid of reason and object.

We are concerned here only with the Unseen in New York—the nocturnal aspects of bird migration. Most small birds migrate at night apparently with two outstanding advantages. The first is avoidance of attacks by hawks and other enemies, and second, the use of hours when feeding is impossible. Students of migration must blame these night activities for creating a mental hazard in themselves, of utter confusion. If all birds migrated in the daytime, migration might be explained, at least in part, as a matter of eyesight. Night voyaging upsets all such theories and we must admit we have no clear-cut explanation of how birds find their way through hour after hour, and night after night of darkness, and over hundreds and thousands of miles of land and sea. . . .

Many years ago (50 to be exact, in 1904) I had a memorable experience watching birds on migration, high in the air, within the limits of Greater New York. In company with Mr. Madison Grant, Secretary of the Zoological Society, I obtained permission from the city authorities to spend a night in the top of the Statue of Liberty. This was about mid-May, a time when migration ought to be at its height. We caught the last boat to Bedloe's Island, and on its return trip it carried away the final sight-seer, reducing the population to the Superintendent, his assistant, Mr. Grant and myself.

My first activity was rather comparable to mountain climbing. It was not the actual mounting of one hundred and sixty-eight steps from the base to the summit, but the difficulty of toting a blanket, lantern, food and binoculars up the narrow convolutions of the circular stairway. I finally had to make two trips, and unloaded in the crown of the noble goddess. As if I were planning an assault on Mount Everest, I made my base camp in the crown and my advance perch or roost in the torch.

In early evening, a downward look toward the water of the bay, three hundred feet below, showed the wakes of tugs and steamers, stretching out in long, well-defined lines, intersecting one another like the strands of a gigantic, waving cobweb. The day had been clear, but as the sun sank lower, clouds collected, and soon there began that most wonderful of earthly sights—an ever familiar, ever new sunset. The sun became obscured but I knew when it sank below the hidden horizon by the sunset guns echoing from fort to fort.

Half an hour later the whole outlook had changed. After the beacon of the statue had been turned on, a feeling of complete isolation became very real, and the distant glimmering lights of the city made this sensation more intense. One felt suspended in midair with no apparent contact with sea or land.

I climbed the vertical ladder on to the narrow duckwalk around the torch itself and prepared to take a short nap before beginning my migration vigil. Hardly had I closed my eyes when a new characteristic of the copper giantess became apparent—she swayed. I was told this oscillation was through a twenty-four-inch arc, back and forth, and that it had something to do with the safety stresses of the whole structure. As long as I remained conscious, the movement was soothing, somewhat like the swinging of a hammock. When sleep closed down, the mobility changed from oscillation to acceleration, and several times I awoke and sat up terrified, certain that the massive figure was hurtling to the ground. I have had a similar sensation three other times, in the midst of the sickening waves of violent earthquakes.

The night had suddenly turned cold, a breeze arose and I changed my pallet to the wooden platform at the head of the stairway. With the rising wind the hollow statue came to life. During the day, with many people passing up and down, the echoes would be confused and not particularly noticeable. With the absence of humanity and the presence of a wind, the sounds became weird and awesome. I dropped a loose bolt which I had picked up, and the reverberations increased by echoes and distance, until, from far down, they sounded like thunder on distant mountains. The scratching of a pin was taken up and magnified until the screakings died out in uttermost coppery hollows. When I laughed and shouted aloud, there resulted a pandemonium of tortured devils yelling back at me. Long after all seemed quiet, a faint squeak, squeak, came softly to the ear, perhaps a mouse feeding on crumbs dropped by some sight-seer.

At eleven o'clock I mounted again to the torch. The wind had quieted down, but haze was drifting up the bay and down from the sky. Every few seconds the sound of bird voices came from overhead; the peet-sweet of a sandpiper, the croak of perhaps a green heron, the thin notes of warblers and the more palpable chirps of sparrows. The haze changed to fog, and now, to the chorus of bird voices, there was added the occasional, distant, sonorous bass of a foghorn. Several times birds called from below my level, and then, without warning, something hurtled past my head, struck, and fell at my feet—a warm, palpitating but dying Magnolia Warbler.

The most surprising event of the entire night was a burst of song from two birds, heard a half-hour apart. The first, I am certain, was a Red-eyed Vireo. Five of the brief, thrushlike phrases came to my ear. The first was dim in the distance, three others were hurried and close, one as the bird actually passed almost within sight. The fifth was half lost in a foghorn.

On October 15, 1887, Leslie's Illustrated Weekly *depicted the night when 1,375 birds crashed into Liberty's torch and died.*

The Statue of Liberty from Battery Park around the turn of the century.

The second song was the unmistakable four-syllabled utterance of a Goldfinch. A single phrase came out of the fog, then the beginning of a second, apparently given as the bird passed, for the call rose into an indeterminate screech as it receded into the distance. I wondered at the emotion—a perfect example of displacement behavior—which prompted such an utterance under such inappropriate conditions.

As the fog increased and condensed in the warmth to almost rain, birds began to pass through the periphery of illumination, then to strike intermittently against railing and glass. I crouched low behind what protection I could find, to avoid being hit. One warbler flew against my coat and sank down panting. They came in waves, a few scattered birds, then a mob, swift and dense as a swarm of golden bees. All appeared bright and shining as they passed. Occasionally a dozen or more would seem to come in obliquely to the general line of flight, and at slower speed. In this case they would all keep on to the light, but put their feather brakes on in time, so that I would have five or six sparrows clinging to me unharmed, wings spread, heads back, panting.

For the period of a few hours I was permitted to share the feelings and activities of birds on migration, sensing altitude, isolation, darkness, wind, speed and the awful confusion and dangers of light-in-fog.

At three o'clock in the morning the fog had lifted, and there was neither sight nor sound of a bird. They had flown down somewhere to a precarious landing in the thinning fog, or had reascended to migration levels. I climbed again into the torch and watched for the first hint of dawn and life. The first came almost imperceptibly as a pale line of gradually brightening light; the latter was startling. A Herring Gull, all gray and white, swung swiftly toward me from the direction of the sea, shrieked when it saw my muffled figure and passed up river. The gull presented a double surprise for at this time of year it must have been a maverick of sorts, and should have been with its fellows on some distant breeding grounds. Prosaic tugs appeared and smoke arose from a hundred chimneys: a new day had begun over New York City.

I descended and joined Mr. Grant. He had been with me for an hour of migration watching, but after that had chosen to finish the night in a guest room at the foot of the statue. Later on, we picked up two hundred and seventy-one dead birds on the ground around the base. We were told of one tragic night when more than fourteen hundred lost their lives. Thanks to the protests of bird lovers and especially half-dazzled pilots of passing vessels, the light of the statue was diminished and rendered indirect, so that, in more recent years, there have been very few avian casualties. A visit today to the great Statue of Liberty must be as memorable as ever, except that access to the torch is no longer permitted to the public.

In the intervening half-century Miss Liberty has witnessed many radical changes within her field of view. Perhaps the most spectacular are the non-migratory airplanes which roar past by day and night, guided by compass, radio, radar and other direction-finding gadgets. Far overhead numberless birds are still passing, exactly as they have for thousands upon thousands of springs and autumns, guided by means which still are a mystery to us.

The
Pheasant Expedition

J. F. Gray. Temminck's Tragopan. "Its home is
in the great heart of China among the oaks and
rhododendrons of high altitudes" (Beebe's caption
in the January 1919 Bulletin). Colorplate from
Beebe's A Monograph of the Pheasants.

*Leaving New York on December 26, 1909,
and returning on May 27, 1911, William
Beebe and his first wife, the novelist Mary
Blair, spent seventeen months in search of
Asian pheasants, visiting twenty countries
and traveling about fifty-two thousand
miles. Carrying heavy cameras and other
equipment, they trekked above fifteen thousand feet in the Himalayas and explored
the dense jungles of Borneo, Sumatra,
Java, the Malay States, and Burma. In
eastern China, they were met by plague,
riots, and violent snowstorms, and in
Mongolia they crossed the bleak deserts
by palanquin and camel. Beebe's studies,
published in the lavish four-volume*
A Monograph of the Pheasants
*(1918–22), still provide the basis for
most taxonomic classifications of pheas-
ant-like birds. At the end of his expedition,
he wrote in the July 1911* Zoological
Society Bulletin, *"Within a very few
years, many of the species of pheasants
will have vanished utterly from the face of
the earth," due to human settlement, forest
destruction for rubber culture, native bird
trapping, and the export of pheasants and
their plumes to Europe and elsewhere.*

Beebe and his wife view the Himalayas (1910).

Chinese headman Sin-Ma-How pointing out where the silver pheasant could be found near the borders of Burma, Tibet, and China.

Beebe with jungle fowl in China.

Mountain haunts of the green peafowl in central Java. "From the tent door, I looked out across a magnificent gorge to a high, misty waterfall beyond. . . . At last came the wholly unexpected sight of three Green Peafowl, two with long trains, shooting like meteors across the rainbowed depths. They appeared, glowed like opals in the low-slanted rays, and vanished" (Beebe's caption in the March 1923 Bulletin).

WILLIAM BEEBE

———

from "The Hills of Hills"
PHEASANT JUNGLES, 1927

*Although Beebe was in Asia in 1910 and
1911 to study pheasants, his adventures in
the jungles of Ceylon, Sikkim, Garhwal,
Burma, Tibet, Yunnan, Pahang, and Borneo
provided him with enough material for
wide-ranging essays, many of which are
included in* Pheasant Jungles. *Much of
this book was written years after the expedition ended, and while Beebe was sometimes
accused of embellishing his experiences, he
also amazed many with demonstrations of
a near-photographic memory.*

The Eastern Himalayan home of six pheasants.

I walked quickly, for I knew my ground, and climbing five or six hundred
feet, reached the ridge breathless, but before the sun rose. Keeping well
hidden on the nearer side, I crept several hundred yards farther on, and, in
the swiftly strengthening dawn light, slipped through a boulder scar to my
chosen hiding place between an outjutting mass of rocks and two ancient
deodars. Beneath me were spruce, fir, deodars, and oaks rising straight as
plummets from the steep slope. Every few yards the trees thinned out into
open, park-like vistas, carpeted with smooth natural lawns. In one place
the grass was starred with myriads of purple and white anemones, but the
dominant blossoms were long-stemmed strawberries which grew eight to
the foot for acres. I had hardly settled myself and swiveled my glasses to
sweep the field ahead when tragedy descended. With a swish of wings
which rose to a roar as they passed, an eagle dropped from nowhere, seized
some small creature, and with hardly a pause launched out over the valley
and out of sight. The tip of a great pinion brushed a shower of dew from a
spruce branch as the bird labored outward, and I found myself staring at
swaying needles and wondering whether what had passed was reality or a
vision. Hardly had the branch settled to rest than a small green warbler flew
to it and chanted an absurdly confident ditty. The unconsciousness of the
diminutive feathered creature increased the unreality of the tremendously
dynamic display of power a second before.

As I mused on this startling introduction to the day's observation, the
narrowness of us humans came to mind more vividly than ever. With such
antitheses to stir the most sluggish blood, how can any real lover of nature
and the wilderness of earth fail to react? My wonder is not with mediocre
work. Many of us can never hope to reach the clear heights of quick dynamic thought, and the genius of generalization which in the last analysis is the
only *raison d'etre* of facts and the search for facts. Most of us must be content to gather the bricks and beams and tiles in readiness for the great architect who shall use them, making them fulfill their destiny if only in
rejection. But I marvel that men can spend whole lives in studying the life
of the planet, watching its creatures run the gamut from love to hate, brav-
ery to fear, success to failure, life to death, and not at least be greatly moved
by the extremes possible to our own existences. Why should science dull
our reaction to the theme of "Louise"? Why should technicalities dry the
emotion when a master makes Beau Brummel live again? Why should paleontology or taxonomy detract a whit from "McAndrew's Hymn" or "the
Jabberwocky"? Must sagittal sections and diagrams ever deaden one's
appreciation of Böcklin and Rodin? Why should a geologist on a ballroom
floor, or a botanist in the front row of a light-opera audience be considered
worthy objects of abstract humor, instead of evincing a corresponding
breadth of real humanness? Is it inevitable that occipital condyles and
operas, parietals and poetry, squamosals and sculpture must be beloved by
different individuals?

But the end of the minute's mood which conceived these wild thoughts
brought me back to my perch among the deodars, and, like an apt moral, to

another antithesis, a tragedy at my finger-tips among the infinitely small. Along the half-decayed bark of a tree fallen across the front of my hiding-place, a huge slug made its way. All unknown to me, this slug was a stranger to scientific mankind, and in the course of time he was to be examined half-way round the world by one learned in the structure of slugs, and to be christened with the name of his discoverer. But we were both wholly unconscious of this present lack and impending honor, quite as much as the race of *Anadenus beebei* is still happy in its ignorance of our altered god-fatheral relations.

The great mollusk crept along the damp bark, leaving a broad shining wake of mucus, then tacked slowly and made its way back. In the mean-time various creatures, several flies and spiders and two wood-roaches, had sought to cross or alight on the sticky trail and had been caught. Down upon them bore the giant slug and, inevitable as fate, reached and crushed them, sucking down the unfortunates beneath its leaden sides, its four, eyed tentacles playing horribly all the while. The whole performance was so slow and certain, the slug so hideous, and my close view so lacking in perspective, that the sensation was of creatures of much larger size being slaughtered.

The comparison of this lowly tragedy of slime with the terrific rush and attack of the eagle from out of the heart of the sky tempted one to thoughts even more weird than I have expressed.

Beebe and assistant heliographing at Sansi Gorge, Burma.

OPALINA'S STORY

This is the story of Opalina
Who lived in the Tad,
Who became the Frog,
Who was eaten by Fish,
Who nourished the Snake,
Who was caught by the Owl,
But fed the Vulture,
Who was shot by Me,
Who wrote this Tale,
Which the Editor took,
And published it Here,
To be read by You,
The last in The Chain,
Of Life in the Tropical Jungle.

I offer a living chain of ten links—the first a tiny delicate being, one hundred to the inch, deep in the jungle, with the strangest home in the world—my last, you the present reader of these lines. Between, there befell certain things, of which I attempt falteringly to write. To know and think them is very worth while, to have discovered them is sheer joy, but to write of them is impertinence, so exciting and unreal are they in reality, and so tame and humdrum are any combinations of our twenty-six letters.

WILLIAM BEEBE

"A Chain of Jungle Life"
JUNGLE DAYS, 1925

Beebe contributed much to the emerging realization of the ecological significance of the food chain, which the English zoologist Charles Elton formalized in his book of 1927, Animal Ecology. *Beebe's interest in connections naturally led him to study who is food for what, and his concentration on a delimited wilderness area helped him make such identifications. The activities of Beebe's department at the Kartabo research station in British Guiana, where this piece was written, were focused on an area no more than half a mile from the station in any direction. But Beebe also made intense studies of the wildlife in a single square yard of jungle, a single tree, or an hour of walking. As a result, Beebe came to know his jungle intimately, and indeed, he talks about the creatures in this food chain as if they were old friends.*

Beebe in field gear, British Guiana.

Somewhere today a worm has given up existence, a mouse has been slain, a spider snatched from the web, a jungle bird torn sleeping from its perch; else we should have no song of robin, nor flash of reynard's red, no humming flight of wasp, nor grace of crouching ocelot. In tropical jungles, in Northern home orchards, anywhere you will, unnumbered activities of bird and beast and insect require daily toll of life.

Now and then we actually witness one of these tragedies or successes—whichever point of view we take—appearing to us as an exciting but isolated event. When once we grasp the idea of chains of life, each of these occurrences assumes a new meaning. Like everything else in the world it is not isolated, but closely linked with other similar happenings. I have sometimes traced even closed chains, one of the shortest of which consisted of predacious flycatchers which fed upon young lizards of a species which, when it grew up, climbed trees and devoured the nestling flycatchers!

One of the most wonderful zoological "Houses that Jack built," was this of Opalina's, a long, swinging, exciting chain, including in its links a Proto-zoan, two stages of Amphibians, a Fish, a Reptile, two Birds and (unless some intervening act of legislature bars the fact as immoral and illegal) three Mammals,—myself, the Editor, and You.

As I do not want to make it into a mere imaginary animal story, however probable, I will begin, like Dickens, in the middle. I can cope, however lamely, with the entrance and participation of the earlier links, but am wholly out of my depth from the time when I mail my tale. The Akawai Indian who took it upon its first lap toward the Editor should by rights have a place in the chain, especially when I think how much better he might tell of the interrelationships of the various links than can I. Still, I know the shape of the owl's wings when it dropped upon the snake, but I do not know why the Editor accepted this; I can imitate the death scream of the frog when the fish seized it, but I have no idea why You purchased this volume nor whether you perceive in my tale the huge bed of ignorance in which I have planted this scanty crop of facts. Nor do I know the future of this book, whether it will go to the garret, to be ferreted out in future years by other links, as I used to do, or whether it will find its way to mid-Asia or the Malay States, or, as I once saw a magazine, half buried, like the pyramids, in Saharan sands, where it had slipped from the camel load of some unknown traveller.

I left my Kartabo laboratory one morning with my gun, headed for the old Dutch stelling. Happening to glance up I saw a mote, lit with the oblique rays of the morning sun. The mote drifted about in circles, which became spirals; the mote became a dot, then a spot, then an oblong, and down the heavens from unknown heights, with the whole of British Guiana spread out beneath him from which to choose, swept a vulture into my very path. We had a quintet, a small flock of our own vultures who came sifting down the sky, day after day, to the feasts of monkey bodies and wild peccaries which we spread for them. I knew all these by sight, from one peculiarity or another, for I was accustomed to watch them hour after hour, striving to learn something of that wonderful soaring, of which all my many hours of flying had taught me nothing.

This bird was a stranger, perhaps from the coast or the inland savannas, for to these birds great spaces are only matters of brief moments. I wanted a yellow-headed vulture, both for the painting of its marvelous head colors, and for the strange, intensely interesting, one-sided, down-at-the-heel syrinx, which, with the voice, had dissolved long ages ago, leaving only a whistling breath, and an irregular complex of bones straggling over the windpipe. Some day I shall dilate upon vultures as pets—being surpassed in cleanliness, affectionateness and tameness only by baby bears, sloths and certain monkeys.

But today I wanted the newcomer as a specimen. I was surprised to see that he did not head for the regular vulture table, but slid along a slant of the east wind, banked around its side, spreading and curling upward his wing-finger-tips and finally resting against its front edge. Down this he sank slowly, balancing with the grace of perfect mastery, and again swung round and settled suddenly down shore, beyond a web of mangrove roots. This took me by surprise, and I changed my route and pushed through the undergrowth of young palms. Before I came within sight, the bird heard me, rose with a whipping of great pinions and swept around three-fourths of a circle before I could catch enough of a glimpse to drop him. The impetus carried him on and completed the circle, and when I came out on the Cuyuni shore I saw him spread out on what must have been the exact spot from which he had risen.

I walked along a greenheart log with little crabs scuttling off on each side, and as I looked ahead at the vulture I saw to my great surprise that it had more colors than any yellow-headed vulture should have, and its plumage was somehow very different. This excited me so that I promptly slipped off the log and joined the crabs in the mud. Paying more attention to my steps I did not again look up until I had reached the tuft of low reeds on which the bird lay. Now at last I understood why my bird had metamorphosed in death, and also why it had chosen to descend to this spot. Instead of one bird, there were two and a reptile. Another tragedy had taken place a few hours earlier, before dawn, a double death, and the sight of these three creatures brought to mind at once the chain for which I am always on the lookout. I picked up my chain by the middle and began searching both ways for the missing links.

The vulture lay with magnificent wings outspread, partly covering a big, spectacled owl, whose dishevelled plumage was in turn wrapped about by several coils of a moderate-sized anaconda. Here was an excellent beginning for my chain, and at once I visualized myself and the snake, although alternate links, yet coupled in contradistinction to my editor and the vulture, the first two having entered the chain by means of death, whereas the vulture had simply joined in the pacifistic manner of its kind, and as my editor has dealt gently with me heretofore, I allowed myself to believe that his entrance might also be through no more rough handling than a blue slip.

The head of the vulture was already losing some of its brilliant chrome and saffron, so I took it up, noted the conditions of the surrounding sandy mud, and gathered together my spoils. I would have passed within a few feet of the owl and the snake and never discovered them, so close were they in color to the dark reddish beach, yet the vulture with its small eyes and minute nerves had detected this tragedy when still perhaps a mile high in the air, or half a mile up river. There could have been no odor, nor has the bird any adequate nostrils to detect it, had there been one. It was sheer keenness of vision. I looked at the bird's claws and their weakness showed the necessity of the eternal search for carrion or recently killed creatures. Here in a half minute, it had devoured an eye of the owl and both of those of the serpent. It is a curious thing, this predilection for eyes; give a monkey a fish, and the eyes are the first tidbits taken.

Through the vulture I come to the owl link, a splendid bird clad in the colors of its time of hunting; a great, soft, dark, shadow of a bird, with tiny body and long fluffy plumage of twilight buff and ebony night, lit by twin, orange moons of eyes. The name "spectacled owl" is really more applicable to the downy nestling which is like a white powder puff with two dark feathery spectacles around the eyes. Its name is one of those which I am fond of repeating rapidly—*Pulsatrix perspicillata perspicillata*. Etymologies do not grow in the jungle and my memory is noted only for its consistent vagueness, but if the owl's title does not mean The Eye-browed One Who Strikes, it ought to, especially as the subspecific trinomial grants it two eye-brows.

I would give much to know just what the beginning of the combat was like. The middle I could reconstruct without question, and the end was only too apparent. By a most singular coincidence, a few years before, and less than three miles away, I had found the desiccated remains of another spectacled owl mingled with the bones of a snake, only in that instance, the fangs indicated a small fer-de-lance, the owl having succumbed to its venom. This time the owl had rashly attacked a serpent far too heavy for it to lift, or even, as it turned out, successfully to battle with. The mud had been churned up for a foot in all directions, and the bird's plumage showed that it must have rolled over and over. The anaconda, having just fed, had come out of the water and was probably stretched out on the sand and mud, as I have seen them, both by full sun and in the moonlight. These owls are birds rather of the creeks and river banks than of the deep jungle, and in their food I have found shrimps, crabs, fish and young birds. Once a few snake vertebrae showed that these reptiles are occasionally killed and devoured.

Whatever possessed the bird to strike its talons deep into the neck and back of this anaconda, none but the owl could say, but from then on the story was written by the combatants and their environment. The snake, like a flash, threw two coils around bird, wings and all, and clamped these tight with a cross vise of muscle. The tighter the coils compressed the deeper the talons of the bird were driven in, but the damage was done with the first strike, and if owl and snake had parted at this moment, neither could have survived. It was a swift, terrible and short fight. The snake could not use its teeth and the bird had no time to bring its beak into play, and there in the night, with the lapping waves of the falling tide only two or three feet away, the two creatures of prey met and fought and died, in darkness and silence, locked fast together.

A few nights before I had heard, on the opposite side of the bungalow, the deep, sonorous cry of the spectacled owl; within the week I had passed the line-and-crescents track of anacondas, one about the size of this snake and another much larger. And now fate had linked their lives, or rather deaths, with my life, using her divining rod, the focussing of a sky-soaring vulture.

The owl had not fed that evening, although the bird was so well nourished that it could never have been driven to its foolhardy feat by stress of hunger. Hopeful of lengthening the chain, I rejoiced to see a suspicious swelling about the middle of the snake, which dissection resolved into a good-sized fish—itself carnivorous, locally called a basha. This was the first time I had known one of these fish to fall a victim to a land creature, except in the case of a big kingfisher who had caught two small ones. Like the owl and anaconda, bashas are nocturnal in their activities, and, according to their size, feed on small shrimps, big shrimps, and so on up to six or eight inch catfish. They are built on swift, torpedo-like lines, and clad in iridescent silver mail.

From what I have seen of the habits of anacondas, I should say that this one had left its hole high up among the upper beach roots late in the night, and softly wound its way down into the rising tide. Here after drinking, the snake sometimes pursues and catches small fish and frogs, but the usual method is to coil up beside a half-buried stick or log and await the tide and the manna it brings. In the van of the waters comes a host of small fry, followed by their pursuers or by larger vegetable feeders, and the serpent has but to choose. In this mangrove lagoon then, there must have been a swirl

Forest near Kartabo.

and a splash, a passive holding fast by the snake for a while until the right opportunity offered, and then a swift throw of coils. There must then be no mistake as to orientation of the fish. It would be a fatal error to attempt the tail first, with scales on end and serried spines to pierce the thickest tissues. It is beyond my knowledge how one of these fish can be swallowed even head first without serious laceration. But here was optical proof of its possibility, a newly swallowed basha, so recently caught that he appeared as in life, with even the delicate turquoise pigment beneath his scales, acting on his silvery armor as quicksilver under glass. The tooth marks of the snake were still clearly visible on the scales,—another link, going steadily down the classes of vertebrates, mammal, bird, reptile and fish, and still my magic boxes were unexhausted.

Excitedly I cut open the fish. An organism more unlike that of the snake would be hard to imagine. There I had followed an elongated stomach, and had left unexplored many feet of alimentary canal. Here, the fish had his heart literally in his mouth, while his liver and lights were only a very short distance behind, followed by a great expanse of tail to wag him at its will, and drive him through the water with the speed of twin propellers. His eyes are wonderful for night hunting, large, wide, and bent in the middle so he can see both above and on each side. But all this wide-angled vision availed nothing against the lidless, motionless watch of the ambushed anaconda. Searching the crevices of the rocks and logs for timorous small fry, the basha had sculled too close, and the jaws which closed upon him were backed by too much muscle, and too perfect a throttling machine to allow of the least chance of escape. It was a big basha compared with the moderate-sized snake but the fierce eyes had judged well, as the evidence before me proved.

Still my chain held true, and in the stomach of the basha I found what I wanted—another link, and more than I could have hoped for—a representative of the fifth and last class of vertebrate animals living on the earth, an Amphibian, an enormous frog. This too had been a swift-forged link, so recent that digestion had only affected the head of the creature. I drew it out, set it upon its great squat legs, and there was a grandmother frog almost as in life, a Pok-poke as the Indians call it, or, as a herpetologist would prefer, *Leptodactylus caliginosus*,—the Smoky Jungle Frog.

She lived in the jungle just behind, where she and a sister of hers had their curious nests of foam, which they guarded from danger, while the tadpoles grew and squirmed within its sudsy mesh as if there were no water in the world. I had watched one of the two, perhaps this one, for hours, and I saw her dart angrily after little fish which came too near. Then, this night, the high full-moon tides had swept over the barrier back of the mangrove roots and set the tadpoles free, and the mother frogs were at liberty to go where they pleased.

From my cot in the bungalow to the south, I had heard in the early part of the night, the death scream of a frog, and it must have been at that moment that somehow the basha had caught the great amphibian. This frog is one of the fiercest of its class, and captures mice, reptiles and small fish without trouble. It is even cannibalistic on very slight provocation, and two of equal size will sometimes endeavor to swallow one another in the most appallingly matter-of-fact manner.

They represent the opposite extreme in temperament from the pleasantly philosophical giant toads. In outward appearance in the dim light of dusk, the two groups are not unlike, but the moment they are taken in the hand all doubt ceases. After one dive for freedom the toad resigns himself to fate, only venting his spleen in much puffing out of his sides, while the frog either fights until exhausted, or pretends death until opportunity offers for a last mad dash.

In this case the frog must have leaped into the deep water beyond the usual barrier and while swimming been attacked by the equally voracious fish. In addition to the regular croak of this species, it has a most unexpected and unamphibian yell or scream, given only when it thinks itself at the last extremity. It is most unnerving when the frog, held firmly by the hind legs, suddenly puts its whole soul into an ear-splitting *peent! peent! peent! peent! peent!*

Many a time they are probably saved from death by this cry which startles like a sudden blow, but tonight no utterance in the world could have saved it; its assailant was dumb and all but deaf to aerial sounds. Its cries were smothered in the water as the fish dived and nuzzled it about the roots, as bashas do with their food,—and it became another link in the chain.

Like a miser with one unfilled coffer, or a gambler with an unfilled royal flush, I went eagerly at the frog with forceps and scalpel. But beyond a meagre residuum of eggs, there was nothing but shrunken organs in its body. The rashness of its venture into river water was perhaps prompted by hunger after its long maternal fast while it watched over its egg-filled nest of foam.

Hopeful to the last, I scrape some mucus from its food canal, place it in a drop of water under my microscope, and—discover Opalina, my last link, which in the course of its most astonishing life history gives me still another.

To the naked eye there is nothing visible—the water seems clear, but when I enlarge the diameter of magnification I lift the veil on another

Field tent used for preparing specimens at Kartabo (1919).

world, and there swim into view a dozen minute lives, oval little beings covered with curving lines, giving the appearance of wandering finger prints. In some lights these are iridescent and they then will deserve the name of Opalina. As for their personality, they are oval and rather flat, it would take one hundred of them to stretch an inch, they have no mouth, and they are covered with a fur of flagella with which they whip themselves through the water. Indeed the whole of their little selves consists of a multitude of nuclei, sometimes as many as two hundred, exactly alike,—facial expression, profile, torso, limbs, pose, all are summed up in rounded nuclei, partly obscured by a mist of vibrating flagella.

As for their gait, they move along with colorful waves, steadily and gently, not keeping an absolutely straight course and making rather much leeway, as any rounded, keelless craft, surrounded with its own paddle-wheels, must expect to do.

I have placed Opalina under very strange and unpleasant conditions in thus subjecting it to the inhospitable qualities of a drop of clear water. Even as I watch, it begins to slow down, and the flagella move less rapidly and evenly. It prefers an environment far different, where I discovered it living happily and contentedly in the stomach and intestines of a frog, where its iridescence was lost, or rather had never existed in the absolute darkness; where its delicate hairs must often be unmercifully crushed and bent in the ever-moving tube, and where air and sky, trees and sun, sound and color were forever unknown; in their place only bits of half-digested ants and beetles, thousand-legs and worms, rolled and tumbled along in the dense gastric stream of acid pepsin; a strange choice of home for one of our fellow living beings on the earth.

After an Opalina has flagellated itself about, and fed for a time in its strange, almost crystalline way on the juices of its host's food, its body begins to contract, and narrows across the center until it looks somewhat like a map of the New World. Finally its isthmus thread breaks and two Opalinas swim placidly off, both identical, except that they have half the number of nuclei as before. We cannot wonder that there is no backward glance, or wave of cilia, or even memory of their other body, for they are themselves, or rather it is they, or it is each: our whole vocabulary, our entire stock of pronouns breaks down, our very conception of individuality is shattered by the life of Opalina.

Each daughter cell or self-twin, or whatever we choose to conceive it, divides in turn. Finally there comes a day (or rather some Einstein period of space-time, for there are no days in a frog's stomach!) when Opalina's fraction has reached a stage with only two nuclei. When this has creased and stretched, and finally broken like two bits of drawn-out molasses candy, we have the last divisional possibility. The time for the great adventure has arrived, with decks cleared for action, or, as a protozoologist would put it, with the flagellate's protoplasm uni-nucleate, approximating encystment.

The encysting process is but slightly understood, but the tiny one-two-hundredth-of-its-former-self-Opalina curls up, its paddle-wheels run down, it forms a shell, and rolls into the current which it has withstood for a Protozoan's lifetime. Out into the world drifts the minute ball of latent life, a plaything of the cosmos, permitted neither to see, hear, eat, nor to move of its own volition. It hopes (only it cannot even desire) to find itself in water, it must fall or be washed into a pool with tadpoles, one of which must come along at the right moment and swallow it with the debris upon which it rests. The possibility of this elaborate concatenation of events has everything against it, and yet it must occur or death will result. No wonder that the population of Opalinas does not overstock its limited and retired environment!

Supposing that all happens as it should, and that the only chance in a hundred thousand comes to pass, the encysted being knows or is affected in some mysterious way by entrance into the body of the tadpole. The cyst is dissolved and the infant Opalina begins to feed and to develop new nuclei. Like the queen ant after she has been walled forever into her chamber, the life of the little Onecell would seem to be extremely sedentary and humdrum, in fact monotonous, until its turn comes to fractionize itself, and again severally to go into the outside world, multiplied and by installments. But as the queen ant had her one superlative day of sunlight, heavenly flight and a mate, so Opalina, while she is still wholly herself, has a little adventure all her own.

Let us strive to visualize her environment as it would appear to her if she could find time and ability, with her single cell, to do more than feed and bisect herself. Once free from her horny cyst she stretches her drop of a body, sets all her paddlehairs in motion and swims slowly off. If we suppose that she has been swallowed by a tadpole an inch long, her living quarters are astonishingly spacious or rather elongated. Passing from end to end she would find a living tube two feet in length, a dizzy path to traverse, as it is curled in a tight, many-whorled spiral,—the stairway, the domicile, the universe at present for Opalina. She is compelled to be a vegetarian, for nothing but masses of decayed leaf tissue and black mud and algae come down the stairway. For many days there is only the sound of water gurgling past the tadpole's gills, or glimpses of sticks and leaves and the occasional flash of a small fish through the thin skin periscope of its body.

Then the tadpole's mumbling even of half-rotted leaves comes to an end, and both it and its guests begin to fast. Down the whorls comes less and less of vegetable detritus, and Opalina must feel like the crew of a submarine when the food supply runs short. At the same time something very strange happens, the experience of which eludes our utmost imagination. Poe wrote a memorable tale of a prison cell which day by day grew smaller, and Opalina goes through much the same adventure. If she frequently traverses her tube, she finds it growing shorter and shorter. As it contracts, the spiral untwists and straightens out, while all the time the rations are cut off. A dark curtain of pigment is drawn across the epidermal periscope and as books of dire adventure say, "the horror of darkness is added to the terrible mental uncertainty." The whole movement of the organism changes; there is no longer the rush and swish of water, and the even, undulatory motion alters to a series of spasmodic jerks,—quite the opposite of ordinary transition from water to land. Instead of water rushing through the gills of her host, Opalina might now hear strange musical sounds, loud and low, the singing of insects, the soughing of swamp palms.

Opalina about this time, should be feeling very low in her mind from lack of food, and the uncertainty of explanation of why the larger her host grew, the smaller, more confined became her quarters. The tension is relieved at last by a new influx of provender, but no more inert mold or disintegrated leaves. Down the short, straight tube appears a live millipede, kicking as only a millipede can, with its thousand heels. Deserting for a moment Opalina's point of view, my scientific conscience insists on asserting itself to the effect that no millipede with which I am acquainted has even half a thousand legs. But not to quibble over details, even a few hundred kicking legs must make quite a commotion in Opalina's home, before the pepsin puts a quietus on the unwilling invader.

From now on there is no lack of food, for at each sudden jerk of the whole amphibian there comes down some animal or other. The vegetarian tadpole with its enormously lengthened digestive apparatus, has crawled out on land, fasting while the miracle is being wrought with its plumbing, and when the readjustment is made to more easily assimilated animal food, and it has become a frog, it forgets all about leaves and algae, and leaps after and captures almost any living creature which crosses its path and which is small enough to be engulfed.

With the refurnishing of her apartment and the sudden and complete change of diet, the exigencies of life are past for Opalina. She has now but to move blindly about, bathed in a stream of nutriment, and from time to time, nonchalantly to cut herself in twain. Only one other possibility awaits, that which occurred in the case of our Opalina. There comes a time when the sudden leap is not followed by an inrush of food, but by another leap and still another and finally a headlong dive, a splash and a rush of water, which, were protozoans given to reincarnated memory, might recall times long past. Suddenly came a violent spasm, then a terrible struggle, ending in a strange quiet: Opalina has become a link.

All motion is at an end, and instead of food comes compression, closer and closer shut the walls and soon they break down and a new fluid pours in. Opalina's cyst had dissolved readily in the tadpole's stomach, but her own body was able to withstand what all the food of tadpole and frog could not. If I had not wanted the painting of a vulture's head, little Opalina, together with the body of her life-long host, would have corroded and melted, and in the dark depths of the tropical waters her multitude of paddle-hairs, her more or fewer nuclei, all would have dissolved and been reabsorbed, to furnish their iota of energy to the swift silvery fish.

This flimsy little, sky-scraper castle of Jack's, built of isolated bricks of facts, gives a hint of the wonderland of correlation. Facts are necessary, but even a pack-rat can assemble a gallon of beans in a single night. To link facts together, to see them forming into a concrete whole; to make A fit into ARCH and ARCH into ARCHITECTURE, that is one great joy of life which, of all the links in my chain, only the Editor, You and I—the Mammals—can know.

TRIALS OF A HERPETOLOGIST

The snake remained locked in my satchel for several days, during completion of my business trip at São Paulo. There was a drought. The streams were dry. Several boys commissioned to get small fish or frogs were unable to catch a single one—and I couldn't find any goldfish for sale. It was my thought, however, that there would be no trouble in getting small fish at Rio. The serpent must wait a couple of days. All I had to do before starting to the coast again was to suggest a design for the serpent shipping boxes. It was my intention to swing the big series to the States without losses invariably attending reptile shipments over such a distance.

Back in the small hotel at Rio—the Gloria—and in the privacy of my room, I inspected the crimson and gold-ringed serpent. It had traveled among the clothing in my satchel. I placed it on the bed, where it glided slowly, peering over the edge. As a test of its appetite, for a fasting serpent will not always start feeding at once, I jumped my finger along the opposite side of the bed, in imitation of a frog. The creature rushed for my hand with open mouth. Something had to be done at once. I would spend the coming morning searching Rio for fish, or even going to the suburbs in search of a frog pond. That handsome serpent was going to shine in New York. The park had never had anything like it. For the time being it was quartered, within a now otherwise empty satchel, in a long drawer of a bureau, the key of which was in my pocket.

I walked and walked around Rio, but couldn't find any aquarium stores. A trip among the markets, in which there were booths where parrots and marmosets were sold, didn't help either. Either my Portuguese was poor, or they spotted me for an American, who might be induced to buy anything; for in the face of my inquiries for small, fresh-water fish, they offered me everything from dogs to monkeys.

On wearily walking back to the Gloria for luncheon my decision was for a couple of hours' rest, then ride to the end of some trolley line to look for a frog pond, if such things existed or were accessible. Not far from the hotel I made a discovery, which looked as if it might solve the problem. There was a fountain, with a large circular bowl; and in this were numerous small silvery fish. Placing a hand in the water I saw they were not very shy. They even swam toward my fingers in investigation.

The thing needed planning, and I sat on the stone coping to think it out. It would have to be a night job, as pedestrians in Rio are too curious to pass anything happening which is out of the ordinary. In the commendable fashion of leisurely enjoyment of life, which North Americans have cast to the winds, Brazilians will even tarry in fair-sized groups to see a man changing a tire. No, the thing had to be done at night, and fortunately there were no benches in the little park for loiterers. Another good point related to several radiating paths. They stretched a considerable distance. Nobody could suddenly pop around a corner—particularly a policeman. The latter was a serious consideration. Policemen in Rio are particularly impressive. They look like soldiers in parade uniform. Just then they were exceptionally vigilant, as a revolution was alleged to be brewing. The President had not ven-

RAYMOND L. DITMARS

from "A Night Job in Rio"

THRILLS OF A NATURALIST'S
QUEST, 1932

The scientific reputation of Raymond Ditmars was established in 1907 with the publication of Reptiles of North America. *He had been in love with snakes from an early age and his personal collection, kept in his parents' home, became the nucleus of the zoological park's collection when he was put in charge of reptiles by Director Hornaday in 1899. That collection grew, in large part thanks to Ditmars' collecting trips to Europe, most of the United States, and Central and South America, during which he was willing to go to great lengths to secure striking and interesting specimens for the zoo's collection. In this description of his ingenious and determined effort to keep a rare fish-eating species of* Liophis *alive until it could be transported from Brazil to the Bronx, Ditmars' enthusiasm for his work, his love of snakes, and his popular touch are evident.*

Ditmars checks a shipment of reptiles to the zoo.

tured from his palace for weeks. A man catching fish in a fountain at night might be harmlessly enough engaged, but could get into a heap of trouble if discovered by a policeman with jumpy nerves. I was, of course, omitting permission to capture fish at this fountain. There was no doubt that if I sought to get a permit, the red tape of Brazilian formalities would drag past the period when the serpent had starved to death. I was figuring on a properly humane act; but it required planning and stealth. I was gratified to note that a suspended electric light—not too near—would render nocturnal operation possible.

There were several details to be planned in doing this job. I thought them out on the way back to the hotel for luncheon. The matter of getting a small net, and keeping it secreted, bothered me. The handle would have to be cut off.

I stopped to light a cigarette in the shelter of the indented door of a hat store, as a breeze was sweeping across Beira Mar. That was a lucky stop! Right in front of me, in the window, was a solution of the net problem. It was a stiff straw hat of the "sailor" shape, the crown of which was of open, lattice design, like network, to admit plenty of air. No more unobtrusive net than a hat worn on one's head could be imagined. . . .

I left the hotel about ten o'clock that evening, carrying a small tin pail in a brown paper bag—and wearing the new hat. The little fountain plaza was deserted, but I had to wait a few minutes for a wide gap in pedestrians. This enabled me to get my pail out of the bag, scoop up some water, and shove the pail against the darkest side of the fountain. The critical moment was approaching—the test of the hat. Several people passed, but paid no attention to me.

There was a big gap. Nothing was in sight, as far as I could see. Going to the edge of the bowl I lowered the hat into the water. The fish inside showed as black forms against the bottom. They were in little groups, almost motionless. One group was close to the edge. I slid the hat under them and they did little more than point their heads one way and move a foot or so. Making a scoop to the surface, I was gladdened to see several of them flapping within the hat. That moment was so intense I can still remember the number. There were three fish in the hat, and no pedestrian in sight. The fish were transferred to the pail. Another scoop brought out a couple, but a pedestrian was now headed for the fountain.

I casually rested my hat on the ledge, lit a cigarette, and waited for the oncoming stroller to pass. The fish flapped quite audibly in the hat.

The promenader approached my side of the fountain, stopped, gazed into the big basin, then passed on. He left in time for me to get the fish into the pail before they expired.

The third scoop was the best. It netted a half dozen fish, but the hat was collapsing. By the time I had these fish in the pail the usefulness of the hat was over. It started to unwind like a live spring and spread around the walk. As I now saw another pedestrian within a quarter of a block, and steadily coming on, I slipped the pail into the paper bag and in as nonchalant a manner as possible, picked it up and steered for the Gloria.

There was but one place to keep the fish, and that was in the commodious bathtub adjoining my room. There were enough fish to give the snake three meals, each several days apart. After that the reptile would need no further feeding on the steamer trip to New York.

How that serpent guzzled the three fish I fed it that evening! The balance of the fountain contingent swam in a foot of water. I made arrangements with a friend down the corridor to use his tub until the fish were gone.

The high spot of that adventure, however, came later.

Finding some bits of bread floating in the tub, it was clear that the chambermaid had discovered the fish and was solicitous about them. After the serpent had eaten four more, and four remained, I removed more bread than usual from the tub.

When the last fish had disappeared, I thought she gave me sharp glances as I passed her along the hallways. Her actions gave me a disturbing idea, and this I determined to clear up by questioning one of the bellboys. He spoke some English and we were pretty good friends, as I had tipped him liberally for doing odd jobs for me.

I told him about the chambermaid, and the fish, and the way she glanced at me, then asked him what she thought I did with them.

"She thinks you ate them," and in his voice was a quaver of doubt, matching the glances of the chambermaid.

Arcturus Adventure

*Though not Beebe's first oceanographic
expedition—nor the world's (there had
been about twenty-four of them since
1870)—the voyage of the* Arcturus *from
February to August of 1925 was certainly
one of the most elaborate and systematic.
Harrison Williams (a trustee) paid most
of the expenses, and Henry D. Whiton
(another) supplied the 282-foot yacht,
which was completely renovated for scientific exploration. A fully equipped laboratory and a spacious conference room were
created for Beebe's scientific staff of seventeen. A photographic darkroom was
installed for developing stills and motion
pictures. The decks were outfitted with long
booms for surface trawling and powerful
engines that could pull up dredging nets
full of specimens from depths up to eighteen thousand feet. Violent storms hindered
operations in the Sargasso Sea, the voyage's first leg, but vast hauls of organisms,
some of them unknown to science, were
collected, examined, photographed, and
sketched once the* Arcturus *passed through
the Panama Canal to the Pacific Ocean
and the Galápagos Islands.*

The Arcturus *anchored at Chatham Bay, Cocos
Island, halfway between Panama and the Galápagos.*

Scientific staff at work in the laboratory of the
Arcturus *(above) and examining sponges on deck*
(left) with Beebe.

Arcturus Lake, a crater lake discovered on Tower Island during the expedition to the Galápagos.

Below: Magnificent frigate birds in the Galápagos.

Team members on the deck of the Arcturus.

Right: Diving gear was used for exploring at a few fathoms. On the Haiti expedition in 1927, Beebe recorded observations with a lead pencil on a zinc plate.

Far right: Staff artist Isabel Cooper's irreverent view of the Arcturus *expedition.*

August 15, 1934. Dive to 3028 feet.

Weather clear, hot, almost no breeze, sea almost dead calm.

Feet	Observations by Beebe
Surface	(Rope tie between telephone cable and steel cable made at 20 feet and each 100 feet.)
20	Can see hull growth by looking up. Red almost gone in spectroscope, only orange left. (First rope tie.)
100	
200	
250	First *Aurelia*.
300	Barton sees pteropod.
310	Beam on.
360	Beam off.
400	Beam on.
420	Beam off.
500	Water a luminous dark blue.
550	Barometer going down a little, lower than 77, just below this line.
570	(Extra rope tie on telephone cable splice.)
600	Only gray visible in spectroscope.
640	One flash, now three more. Beam on. Copepods abundant. Sagitta, pale ones, and larval fish.
700	A mist of copepods and other plankton. Turquoise one half the distal length of beam of light, this considerably more than on Dive 30.
720	8 inch fish shot past.
760	String of salpa or siphonophores.
800	
840	6 Cyclothones close together. Leptocephalus, 5 inches, with 2 black spots, swimming right into beam.
900	Beam out. Oxygen 1900 pounds. Humidity 55%. Temperature 85°. Hose all right, door all right. Barometer 76½.
970	Walls getting very cold. No fish, only little lights now and then.
1000	6 or 8 lights, pale greenish color; it is a shrimp with 6 greenish lights. Beam on, and off.
1050	Fish with 6 lights in a row, near front of body. Circle below eye of pale yellow, and 5 or 6 separate lights behind, rest of body a long slender tail.
1100	Lights getting thicker, 4 or 5 at once.
1150	*Aurelia*, unexpected at this depth. Large pale green light just glowing.

WILLIAM BEEBE WITH
GLORIA HOLLISTER

from *"Unedited Telephone Observations on
Dive Number Thirty-two"*

HALF MILE DOWN, 1934

A new chapter in deep sea exploration opened in 1930 when Otis Barton designed the first bathysphere. Weighing some five thousand pounds, this steel diving sphere had a four-hundred-pound door and cylindrical windows made of fused quartz eight inches thick. An insulated cable supplied electric power for the bathysphere's headlight and telephone communication with the mother ship above. In 1930, 1932, and 1934, Beebe, Barton, and others in the group made thirty-five deep descents, during some of which Beebe made detailed observations of many previously unknown species; he also noted the phenomenon of spectral colors disappearing, one after the other, as the bathysphere descended. Gloria Hollister transcribed Beebe's observations, and a portion of those made during the record 1934 dive to 3,028 feet, financed by the National Geographic Society, are excerpted here.

Today, the bathysphere may be seen at the Society's Aquarium for Wildlife Conservation in Brooklyn.

1170	A net-work of light.
1200	A fish, 4 inches, lighted up all over, grayish silver like Ptax, must be luminous mucus. No spectroscope reading possible.
	No hose has come in bathysphere. [Beebe kept a close watch on the "stuffing box" through which the hose carrying telephone and electrical wires entered the bathysphere. The hose moved very little during the descent, and so leaks were avoided.]
1220	Fish, appears as only a flash of light and an indefinite outline. Here comes a beauty, 3 inch fish, with pale greenish light, must be on side of fish.
1250	A very big flash.
1300	Beam on.
	A fish swam right up to window and moved about. It had decided lights coming out of sides, and big nostril-like lights.
	3, 8 inch fishes, with head lights pale green, looks like big *Diaphus* but bigger than largest Myctophids.
1380	Many streaks, these are sagitta, the light kind. Many copepods.
1400	Turquoise creeping up, rich pale blue, 8 or 10 salpa hung together. Beam off.
1500	Oxygen reading 1300, still feeding at 1 litre per minute. Barometer 76. Humidity 55%. Temperature 86°. Probable reason for temperature being high is because it is so close to the hot chemical trays. I am moving device to a forward hook on same side.
1530	Beautiful Melanostomiatid, 6 to 7 inches, and another and another, grayish skin. Can see whole outline but not from own lateral lights.
1600	Many worms, can see lights on window glass, as many as 50.
1620	Another light. Big fish after 2 others, the pursuer is 3 or 4 times larger. Now another pale lemon yellow light. Think it is a shrimp.
1680	Saw shrimp sending out light, when near glass, they turned sideways as they hit and I saw them, in their own lights, send sparks out like skyrockets. This explains much that has puzzled me, and is the biggest discovery yet.
1700	Faint glow of light on window ledge.
1770	No telephone hose has slipped in.
1790	*Argyropelecus.*
1800	Life getting thicker.
	Here's a fish with nothing but teeth illumined, mouth 1 inch across, does not close completely. Teeth are lighted from the bottom upward with black between.
1810	Siphonophore, 6 to 8 inches, with all net-work lighted up and oval in shape. Now a copepod which looks like a fish's light, but is not luminous.
	3 more fishes, 18 inches, with irregular lightning-like line around side, and another one which may be same kind.
	We have colored plate of these but this is record size.
1900	Sides of bathysphere as cold as the devil. Whole atmosphere perfect.
1950	Fish crash again and again, no, it is shrimps throwing out light, letting it go every time they hit the glass.
1990	Beam on.

Big fish seen above are *Lamprotoxus*. Remember this.

2000	Lights here are great. 1650 pounds oxygen, humidity 60%, temperature 86°.
2030	Lots of lights that come and go.
2060	4 to 5 inch big Myctophids.
2090	Now ghostly things in every direction, like meteors in every direction.
2100	Colors of lights are pale blue, pale lemon yellow, and pale green. Now 2, 12 inch fish, one lights up the other, then both light up. Their lights are under control. Big cheek lights are lights along sides, both fish elongate like Melanostomiatids.
2150	Big siphonophore, and now 4 or 5 inch fish and something wiggling like mad.
2200	Shrimp explodes in midwater, no trace of any color. Oxygen 1550 pounds, temperature 85°, humidity 60%, barometer 76½. Have never seen such a dark place, it is the darkest in the world. Can see radiolite markings on the barometer glass in bathysphere.
2290	15 Myctophids in a school.
2300	
2330	Little forms, like separate sparks, like net-work. Can this be the fluid, luminous tissue let out in the water by shrimps?
2400	2 twin lights, light up. Beam on.
2430	Turquoise extends over four-fifths of beam, very delicate color.
2450	Big fish or cetacean came quite near, could just see his outline. Was at least 20 feet long, one-third of this deep. It is icy cold in here.
2500	Beam off. Barton says not more than one-quarter inch of hose has slipped in. Oxygen 1500 pounds, humidity 63%, barometer 76.
2540	Another shrimp. Ctenophore completely lighted up. Another big shrimp at window, whole thing very clear now about the luminous substance they shoot out.
2600	Beam on, and off.
2640	
2650	Millions of sparks when hit window. Big 12 inch heteropod, like *Firola*. Luminous all over but no luminous spots. Another big shrimp shooting out luminous material which looks like a veil.
2690	The walls of bathysphere are icy cold.
2700	Hose in about one-half inch only. Oxygen 1450 pounds, barometer 76, temperature 80°.
2775	So black outside can't look, and what lights! A fish with long, slender, pointed tail, this a big fish.
2800	Here's a telescoped-eyed fish, it's *Argyropelecus*, and its eyes are very distinct. Barton sees something like a huge necklace of silvery lights. Now another big shrimp.

Gloria Hollister communicated with Beebe on a telephone line, recording every exclamation, fact, and order for the winchman, as well as time, depth, and position.

	Beam off.
	Marvelous outside lights. Water filled with lights, more so than on our last dive at 2500 feet.
2900	Now a curved, pale-green light under eye, eye lighted up by it. It is crescent-shaped. The fish at least 3 feet long. 5 inch Myctophids, swimming so slowly that I can see whole light pattern. Several close lines of lateral lights, and constantly lighted plates. *Lampadena*, sure, try to look up species.
2940	Not a flash in sight.
2950	Now a light coming toward me.
3000	Siphonophore, a big one.
	Oxygen 1400 pounds, barometer 76, temperature 77°, humidity 62%.
3028	Beam on.
	Beam off.
	Long lace-like things again.
	Salpa-like with big head and long slender tendrils. Now another one.

❄

WILLIAM BEEBE

from "Appendix H: Summary and Conclusions"

HALF MILE DOWN, 1934

(a) Abundance

A vertical haul with a meter net in these waters yields but a meager amount of life. A thin scattering of plankton with perhaps a few Cyclothones and Myctophids. Even a horizontal haul of four hours at any depth produces at the most a pint of plankton and ten to thirty fish, all small, except perhaps one or two twelve inches or so in length. Yet every descent and ascent of the bathysphere showed a fauna, rich beyond what the summary of all our 1500 nets would lead us to expect. Bermuda is in the Sargasso Sea, which is accounted an arid place for oceanic life, but my observations predicate at least an unsuspected abundance of unknown forms. . . .

(b) Illumination

. . . Under cloudy conditions I have detected sparks of light in the bathysphere dives as far up as 400 feet. From 2000 feet down, animal light is the only source of external illumination. The nonhalation of these lights was marked throughout. This must be due to the clarity of the mediums traversed by the light. At times there were flashes from unknown organisms so bright that my vision was confused for several seconds. Often the abundance of lights was so great that the comparison was unavoidable with the major stars on a clear, moonless night. The constant movement tended to confuse direct, concentrated vision, but by continual effort I managed to follow definite, related groups of lights, and in many cases could ultimately make out the outline of the fish.

Occasionally the head of a fish would appear conspicuously against the surrounding black, illumined by some unknown source of indirect lighting. Eyes especially stood out with no definite source of light visible. When

The Ready, *mother ship for the bathysphere dives, was once a British man-of-war.*

teeth were thus silhouetted I knew it was from a luminous mucus which covered them. Cheek lights flashed and dimmed, or vanished altogether, showing some control other than the usual disappearance into an opaque, epidermal trench. The visibility of hundreds of minute photophores scattered over the surface of the body of certain Melanostomiatids was unexpected. These are inconspicuous, minute, and in living trawled specimens show no sign of luminosity.

On early dives and on the first observations of Dive Number Thirty, I reported small, dim fish of uncertain form as not uncommon, and frequently fairly close to the sphere. Also, that from time to time some organism struck the glass and exploded. I discovered on the last dive that the cause of these phenomena was the fluid ejected by shrimps, *Acanthephyra* and others. Two kinds of emanation were observed, one, a homogeneous, luminous cloud which diffused with great rapidity at first and then hung suspended for a considerable time as a faintly luminous area. The other was a discharge of a multitude of very bright sparks, which died out much sooner than the first type. These sparks were much more startling, making us jerk back our heads as from a blow when they occurred close against the glass.

I cannot hazard even a guess as to the number of blind, unlighted organisms which passed, or those whose lights were dimmed as long as they were in the vicinity of the bathysphere. The number of creatures illumined, the number of functional photophores on individual fish, and the strength and colors of these lights—all these have been far beyond all my expectations.

(c) Activity

It has been thought that the activity of fish and other organisms is less at great depths than at the surface, and the bizarre shapes, globular and angular, of many abyssal forms would seem to support this theory. In the many cases where I was able to watch fish and other creatures in motion down to a half mile, there was no hint of slowness, other than that imposed by the absence of stream lines. This was foreshadowed by the fish from our nets, taken from a half to a full mile, which we have kept alive in refrigerators and have filmed. These have swum about, and snapped at my fingers with as much accuracy of balance and swiftness as surface fish.

Else Bostelmann rendered what Beebe saw in the ocean depths, taking some liberties. Right: "Giants of the deep greet the bathysphere," the National Geographic *caption reads. "Sighted at 2,000 feet below sea level, this big creature was named* Bathyspherae intacta, *or the Untouchable Bathysphere Fish. It has not yet been caught in the nets." Below: "An 'air raid' half a mile below the nearest air!" Scarlet arrow fish attain their color at great depths.*

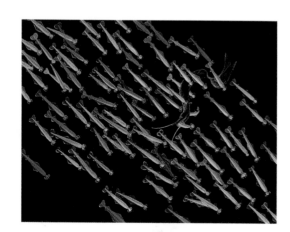

(d) Size

A 12-inch fish is accounted a giant in our trawling operations. The largest we have ever captured was a deep-sea eel more than $4^1/2$ feet long. On my dives there was a decided increase in general average of the size of fish the farther we descended. . . .

(e) Vertical Distribution

. . . It is sufficient to say that in almost every group of organisms, I saw individuals, from the bathysphere, at much higher levels than we have ever trawled them. This may be due in part to the ease with which creatures in the upper, more lighted levels, perceive and avoid the slow, oncoming nets. Yet the fact holds good as well for organisms in the deeper, lightless strata.

It would be futile to attempt any explanation of this great discrepancy in size, distribution, illumination, etc., between trawling captures and bathysphere observations. I never anticipated it, and I have no adequate theory to account for it. The fact remains that a much more abundant and larger-sized fish fauna exists in these waters than is in any way adumbrated by six years of trawling with the best possible oceanographic collecting outfit.

*Beebe and Otis Barton, the inventor of the bathysphere,
after their descent to 1,426 feet on June 30, 1930.*

The bathysphere emerges from a test dive in 1932.

The trail was rough but wide and fairly clear, and it was different from any other jungle trail I had ever seen—it was straight, impossibly straight. The explanation came later from a young American engineer who told us that it was the first rough survey line for a United Fruit narrow-gauge railway. It would some day receive bananas from great . . . plantations in Golfito and carry them straight through the jungle, over two low ranges, into the next bay to the south, which is in Panama. So the wonders of this jungle became all the more precious, because so soon they would be thinned out and frightened, and in place of great trees and lovely orchids and birds there would be men and dogs, bananas and paydays. Ultimately, some men, somewhere, would be able to deposit large sums of money in their banks, but they would never know or care how much more attractive and scenic were macaws and jungle lilies than chickens and miles of banana plants, how infinitely sweeter the voices of tinamous and wild pigeons, than the barking of curs and the roar of outboard motors. But if I keep this up, I shall dissolve into sentimentality, and weep into my journal!

WILLIAM BEEBE

from "Golfito: Bay of Jungles"
BOOK OF BAYS, 1942

William Beebe in his office at Simla, Trinidad (1952).

A New Global Vision

Madison Grant followed Henry Fairfield Osborn as president of the Society in 1925, serving until 1937, and William Hornaday retired as director of the zoological park in 1926. The Society had entered a period that even then seemed like an interregnum. Townsend remained at the aquarium's helm until 1937, and Beebe continued as the Society's vital connection with nature, but the founding generation was about to die out.

Presiding over the zoo from 1926 to 1940 was Dr. William Reid Blair, who had been appointed the country's first full-time zoo veterinarian in 1902, and then in 1922 became Hornaday's assistant. After Hornaday, the pace of combat inevitably slowed, particularly in the 1930s, when the Society and the careful, conservative Blair threaded their way through the Great Depression. Yet the zoo and aquarium were popular centers of respite in New York during that period, and Blair was involved in several significant projects, including the creation of a new zoo education department in 1929. Blair also helped restore the European bison in Germany and Poland through a program based on Hornaday's earlier interest, and he represented the Society, with Lee Crandall and others, on the American Committee for International Wild Life Protection, which was headquartered at the Bronx Zoo from 1938 through the late 1960s.

By 1940, the Society was ripe for new leadership. Osborn, Hornaday, Grant, and W. Redmond Cross, the Society's president from 1937 to 1940, were dead. Membership was falling. Other zoos, notably those in St. Louis and Chicago, had stolen a march on the great Bronx institution with their moated, barless outdoor exhibits, following the design and animal management innovations of Carl Hagenbeck at his Stellingen Zoo in Germany. And, most importantly, the world was changing. Politically and ecologically, under the threat of totalitarian regimes and resource exploitation, the earth was proving to need protection on an international scale.

New leadership came in the form of Fairfield Osborn and Laurance S. Rockefeller, who were elected, respectively, president of the Society and chairman of the executive committee by the Society's board of trustees on June 25, 1940. Osborn had been a trustee since 1922 and was elected secretary in 1935, the year of his father's death. He directed the Society's entry in the 1939 World's Fair in Flushing Meadows Park, which featured Pandora, the giant panda, who had come to the zoo from China in 1938; an aquarium demonstration of electric eels; and a display of Florida marine life. Rockefeller had joined the board in 1935. The two worked closely until Osborn's retirement in 1968, after which Rockefeller served as president for two years.

Changes came quickly with Osborn and Rockefeller in place. African Plains, the zoo's first moated exhibit, was planned and constructed in just eighteen months, opening on May 1, 1941. It was financed, anonymously at first, by Marshall Field, a trustee and longtime supporter of Beebe's work. The moats made possible the creation of a savanna landscape, complete with antelopes, zebras, lions, and an array of other species. This was part of a zoogeographic plan for the zoo put forth by Osborn that would stress, rather than isolated, individual species, the diversity and integrity of habitats as they exist in nature.

A few months later, however, the Society's grand plans to re-create the aquarium had to be abandoned when Battery Park was closed for the construction of the Brooklyn-Battery Tunnel. These plans were to be realized, in another form and another place, sixteen years later, with the remainder of the aquarium collection and staff, which had moved for this duration to the Lion House at the zoo.

With the onset of World War II, much else had to be abandoned—or postponed—as well. During the war, visitors continued to flock to the zoo (more than two million each year), and Society scientists were engaged in a number of government-sponsored medical and conservation projects. Finally winning the war produced a certain optimism and confidence in human possibilities, symbolized by the formation of the United Nations in 1945. But the war's global destructiveness, climaxing in the instant obliteration of large areas of Hiroshima and Nagasaki, also produced a doomsday uncertainty that has been with us ever since. Osborn took the long and painful victory as another call to action. Lively, innovative prewar plans and ideas were now pursued with a much larger understanding of how they might contribute to the earth's future.

If William Hornaday defined the Society's first great era, leading the battle for wildlife protection, Fairfield Osborn defined its second, leading the battle for global responsibility. Whereas Hornaday, the midwestern hunter, fought with steady scorn those who opposed him, Osborn, the urbane New Yorker, fought with persistent persuasion. Two world wars and a growing perception of ecological interdependence altered the terms of survival, and Osborn was one of the first to fully understand the differences. The problem was to save not only wildlife but the vast complex of life-supporting resources being polluted and destroyed by human exploitation.

The Society's exhibition at the 1939–40 World's Fair drew about four hundred thousand people.

*Fairfield Osborn opens the Penguin House in 1950,
with John Tee-Van and Laurance S. Rockefeller
looking on.*

For his joyous promotion of the zoo and aquarium, he was known as "the
greatest showman since Barnum." Under his direction, the zoo experience
was enlivened by greater naturalism in exhibitions and more education.
And the new aquarium was finally opened in Coney Island in 1957, after
many years of planning by Osborn, Rockefeller, and others, under the
direction of Christopher Coates, who had worked at the aquarium since
1930 and became its curator in 1943.

He also wrote that "it was never intended, from the beginning, that the
Zoological Society's interests should be bounded by the fences around
the Zoo and the Aquarium." His first book, published in 1948, anticipates
by many years the concerns of the environmental movement of the 1960s,
not only quantifying the threats of overpopulation, pollution, waste, and
war, but raising issues of moral responsibility. *Our Plundered Planet* (a title
suggested by William Beebe) was a clarion call and the beginning of
Osborn's leadership in the conservation movement. He worked with various groups, including the U.S. Department of the Interior, UNESCO, and
the American Association for the Advancement of Science.

In 1947, Osborn had already created a conservation division in the Society to explore these issues and help bring some sanity to resource use. A

*Fairfield Osborn (second from right) and other
international conservationists in the 1960s,
including Sir Peter Scott (second from left), chairman of the World Wildlife Fund—International,
and Carl Buchheister, president of the National
Audubon Society (center front).*

year later this division became the Conservation Foundation, and Osborn served as its president from 1948 to 1961. In papers, conferences, films, and books, the foundation took on a range of specific environmental problems. Among its collaborations with the Society were studies of wildlife decline in Alaska, the effects of pesticides on animals (several years before Rachel Carson's seminal *Silent Spring*), and the ill effects of eradicating small mammals, including prairie dogs and black-footed ferrets, in the West.

Partly to advance this broader concept of conservation, the Society embraced investigative science as never before. Hornaday and Townsend had never been overly supportive in this area, but Osborn gave research his full blessing at the zoo and particularly at the aquarium, where the work of Christopher Coates with electric eels, Myron Gordon with fish genetics, and Ross Nigrelli with drugs derived from marine organisms flourished. In 1967, the aquarium's active program was amplified in a new building named after the president—the Osborn Laboratories of Marine Sciences.

The Society's work stretched to Wyoming, where in 1946 the Jackson Hole Wildlife Park was established on land donated by John D. Rockefeller, Jr., and Laurance Rockefeller. For many years, the Society operated the Biological Research Station there, jointly with the University of Wyoming from 1953 to 1975.

Thus the seeds of the Society's modern field program were planted. The Society had conducted field studies since 1897, but in the 1950s they took on a new urgency and direction. Support was given to Olaus Murie, who as a scientist for the U.S. Bureau of Biological Survey had for many years opposed their program of eradicating predators. With his wife, Margaret, and a young assistant named George Schaller, Murie explored the southern slope of the Brooks Range in Alaska. Their recommendations led to the establishment of the Arctic National Wildlife Refuge in 1960, the largest protected area in the United States.

In the late fifties and early sixties, the Society expanded its work in Africa and South America. George Schaller was involved in a landmark study of mountain gorillas, at first with University of Wisconsin ethologist John Emlen, in 1959. Osborn himself traveled to Kenya, Tanganyika (Tanzania), Uganda, and the Belgian Congo (Zaire) to assess the conservation needs of those countries in 1960, and, ever since, the Society has been instrumental in setting up conservation programs and establishing major wildlife parks there. Backing came from the African Wildlife Fund, which was set up by the Society in 1959 and drew increasing support and involvement from trustees and others. In Tanzania alone, Arusha National Park was set up in 1963, Ruaha in 1966, and Tarangire in 1969.

Also in 1960, Curator of Birds William Conway trekked through Argentina with trustee Robert Goelet, beginning a long-range scientific presence and a relationship with conservation supporters there that resulted in the creation of six coastal reserves by 1964, including Punta Tombo and Península Valdés, and many others since. Meanwhile, a new $10 million general development fund was begun in 1961 mostly to create new, more naturalistic habitats at the zoo and aquarium.

This proliferation of efforts on several fronts at once seemed to be what Fairfield Osborn had in mind with his emphasis on global issues and the Society's obligation to address them.

Jackson Hole Wildlife Park, Wyoming, where the Society established a field station in 1948.

Following pages:
Elephants in Kenya's Amboseli National Park.

FAIRFIELD OSBORN

from "We Must Reverse the Tide"

ANIMAL KINGDOM, BULLETIN
OF THE NEW YORK ZOOLOGICAL SOCIETY,
DECEMBER 6, 1945

The tide is still running out. Forests are being depleted, soils and water sources are deteriorating. This is true not only in the United States but in many other parts of the world. If these primary natural resources continue to disappear, the gains that have been made in wildlife preservation will be forfeited. As for man himself, his world will become to an increasing degree a world of want.

How can such conditions be explained? Principally because there is no general understanding of the complete interdependence of plant life, animal life, water supply and soils. Great advances in knowledge concerning this complex subject have been made. A new science, known as Conservation, has come into existence.

The cure for the present critical situation must come through basic education and informed public opinion. As to basic education, the principles of Conservation should be integrated into the general curricula of our schools and colleges and not isolated as a "special course." The teaching of history would be illuminated by analyzing to what extent the exhaustion of living resources contributed to the fall of civilizations and to wars between nations. Courses in chemistry and engineering would be vitalized were they oriented to the needs of effective management of Nature's resources. By the same token, courses in biology would become far more purposeful if they provided a better understanding of the interrelationship of all living things. . . .

Conservation is no longer a "side show"—it is the "big tent" of human existence.

Pesticides—crop dusting in Texas (1955).

OSBORN'S PLUNDERED PLANET

FAIRFIELD OSBORN

from "The Dim Yet Potent Years"

OUR PLUNDERED PLANET, 1948

It is a curious fact that mankind appears to justify the killing of his own kind by assuming that it is a "law of nature." There are a lot of current misconceptions about the laws of nature, of which this is one of the most erroneous and fateful. Political ideologies have been based upon it with results that have come near to destroying human civilization. The theory that war is a biological necessity, that it is nature's method of controlling population and assuring the survival of the strong and the elimination of the weak, is inaccurate and insupportable. Within the last century, when wars have been common all over the world, the human population of the earth has almost doubled.

The principle of "the survival of the fittest" has quite a different meaning than that commonly attributed to it. Darwin's conclusions were drawn from his long observations of the methods of living things, which led him to conclude that those kinds survived who were best able to adapt themselves to their environment, not those who were most competent in mass murder. It is further to be observed that when all of the larger and higher types of mammalian animals are considered, the carnivores, namely those that live upon the lives of others, are merely outliers among the great animal populations—a minority party indeed. It is estimated that the number of carnivores or killers would not exceed one per cent of the total animal populations as they originally existed in Africa or North America—that is before man decimated the wildlife of these continents. Only in exceptional cases in higher forms of animal life is there organized killing within a species itself, and even combat is rare except in defense of members of the immediate family or social group, or when males are seeking dominance. . . .

Publication of Our Plundered Planet *was well timed to promote the official beginning of the Conservation Foundation on March 30, 1948. Conceived by Fairfield Osborn as a division of the Society, the foundation soon involved a roster of prominent scientists dealing with world problems in soil and water resources, forests and vegetation, wildlife, and human population growth. Called "perhaps the most convincing account of man's material plight that has yet appeared" by the New York* Herald Tribune, *the book served as the philosophical basis for the foundation's program in research, education, and communication. More completely than anyone at the time, Osborn expressed his understanding of organic wholeness on the planet. His image of life as a circle we are in danger of breaking served as a powerful metaphor for the foundation's activities.*

At a radio panel discussion later in 1948, Osborn noted one of the central contradictions of our time: "We are bouncing radar beams off the moon at a time when we are gradually reducing our own world to the condition of sterility of that romantic planet. We have seemingly discovered the secrets of the universe but we have not as yet persuaded ourselves that we must adhere to the principles that ensure the existence of all living things, man included."

Erosion—gullying caused by cattle overgrazing in Monolith, California (1932).

Through the development of the physical sciences, funneled into vast industrial systems, [man] has created and continues to create new environments, new conditions. These extensions of his mind-fertility and his

Industrial pollution—Smithfield Street in Pittsburgh, blanketed by smog (1940).

Automobile culture—Los Angeles freeway interchange in the 1950s.

Overpopulation and poverty—favelas in Rio de Janeiro.

mind-restlessness are super-imposed, like crusts, on the face of the earth, choking his life sources. The conditions under which he must live are constantly changing, he himself being the cause of the changes. In this metamorphosis he has almost lost sight of the fact that the living resources of his life are derived from his earth-home and not from his mind-power. With one hand he harnesses great waters, with the other he dries up the water sources. He must change with changing conditions or perish. He *conquers* a continent and within a century lays much of it into barren waste. He must move to find a new and unspoiled land. He must, he must—but where? His numbers are increasing, starvation taunts him—even after his wars too many are left alive. He causes the life-giving soils for his crops to wash into the oceans. He falls back on palliatives and calls upon a host of chemists to invent substitutes for the organized processes of nature. Can they do this? Can his chemists dismiss nature and take over the operation of the earth? He hopes so. Hope turns to conviction—they *must*, or else he perishes. Is he not nature's "crowning glory"? Can he not turn away from his creator? Who has a better right? He has seemingly "discovered" the secrets of the universe. What need, then, to live by its principles!

FAIRFIELD OSBORN

from "Life Begets Life"
OUR PLUNDERED PLANET, 1948

How do we happen to delude ourselves that certain *inventions* or accomplishments are man's alone? Radar, direction finding either by supersonics or, as is now suspected, by electromagnetic waves, long nonstop flights, dives to great ocean depths, feats of engineering. Man is not the first to achieve these things. They have been developed and practiced by various kinds of animals during countless millennia, even before man appeared upon the earth. This fact is not cited as a humbling thought, nor in denial of the obvious and complete supremacy of the human mind. It is merely a truth that symbolizes a relationship between man and other living things. In its own fashion it bespeaks the unity of all life. . . .

With such thoughts in mind it is difficult to bring oneself to speak of animal life merely from the point of view of its utility or, let us say, of its functional contributions to the fertility of the earth. Yet, while based on the belief that all kinds of wild living things are a joy to the eye, as well as fascinating subjects to study, and that it is wrong wantonly to destroy them, this book is not written primarily for any aesthetic or ethical purpose. The matter can be resolved by recognizing that when killing of other creatures is done without an understanding of what they are contributing to the life scheme, man is contributing to his own life deterioration. Some of the killing that man does of other creatures is all right; it is close enough to the pattern of life as a whole—reasonably close enough, that is—to justify itself. But the rub comes when we kill without knowing enough about the aftereffects. There is no risk in making the flat statement that in a world devoid of other living creatures, man himself would die. This fact—call it a theory if you will—is far more provable than the accepted theory of relativity. Involved in it is, in truth, another kind of principle of relativity—the relatedness of all living things.

As a somewhat extreme illustration, among many others, take that form of life that man likes the least—of which the unthinking person would at once say, "Kill them all." Insects. Of the extraordinary number of kinds of insects on the earth—about three quarters of a million different species have already been identified—a small minority are harmful to man, such as the anopheles mosquito, lice, the tsetse fly, and crop-destroying insects. On the other hand, innumerable kinds are beneficial and useful. Fruit trees and many crops are dependent upon insect life for pollination or fertilization; soils are cultured and gain their productive qualities largely because of insect life. Human subsistence would, in fact, be imperiled were there no insects. On the other hand, insects, capable of incredibly rapid reproduction, have been freed by man himself of many natural controls such as those once provided by birds, now so diminished in numbers, or by fish, once a potent factor in insect control no longer existing in countless lakes, rivers and streams now so polluted that aquatic life has disappeared. . . .

It is apparent that many of the lower forms of animal life—ranging from protozoa up through the insects and other invertebrates even to the reptiles, fishes, birds and certain small mammals—play an essential part in the economy of nature. On the other hand, it is far from easy to prove that some of the higher orders or families of mammals are necessary to the life scheme of the earth, at least of this earth today, when human beings are so numerous and their demands for both space and subsistence so pressing....

The matter can be approached by recognizing the general principle that the sustained richness and productivity of the earth depends upon there being returned to it the organic material that grows from it. This *order of nature* can be expressed by the symbol of a circle. Formerly all wild animal life was an inherent part of that organic circle. Our present domestic animals represent a minor portion of the organic whole that is not permitted to return to the earth of its origin. They end up in the consuming centers, their residues in disposal plants or carried to the ocean. The broader implications are that this holds true of a large proportion of the earth's products today—both animal life and plant life, including vast quantities of forest products. There is one steady movement of organic material to towns and great cities and industrial centers—there to be consumed or disposed of as waste but never to go back to the land of origin. We are hacking at the circle expressive of the organic unity and productive processes of nature. The question is, Will we one day actually break that circle?

The animals of the earth! They are dependent on man's sufferance now. Late years are brighter for them. There is a growing public consciousness that whether or not we need them for utility's sake we must protect them. National Parks and refuges have been set aside for them in our country and in many others. But civilization and the rising needs of increasing numbers of people are pressing hard upon the last remaining wildernesses. Man must live, but one wonders sometimes, in faraway moments, whether there is not a primal form of ethics involved. Should not man perhaps, even for his own peace of mind, think of himself not as the consumer alone but as the protector? Like companions of an earlier life, if we forget them they are gone forever. It is man's earth now. One wonders what obligations may accompany this infinite possession.

LAND AND POPULATION

It would seem, at first glance, as if Central and South Africa must be a "new" country with vast unexplored areas, capable of productive development. Actually this is far from the case. Land deterioration through erosion is widespread and great portions of the cultivable areas have already been considerably damaged. Africa illustrates perhaps more vividly than any other continent the ill effects of transplanting European cultures, and specifically European methods of using the land, to other regions of the earth, especially those lying in tropical or subtropical areas. What has happened in Africa confirms the axiom that methods of land use suitable to one social system or to one climate or region are not necessarily so elsewhere, and may, in fact, prove extremely harmful. Above all, Africa compels one to recognize the dire results of using the land to gain cash profits rather than as the source of basic subsistence.

Take it or leave it, nature gives no blank endorsement to the profit motive. For several thousand years it has won the argument on this point. How many times does this have to be proved to us? It might be justifiable for man to continue the argument indefinitely were it not for the

FAIRFIELD OSBORN

from "Mediterranean Lands and Africa"
OUR PLUNDERED PLANET, 1948

Osborn perceived conservation problems as global from a perspective that was not available to Hornaday. He moved naturally from one continent to another, pointing out the common interests and needs of all people. "No longer," he wrote, "can 3,000,000 people in India die of starvation, as they did in 1943, without a specific and cumulative effect on an Englishman in Sussex." Colonialism itself was understood as a rending of the organic fabric, the irony being that despite foreign disruptions of indigenous life, human populations exploded.

fact that it is waged with mounting injury to people everywhere.

Before the arrival in Africa of European colonizers the native peoples had their own way of using the land. Approximately 120,000,000 people were living in an area almost four times that of the United States. Even allowing for the uninhabitable areas there was adequate room for the native peoples and they were not in the habit of taking more from the land than it could give, which is another way of saying that they gained their basic subsistence without thought of cash profit or of the wealth that might be gained through exporting land products. The methods of land use employed in various regions of Africa are well worth observing if only for the reason that they illustrate the ability of human beings to live on the land in what may be thought of as practically natural conditions. With the coming of European colonizers, two major changes took place: first, the native peoples were not infrequently forced from the fertile valley lands so that they were compelled to burn and cut forests in order to create clearings for their crops. While the pressure resulting from increasing numbers of people using the land has made itself felt, probably the most unfavorable recent

Water pumping stations for Masai cattle were established with Society help in 1959–61 to prevent overgrazing on the savanna. Royal Little, the principal supporter, here visits Roy's Bore Hole in Tsavo National Park.

development is resulting from the introduction by European colonizers of new crops such as cotton, coffee and tobacco, cultivated in order to bring cash returns through export. Naturally the native peoples in certain regions are quick to observe the ways of the colonizers and become interested on their own account in sharing in the returns. New desires are stimulated to acquire the kind of things that Europeans own that cost money, whether it be clothes or bicycles or just a bottle of gin. As a result, the natives are tempted to a greater and greater degree to mine the land for the cash that it will produce.

Monoculture—
tea plantation
that replaced a
forest in Kenya.

Another strong influence in hurting the land has been the system of taxation imposed by governing European powers. Often taxes imposed on native peoples amount to one twelfth or even one sixth of a man's total earning power. In Nyasaland [Malawi], for instance, the native peoples were practically forced into tobacco culture in order to meet government taxation. The growing of crops for sale, which are almost without exception export products, obviously provides a revenue to the controlling governments not only in tax money but in the value of raw materials exported. Taxation has been thought of as a most effective means of forcing the native out of his naturally contented state, a process that for some reason is considered necessary in attaining a condition of "higher civilization." From another angle taxation is used as a thin veneer to cover forced labor or economic slavery. One observer bitterly comments that every European influence, whether government, school, church, trader or rumrunner, pushes the African in the direction of money crops. The further the native is from the market, the more effective the tax plan is in forcing a change in the type of agricultural production. Native owners of cattle have not felt the squeeze so greatly and have had to make fewer adjustments, but they have been more heavily taxed because their wealth is more evident and more easily convertible into cash.

One should not be led to conclude that these trends and influences and conditions are by any means general, for the African by weight of numbers has held largely to his original customs and methods of land use. Agriculture is so much a part of the soil and the physical environment that it cannot be as easily displaced as can less basic activities. Consequently the production of food for man and beast in Africa, when one looks at the continent from a distance, still continues, in the main, to be by methods developed by the Bantu and other native races. Nevertheless, the pressure of these new and destructive influences is steadily spreading and the entire trend is towards an increasing destruction of the natural living resources of this great continent.

HUXLEY'S RESPONSE

ALDOUS HUXLEY

Letter to Fairfield Osborn

ANIMAL KINGDOM, BULLETIN OF
THE NEW YORK ZOOLOGICAL SOCIETY,
APRIL 1, 1948

Dear Mr. Osborn:

I have to thank you for having given me the opportunity of reading your very interesting book. I airmailed a few words to Little, Brown last Tuesday, and hope that they will have got them in time. The great question now is: will the public and those in authority pay any attention to what you say, or will the politicians go on with their lunatic game of power politics, ignoring the fact that the world they are squabbling over will very shortly cease to exist in its old familiar form, but will be transformed, unless they mobilize all available intelligence and all available good will, into one huge dust bowl inhabited by creatures whom progressive hunger will make more and more sub-human? I have been trying to put this question to the general and specialized publics for the last year or two—even succeeding in planting it in the Bulletin of the Atomic Scientists this summer, pointing out that, while mankind could do very well without atomic energy, it cannot dispense with bread. But hitherto I have had no audible response from any quarter. I hope very much that you, with your scientific authority and your beautifully organized collection of facts, will be able to make some impression in influential quarters. But, alas, in view of what politicians and the voting public are like, hope must always be mingled with a great deal of doubt.

My own interests in recent years have turned increasingly in the direction of philosophy and mystical religion, and I see this problem of Man's relation to nature as not only an immediate practical problem, but also as a problem in ethics and religion. It is significant that neither Christianity nor Judaism has ever thought of Nature as having rights in relation to man, or as being in some way intrinsically divine. You will find orthodox Catholic moralists ascertain (on the basis of those extremely unfortunate remarks in Genesis) that animals may be treated as things. (As though things didn't deserve to be treated ethically!) The vulgar boast of the modern technologist to the effect that man has conquered Nature has roots in the Western religious tradition, which affirms that God installed man as the boss, to whom nature was to bring tribute. The Greeks know better than the Jews and Christians. They know that hubris towards Nature was as much of a sin as Hubris towards fellow men. Xerxes is punished, not only for having attacked the Greeks, but also for having outraged Nature in the affair of bridging the Hellespont. But for an ethical system that includes animate and inanimate Nature as well as man, one must go to Chinese Taoism, with its concept of an Order of Things, whose state of wu-wei, or balance, must be preserved; of an indwelling Logos or Tao, which is imminent on every level of existence from the physical, through the physiological, up to the mental and the spiritual. In many passages, particularly of the Specimen Days in America, Whitman comes very close to the Taoist position. And because of Whitman and Wordsworth and the other "Nature mystics" of the West, I feel that it might not be too difficult for modern Europeans and Americans to accept some kind of Taoist philosophy of life, with an ethical system comprehensive enough to take in Nature as well as man. People have got to understand that the commandment, "Do unto others as you would that they should do unto you" applies to animals, plants and things, as well as to people; and that if it is regarded as applying only to people (as it has been in the Christian West), then the animals, plants and things will, in one way or another, do as badly by man as man has done by them. It seems to me that, if we are to have a better policy towards Nature, we must also have a better philosophy.

Yours very sincerely,
Aldous Huxley

Also a crusader for changing consciousness, Aldous Huxley appreciated Osborn's forthright message. In his early novels, Huxley depicted with bitter satire the social and spiritual bleakness of England after World War I; he took on the future in Brave New World *(1932). After moving in 1937 to Los Angeles, where he died in 1963, he turned to mysticism and non-Western religious philosophy as a hopeful way out of the modern predicament.*

The Zoogeographic Idea

When African Plains opened on May 1, 1941, it was the Bronx Zoo's first realization of "a new conception of zoological park planning, involving the principle of exhibiting animals by continents *rather than by* orders *or* families," *as President Fairfield Osborn declared. The zoogeographic approach was meant to convey to the public, through dramatic, naturalistic habitats, a clearer understanding of the distribution of life forms. The idea was immediately incorporated into a master plan for the zoo drawn up in 1941 by W. K. Harrison & J. A. Fouilhoux, the architectural firm that had just designed African Plains. All the continents were to be represented in intensively developed areas, and the plan also included a children's zoo (already completed in 1941) and the Farm-in-the-Zoo (opened in 1942), both of which were not only crowd pleasers but also active ventures in education. The comprehensive scheme set the direction for future exhibition and educational planning, though most of the continental areas were eventually developed in different locations around the zoo.*

Above: From the 1940s into the '60s, Helen Martini was in charge of the zoo's nursery, providing care for many rare animals, including three Bengal tigers born in 1944.

Above right and right: The Bronx Zoo's first Children's Zoo, opened in 1941, evoked children's games and stories—a Wishing Seat, Kanga's House, Hickory Dickory Dock, Brer Rabbit—and included many opportunities to pet and feed animals.

Opposite: Thanks to Mme. Chiang Kai-shek, John Tee-Van brought two baby giant pandas to the Bronx Zoo by plane, ship, and train, crossing the Pacific as the Japanese attacked Pearl Harbor (inset). Pandah and Pandee, female and male, flourished at the zoo, growing from about sixty pounds when they arrived on December 30, 1941, to about 150 pounds eight months later.

Above: The Farm-in-the-Zoo, opened in 1942, provided enjoyment and instruction as well as wool, eggs, milk, and other products appreciated in the war effort.

Thousands of people poured through the stockade gateway with its colorful maps of Africa to celebrate the opening of African Plains on May 1, 1941.

Six young male lions on their rocky island in African Plains.

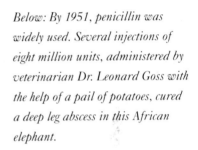

Below: By 1951, penicillin was widely used. Several injections of eight million units, administered by veterinarian Dr. Leonard Goss with the help of a pail of potatoes, cured a deep leg abscess in this African elephant.

Left: Curator of Reptiles James Oliver (1951–58) made the Reptile House a series of living habitats. Oliver later became director of the New York Aquarium (1970–76).

African Plains has since been expanded, but the lions, nyalas, and other savanna wildlife remain neighbors, safely separated by moats.

KEEPING A PLATYPUSARY

The first skin of a platypus arrived at the British Museum in 1798, but it was not until 1884, when an English zoologist obtained eggs of both the platypus and the echidna in Australia, that the little duckbill was finally acknowledged as a primitive, egg-laying mammal. The protracted controversy concerning its nature is not surprising. Who *would* believe that a mammal laid eggs—and especially so improbably concocted a mammal, with silky fur, a broad and ducklike bill, webbed feet, and rooster-like spurs on its hind legs?

Considering the immense interest of such an animal, it is not remarkable that efforts were made to keep the platypus in captivity. In 1910 Harry Burrell, the "platypus man," began the experiments that laid the foundation of our present knowledge and finally resulted in the successful transportation of living platypuses to America. Burrell constructed a portable contraption that he called a "platypusary," consisting of a small tank and an attached labyrinth of tunnels through which the animal had to pass to reach its nest. The important feature was a series of rubber gaskets placed in the tunnels. These served to squeeze the water out of the platypus's fur as it passed through. Without them the nest would become wet, and the animal, unable to dry its coat, would be in risk of pneumonia.

Burrell's platypusary was well thought out, for it reproduced to some extent the animal's natural habitat. Semi-aquatic, the platypus seeks its food in the water—small crayfish, or "yabbies," aquatic insects, and worms—and then retires to burrows in the banks of streams for shelter and nesting. The platypusary had what the platypus wanted—a tank in which to feed, a tunnel, gaskets to scrape the fur dry as the sides of a natural tunnel would do, and a nesting chamber.

Some years after Burrell perfected his contraption, the late Ellis S. Joseph, a well-known dealer in animals, joined forces with him. In the spring of 1922 Joseph embarked aboard the *USS West Henshaw* with five male platypuses in a bulky platypusary and a large supply of earthworms for use as food for the animals. He reached San Francisco some six weeks later with one platypus but no earthworms, an early intimation of the enormous food capacity of these little animals.

After a stop to renew the food supply, Joseph proceeded to New York by train and reached the New York Zoological Park on July 14. Here the difficulties of maintaining the food supply immediately became apparent, and William T. Hornaday, at that time director of the Zoological Park, complained in print that the cost was from $4.00 to $5.00 a day. He gave as one day's ration ½ pound of earthworms, 40 shrimp, and 40 grubs—an amount that in the light of more recent experience seems hardly adequate. "Really, it seems incredible that an animal so small could chamber a food supply so large," he wrote. "I know of nothing to equal it among other mammals."

Each afternoon during its sojourn here the platypus was exhibited daily for one hour, long lines of visitors filing slowly past the open tank of the platypusary. The highly nervous temperament of the animal caused it to swim, scramble, and climb incessantly. On occasion, the keeper in charge

LEE S. CRANDALL
IN COLLABORATION WITH
WILLIAM BRIDGES

from "The Platypus, or Duckbill"
A ZOO MAN'S NOTEBOOK, 1966

Lee Crandall's career at the Society did not end with his retirement as general curator in 1952. Until within six months of his death in 1969, he continued to work in his zoo office five days a week. He wrote his great tome, The Management of Wild Mammals in Captivity *(1964), over a ten-year period from his extensive index-card files at the zoo. It covered 1,382 animals, whereas the shorter popular version,* A Zoo Man's Notebook, *published two years later, deals with just forty-seven. It seemed that Crandall remembered everything he had ever learned about every animal he had ever known, enough to correctly recall, after some thirty years, the color of the eyes of a bird he had seen in the London Zoo in the 1930s.*

Lee S. Crandall with a young agile wallaby.

The duck-billed platypus was first shown at the zoo—and outside Australia—in 1922.

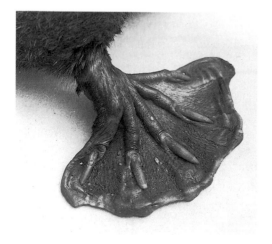

With webbed feet and a duck bill, the platypus is well suited to bottom feeding in rivers and streams.

did not hesitate to pick up the platypus and hold it—as long as he could—for the closer inspection of special guests. All of this, at the time, seemed perfectly reasonable, and the survival of the animal for the forty-seven days was considered to be an unexpectedly good result.

In the next twenty-five years there were further experiments in Australia with keeping platypuses in captivity. In 1944 the Australian naturalist David Fleay actually succeeded in breeding the animal. To his pair, named Jack and Jill, a youngster named Corrie was born—or hatched!—after the extraordinarily brief incubation period of six to ten days.

Encouraged by this triumph, the New York Zoological Society decided to attempt another platypus importation. After a long wait in Australia for the construction of traveling platypusaries, accumulation of the necessary supply of earthworms, and, most important of all, securing of official sanctions, Fleay and his wife embarked for Boston in the spring of 1947 with one male and two female platypuses. After an arduous journey of twenty-seven days, during which the food supply was reinforced by the addition of fresh worms at Pitcairn and at Panama, the ship reached its destination, and the platypuses were convoyed to New York by motor. Three days later they went on exhibition in the New York Zoological Park in a permanent platypusary we had constructed for them.

It had all seemed so simple back in 1922 when the delicate and temperamental nature of the platypus was not recognized. Now that we knew more we realized that exhibiting a platypus even for one hour a day was not a simple matter. We soon found that 60° F. was the critical low temperature for the water in the tank; they liked it even warmer and below this point became reluctant to enter the water. A small electrical water-heating unit had to be installed in the platypusary.

When first allowed to enter the tank, the platypuses gave the usual indications of discontent, rolling over and over in the water and trying frantically to climb the corners. David Fleay considered that the disturbance was caused by the lack of overhead cover. We then arranged a green canvas, lined with white, above the pool to reduce the light, but the white lining had to be replaced before the animals were satisfied.

Fleay had named our animals Cecil, Betty Hutton (soon shortened to Betty), and Penelope. Because of the danger to Betty and Penelope from an injection of venom from Cecil's spurs, the male alone and the two females together were exhibited for one hour on alternate afternoons.

At 4:00 P.M. the slides that closed the burrow openings were opened so that the animals could leave or enter at will, and their food was placed in the water. From dusk to dawn the platypuses were almost continually active, filling their cheek pouches under water and floating on the surface to break up and swallow the prodigious quantities of food consumed.

Normal daily rations for one platypus consisted of one pound of earthworms (about two hundred adult "night crawlers" and another large species of earthworm), two dozen live crayfish, one or two leopard frogs, two eggs steamed in a double broiler, and perhaps a handful of cockroaches or mealworms. All these items added up to at least double the amount of food that had been considered adequate in 1922. On this regime our three platypuses throve during the summer of 1947 and, by turnstile count, were viewed by just over two hundred thousand of our visitors.

A smaller version of the permanent platypusary was built in the basement of one of the zoo buildings for winter quarters, and the animals settled down quickly. When exhibition in the outdoor platypusary was resumed in the spring of 1948, Betty was obviously out of condition, although her weight remained at 1.98 pounds, her apparent normal. Gradually she began to lose, and in September of her second year with us she died.

Cecil and Penelope continued in the alternation of summers out of doors and winters indoors until the spring of 1951, when it became apparent that we should give serious thought to breeding possibilities. Always mindful of Cecil's venom glands and the spurs on his hind legs, we had built a separating wall between the male and female quarters in the winter platypusary. But eventually telltale tracks on the dusty floor revealed that one or both had found a way out through an unsuspected crack. When one morning Cecil was found asleep in Penelope's nest and Penelope curled up in Cecil's, friendly relations seemed obvious. Our hopes of duplicating Fleay's breeding success rose.

No behavior indicating anything beyond casual friendship and tolerance occurred, however, until the spring of 1953.

On May 21, at the close of Penelope's exhibition hour, she refused to return to her burrow as she customarily did. Cecil was then liberated to his side of the divided pool, in preparation for feeding, when Keeper Blair noticed that Penelope was scratching desperately at a wooden corner of the pool. Blair then removed the partition and the two animals almost immediately went into the circular mating maneuver that David Fleay had described for his Jack and Jill, Cecil grasping Penelope's tail firmly with his bill. When his grip finally loosened there was a brief pursuit, ending with Penelope floating quietly on the surface while Cecil preened her fur with his bill. This cycle was repeated four times up to 10:30 P.M., but no actual copulation was seen. For the next several days Cecil continued courting and Penelope showed no fright reactions, but the circling maneuver was not seen to be repeated.

David Fleay had written a precise and detailed timetable of the behavior of his platypuses before the appearance of young Corrie, and throughout the summer of 1953 Penelope's actions closely paralleled it. She began excavating the earth mound we had provided for her (corresponding to the bank of a stream in her native Australia), and when she showed disturbance at Cecil's company he was removed. She dragged dried eucalyptus leaves (obtained in quantity from the zoo's neighbor, the New York Botanical Garden) into her burrow, and finally she retired into the burrow for days at a time without emerging. When she did emerge she fed voraciously. Just as a test, in the early fall we gave her all she would eat: 2½ pounds of earthworms, 2 frogs, and 2 cooked eggs, no crayfish being available. This prodigious meal was completely consumed.

By Fleay's timetable, interpreted in the light of Penelope's behavior, her eggs should have hatched on July 16. Fleay's Corrie emerged from the nest seventeen weeks after hatching, but we could not wait that long. Sixteen weeks from July 16 brought us to November 5, and cold weather with heavy snow was forecast for the following day. Penelope and her baby had to be dug out and removed to winter quarters.

And so the mound was carefully excavated. At the end of two hours of digging, Penelope alone was unearthed, with no sign of young, no proper nest, or even remains of the many leaves that she had carried underground from the pool. Why she should have paralleled Jill's cycle without result remains unexplained. The platypus is known to hibernate in some parts of Australia; we can only guess that Penelope's retirement in July was for hibernation rather than incubation.

After creating such a peak of hope and excitement, Cecil and Penelope returned to serene normality. Penelope somehow escaped from the Platypusary on August 1, 1957, after she had been with us for 10 years, 3 months, 7 days. Cecil was found dead in his nest tunnel a few weeks later, after 10 years, 4 months, 24 days with us. Their life spans do not constitute a record for longevity—Fleay's Jack, with at least 17 years, holds that—but certainly they improved on our 47-day experience with the first platypus in 1922.

Any practicing naturalist can astonish his friends with stories of complex life cycles and intricate food chains—Darwin's classic example of the relationship between cats and clover is a familiar example. But the parasitologists can tell the best stories, because some of their little animals will go to almost fabulous lengths to perpetuate their kind.

Take *Leucochloridium paradoxum.*

It is a minute parasite, a fluke, and its life fluctuates between a bird in a tree and a snail on the ground. Now admire the subtlety of its path.

Its reproduction begins in the intestine of a baby bird—a Sparrow, for example. The adult flukes lay vast numbers of eggs which pass out in the nestling's excrement and are thus strewn over bushes and on the ground.

Along come snails—many kinds—and feed upon the excrement. That is the end of the road for most of the eggs; they are simply eaten and digested. But *in one kind* of snail the eggs hatch into wriggling larvae and start their journey through the snail's body. They are pretty little things at this stage, even though they can only be seen under a microscope—striped green and white, with bright red tips.

These decorative mites burrow through the tissue of the snail and crowd into the tentacles. Such vast numbers of them jam into the delicate, extensible "feelers" of the snail that the tentacles are swollen and cannot be drawn back under the shell.

The skin of the snail's "horns" is stretched taut and thin and through its transparent sides the bright red tips and the green-and-white stripes of the parasites are clearly visible. They wriggle continuously and thus the tentacles seem to move and twinkle with ruby light.

ROSS F. NIGRELLI

"The Subtlety of Leucochloridium paradoxum*"*

ANIMAL KINGDOM, BULLETIN OF THE NEW YORK ZOOLOGICAL SOCIETY, JUNE 4, 1945

Research at the New York Aquarium was given its biggest push by Charles M. Breder, Jr., who joined the staff as aquarist in 1921 and became director when Townsend retired in 1937. Pathologist Ross Nigrelli arrived in 1934 and through the next three decades became one of the world's preeminent experts on fish diseases, virus-induced tumors in fish, and the effects of pollution, salinity, and water temperature on aquatic organisms. Nigrelli served as director of the Osborn Laboratories of Marine Sciences from 1964 to 1973 and as director of the aquarium from 1966 to 1970.

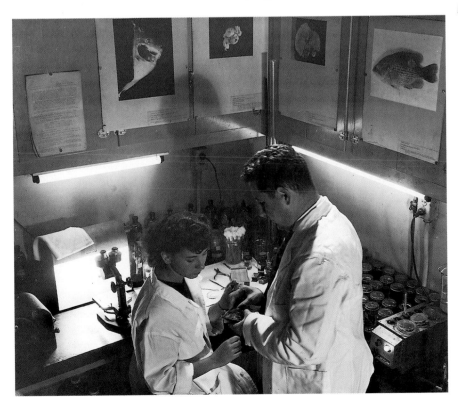

Ross Nigrelli and assistant in his aquarium lab.

What more likely to attract the attention of an adult Sparrow, perched on a limb and spying out the ground for its hungry nestlings?

The Sparrow flies down, the snail in alarm draws itself back into its protecting shell—and only the weaving, pulsating, tempting red tentacles remain exposed. The Sparrow nips them off.

If the Sparrow happens to be hungry itself, it may swallow the little bags full of parasites—in which case, again, it is the end of the road, for the strong digestive juices of an adult Sparrow destroy them.

But if it unselfishly carries them back to the nest and pops them into the mouths of its ravenous nestlings, the chain is complete; in the milder secretions of the nestlings' intestines, the larvae quickly develop into adults—which lay more eggs—which pass out in the excrement—which the right kind of snail eats—and the cycle is beginning all over again.

What happens to the snail who has been detentacled?

Nothing much; it simply grows new "horns," which fill up with parasites again, which another Sparrow nips off. And so *Leucochloridium paradoxum* continues to survive.

The paradox is that it has to be eaten in order to survive.

EXPLORING MARINE DRUGS

JAMES W. ATZ

"Beneficent Poison from the Sea?"

ANIMAL KINGDOM, BULLETIN OF THE NEW YORK ZOOLOGICAL SOCIETY, DECEMBER 1952

James Atz was hired by Charles Breder in 1937 and later became curator of the aquarium in the early 1960s, before moving on to the American Museum of Natural History. He wrote frequently for the Society's magazine, Animal Kingdom, *in the 1940s and '50s. An accomplished endocrinologist and geneticist, Atz collaborated with Grace Evelyn Pickford on* The Physiology of the Pituitary Gland in Fishes, *published in 1957 by the Society. By 1992, it held the record as the most-cited book in the scientific literature, with citations in more than 650 publications.*

It is hard to believe that any creature as unprepossessing as a sea cucumber could ever be a benefactor of man, but that is what one West Indian species gives promise of becoming under the guidance of Dr. Nigrelli, the Aquarium's Pathologist, and other zoologists, biochemists and pharmacologists. Sea cucumbers generally have been neglected by scientists and laymen alike. Until just a few months ago, no one except the very few sea cucumber "experts" would have dreamed of calling them exciting or promising animals for laboratory and medical research.

At that time Dr. Nigrelli took a month's leave of absence from his duties at the Aquarium and flew down to the island of Bimini in the British West Indies, sixty miles due east of Miami. There on the edge of the Gulf Stream, amidst the rich West Indian marine fauna, the American Museum of Natural History maintains the Lerner Marine Laboratory. Dr. Nigrelli had been a guest at the laboratory on two previous occasions, and he had three or four scientific problems on his agenda, one of which concerned the sea cucumber that is locally abundant in waters surrounding the island.

This species, whose scientific name is *Actinopyga agassizi*, exhibits the typical sea cucumber appearance and demeanor—that is, it looks and acts like a not-too-animated sausage. Numbers of these dark brown or reddish creatures can be seen through the crystal clear Bimini waters, very slowly moving about on white coral sand banks not far from the laboratory. Large specimens may be fifteen inches long with a diameter of five or more inches. The first time you handle one of them you receive the impression of an overgrown sock packed with mud, or perhaps a large, waterlogged loaf of brown bread. Soon, however, you become aware of the strong muscles in the animal's body wall and perhaps you can feel the hundreds of tiny tube-feet by which it ordinarily moves along the bottom. These are hydraulically operated through a complicated water vascular system consisting of innumerable canals, sacs and valves. For although the sea cucumber may look rather simply put together from the outside, inside it is in reality marvelously complex.

Its behavior is no less wonderful than its anatomy. It breathes by means of "respiratory trees," which are long, branched tubes attached to the cloaca. In breathing, water is rhythmically passed in and out through the *posterior* opening of the alimentary tract. Perhaps the most remarkable of all the sea cucumber's peculiarities is the way it defends itself by means of its own viscera. When sufficiently irritated, the animal contracts the muscles of its body and actually ruptures the walls of its own cloaca through which then shoot out the respiratory trees and sometimes the entire gut. In some species there is a special set of tubelike organs, called the Cuvierian organs, attached to the base of the respiratory trees. These, too, are thrown out of the body, and when they come into contact with sea water they swell up and form thousands of sticky white threads, enough completely to ensnare a large lobster, for instance. Such sea cucumbers are aptly called cottonspinners. After practicing this extensive self-mutilation, the sea cucumber is able to regenerate its lost organs completely.

The Cuvierian organs of the Bimini sea cucumber do not expand in sea water, but Dr. Nigrelli discovered that they nevertheless function defensively. In fact, it was the strange defensive behavior of this animal that he set out to study last June. For some time it had been noticed by Dr. Nigrelli and other workers at the Lerner Marine Laboratory that putting sea cucumbers into tanks with fishes frequently resulted in the death of the fishes. Whenever the sea cucumbers eviscerated themselves, all the fishes invariably died, but occasionally they died in the presence of intact cucumbers. Whatever the sea cucumbers gave off must have been extremely deadly, because fishes many tanks away (but receiving circulating water from the cucumber tank) were killed as readily as those in immediate contact. To find out the source and nature of this powerful substance was the number one problem on Dr. Nigrelli's program of research.

One of the reasons why Dr. Nigrelli was so interested in sea cucumber "poison" was that it seemed to offer an excellent opportunity to demonstrate a theory of his concerning the interrelationships of life in the sea. In brief his idea is this: In the struggle for existence among all the multitudinous forms of marine life, some of these creatures must have developed *chemical* means of overcoming their enemies. Accordingly, the ocean and ocean life should be the source of numerous, biologically powerful substances—especially in shallow tropical waters where the number of marine species is greater by far than anywhere else. This theory is simply an application of a concept originated by two Nobel Prize winners, Dr. Selman Waksman and Sir Alexander Fleming. Dr. Nigrelli believes the chemical "warfare" that Waksman and Fleming demonstrated as constantly going on between microorganisms, especially those of the soil, also goes on in the sea, and among both large and small marine creatures.

At the Lerner Laboratory, the first thing that Dr. Nigrelli found out was that a fluid given off by the Bimini sea cucumber at the time it shot out its "insides" contained very toxic material. He then tested different parts of

A *Caribbean sea cucumber,* showing tentacles for capturing food at the anterior end and short, mobile tube feet covering the body.

Some of the aquarium's most interesting research involved medicines from the sea, which is comparable to the rain forest in its biological diversity and vulnerability. Much of this research was conducted by Nigrelli and George D. Ruggieri, who served as director of the Osborn Laboratories of Marine Sciences from 1973 until his death in 1987 and the aquarium from 1976 to 1987.

Holothurin, investigated by Nigrelli over many years, was shown to inhibit the growth of tumors in mice, but more recent research in Japan has been inconclusive so far. Only about .5 percent of our lab testing agents and medicines—including anticoagulants and antivirals—come from the sea, but there is always hope of a vast storehouse waiting to be tapped.

the animal to discover what organ or tissue was producing this poison. The skin and various internal organs proved only slightly toxic, except for a group of small, pink, finger-like structures, the Cuvierian organs, which turned out to be the most poisonous of all. There was no doubt that this was the principal, if not the only source of the deadly stuff. Even Dr. Nigrelli was amazed at the material's strength. One ounce of a crude extract of Cuvierian organs diluted in more than 750 gallons of sea water killed fish in twenty-three minutes.

When Dr. Nigrelli returned from Bimini, he brought with him a bottle of dried Cuvierian organs for further biological and chemical analysis. A name for the strange new substance was needed, so he called it *Holothurin*, after the Class Holothuroidea to which the sea cucumbers belong. Holothurin has proved to be one of the most powerful and wide-reaching of all animal poisons. All kinds of animals are apparently susceptible to it—from protozoans (microscopic one-celled animals) to mammals—and in extremely small doses. It also affects certain plants.

No one yet knows how useful Holothurin will turn out to be, but it is worth noting that some of our most valuable drugs, such as strychnine and belladonna, are naturally-occurring poisons. . . .

Even if Holothurin should prove unsuitable for medical use, Dr. Nigrelli feels that he has come a long way toward demonstrating his theory of chemical antagonists in the sea. Moreover, there are other sea cucumbers known to be poisonous. At least one species is used by natives of the Pacific islands to stun fishes. Another is said to be so toxic that mere contact of its Cuvierian organs with the skin produces painful inflammation. And then there are all the other poisonous animals of the sea—some known, many still to be discovered. Among them may well be found important pharmaceuticals.

Conservationists have looked to the sea as mankind's great larder of the future. Dr. Nigrelli believes it may well turn out to be a medicine chest.

Brooklyn's Aquarium

Two young Atlantic walruses could be seen from the boardwalk in 1956, before the aquarium opened.

By the time the old aquarium in Battery Park was closed in 1941, the new master plan for the Bronx Zoo already included a grand new aquarium projected on a site next to the Bronx River. It was not to be. It was not until after the Korean War, in 1953, that a contract was signed by the Society and the parks department of New York City to share the costs of building a new aquarium—facing the Atlantic Ocean in Coney Island. Work was begun on the first stage of a grand design by Harrison, Fouilhoux & Abramovitz and Aymar Embury II in 1954 and completed in 1957. This first stage provided the core around which many exhibits have been added since, in different configurations than those of the early master plan.

Fairfield Osborn, with John Tee-Van on left, helps a penguin at the aquarium's official opening on June 5, 1957.

When the aquarium closed at the Battery in 1941, Christopher Coates took his study of electric eels to the Lion House basement, where his work was useful to the war effort. Here he prepares to measure the charge given off by an eel, which could register more than five hundred volts. His research of thirty years, begun in the early 1930s, contributed to our understanding of the nervous system.

Laurance S. Rockefeller and aquarium Director Christopher Coates in 1961.

Sea lions being fed by an attendant, ca. 1960.

FAIRFIELD OSBORN

from an address before the 67th Annual Convention of the General Federation of Women's Clubs

DETROIT, MICHIGAN, JUNE 3, 1958

We are more prodigal and wasteful of the resources that are drawn from the earth than any nation in the history of man. We also seem to take pride in our extravagant use of materials. We should not forget that the eyes of the world are upon us. Other nations are fully conscious of our ways of living and jealousy of our position and practices is spreading. We cannot stand alone, and I frequently wonder how long the rest of the world will let us go on as we are. Not indefinitely, surely. The idea that the riches of the earth must be shared is a growing belief—most potent in the backward, poverty-stricken countries. . . .

The pressing need for ever increasing amounts of raw materials throughout the world is compounded by the extraordinarily rapid and continuing growth of populations in virtually every country. The extent of this population increase is difficult to realize because the numbers involved border on the astronomical and are therefore hard to grasp. Take these statistics, for instance:—there are 400 million more people on the earth today than there were *only* a brief 10 years ago. . . .

Who can deny that the pressures resulting from this extremely rapid increase in human numbers are not a principal cause of world unrest? Quite apart from their social and political consequences, population increases are certainly pressing harder and harder on the world's store of natural resources.

Coming back to our own country, what are we Americans to do? There are two choices—first, continue as we are and hope we can get away with it; second, revise our standards and readjust our goals so that we may be looked upon as a prudent nation rather than a prodigal one.

I am speaking mostly as a conservationist but somewhat as a moralist. Conservation is not only an economic process but contains strong ethical objectives. There is something ethically wrong in the wastage of the earth's bounties. The slogan of America is aimed at the constant increase of our national economy. Why? Are we really any better off or any happier with a glut of material possessions? The history of civilization provides an unequivocal "no." Go through your history books and see what became of one nation after another that has attempted to build a permanent national society principally on *material* wealth. It is hard to fathom why great nations in the past have lost their place in the world. Looking back, we can observe the gradual dissolution, one after another, of the Roman Empire, the Spanish Empire, and the British Empire. There is always, of course, more than one cause for the decline of great empires, but an essential one is unquestionably the loss of adequate natural resources. Each of these three great empires did indeed make remarkable contributions to civilization through the development of the processes of law, of methods of government, or through the encouragement of the arts and sciences. Yet in each instance the emphasis of these former great powers was placed primarily upon material wealth as an end in itself. This purpose assured none of them of permanency—nor will it this country of ours. . . .

THE MOST DANGEROUS
ANIMAL IN THE WORLD

YOU ARE LOOKING AT THE MOST DANGEROUS ANIMAL
IN THE WORLD. IT ALONE OF ALL THE ANIMALS
THAT EVER LIVED CAN EXTERMINATE (AND *HAS*)
ENTIRE SPECIES OF ANIMALS. NOW IT HAS ACHIEVED
THE POWER TO WIPE OUT ALL LIFE ON EARTH.

A message in the Great Apes House.

The cure cannot come through political leadership because every politician is bound to promise "bigger and better." The cure cannot come from business and industry because the aim of every business is to "beat last year's record." Times call for a tremendous readjustment in our national point of view. The cure can come from the American citizens, individually and collectively.

CHAPTER 4

FIELD SCIENCE COMES OF AGE

From the Society's earliest days, important conservation efforts have been based on field science. Society studies in Alaska in 1897 and 1901 indicating the decline of game species laid the groundwork for William Hornaday's successful advocacy of federal laws to restrict hunting there. Charles Townsend's work on fur seals, whales, Galápagos tortoises, and Guadalupe elephant seals was done to help save them. And William Beebe's jungle and ocean expeditions, while less purposeful in this respect, celebrated biodiversity in a way that had important consequences for modern field science and conservation.

Still, most fieldwork prior to World War II presumed human dominance. Then, perhaps the impact of the war, nuclear destruction, and environmental degradation, as so vividly grasped by Fairfield Osborn, made such dominance seem less desirable. In any case, new attitudes toward studying nature in nature soon emerged in the work of several people, most notably a young Society-supported scientist named George Schaller. In his thoroughness, inclusiveness, and purpose, Schaller helped create what has become known as conservation biology—conservation through science.

Inherent in all Schaller's work is respect for nature's own processes and revulsion against claims of human superiority. Like a good teacher, he has been concerned primarily with learning from the places and creatures he studies. Each species, and each individual within that species, is to be understood on its own unique terms, rather than as a cipher in a system or a unit of bioenergy.

At the center of this transformation is a consciousness, measured by humility, that expands in several directions at once. Schaller is not simply an expert on lions or giant pandas or mountain gorillas, or any other of the species or habitats about which he has produced one landmark study after another. He is also an intimate and advocate of their lives, and as such is free to develop a full picture of how they live and what they need to flourish rather than how they can be tolerated in a human-dominated world.

Because the idea is to know as much as possible about how a species survives in an environment, how it relates to other living things and to the whole, Schaller's science achieves a new level of detail and comprehensiveness. Day after day, month after month, he records and tabulates everything he observes about an animal. And yet, though this assembling of facts is essential, it is only the beginning of understanding. The image created through fieldwork is necessarily skewed by the questions asked. In his approach, it is necessary to seek another level of comprehension, through empathy, or even identification with the animal being studied. As Schaller has one of his giant pandas say, "Most aspects of my life cannot be written in the language of mathematics." Besides, the panda continues, "It's not *your* perception of reality that matters."

The goal is not to tie up a neat little package of data, but to spend months, or even years, opening up the possibilities of knowledge, and then at some point to leave so that others might continue, the importance of the work having been established. Schaller forged such a path, conducting, in roughly three- or five-year cycles from 1959 on, seminal studies on mountain gorillas in Rwanda and Zaire, tigers and their prey in India, lions and their prey in the Serengeti, mountain goats and sheep (and snow leopards) in the Himalayas, jaguars in the swampy Pantanal of Brazil, giant pandas in China, and the wildlife of the Tibetan Plateau and of the Mongolian steppes. In most cases, each of these experiences has resulted in several studies and two books, one devoted to scientific observations, the other to personal experiences and thoughts. Thus, Schaller completes the circle of concern, or at least draws it, by fixing crucial places and species in both the scientific and the public imaginations.

Perhaps the most telling expression of Schaller's reinvention of the field is his fascination with and treatment of predators and other formerly reviled creatures. His early mentor in Alaska, of course, was Olaus Murie, who had long objected to the practice, elevated to a government policy, of killing predators in massive numbers to save their prey. Schaller went further. In succession, he took on gorillas (not predacious monsters of the jungle at all, but primarily herbivorous), then lions, tigers, snow leopards, and jaguars. By entering the predator's world, he helped emphasize, both as a Western scientist and a seeker of knowledge, their importance, and he created a space for them in our imagination that it is now difficult to deny. After his first encounter with a snow leopard in the Hindu Kush, he wrote, "I am well aware that a wilderness that has lost its large predators, whether wolf, snow leopard, or other, lacks an essential ingredient. I can feel the difference; there is less vitality, less natural tension." And there is more to science than numbers and problem-solving.

Schaller's adventures in the early 1960s, his empathetic approach, and his meticulous development of data over long periods provided a model for the Society's growing program in wildlife research and conservation. His work in Africa, along with support for wildlife reserves stimulated by the interest and contacts of Fairfield Osborn and others, was contemporary with the emergence of independent nations across the middle of the continent. Hopes seemed parallel for natural and national integrity, though new problems for both would arise soon enough. Indeed, the Society's work with the new governments from the beginning helped formulate much-needed conservation plans and strategies in which the Society continues to play a crucial role today.

The international program's course was set in 1966, under the Society's new general director, William Conway. In that year the Society's Institute of Research in Animal Behavior was established in collaboration with Rockefeller University, joining field science with explorations of the mechanisms of animal behavior. The latter type of research—on echolocation in bats, the effects of the sun on bird navigation, and other subjects—was conducted at the Bronx Zoo. In the field, the Society hired three biologists to conduct major long-term projects: Schaller, who had already started his great Serengeti study; Thomas Struhsaker, who worked on primate populations and rain-forest dynamics, first in West Africa and later in Uganda's Kibale Forest; and Roger Payne, who advanced our understanding of communication in the great whales, becoming a key figure in the battle to restrict international whale hunting.

George Schaller with a giant panda in Wolong Reserve, China (1981).

The Society's conservation committee was reconvened in 1969 under trustee Charles Nichols, Jr., who had been active in promoting Society involvement in Africa, and a major expansion of the international program began in 1972. Schaller, while studying the world's greatest variety of sheep and goats, in Central Asia, became coordinator of field science on five continents. The Society's presence was becoming more distinctive, associated with and responsible for, in the manner of Schaller himself, key species and key areas.

Among them were African elephants and the East African savannas where they live. With Society support, Iain Douglas-Hamilton began elephant surveys in 1976 that are still the basis for measuring the species' drastic decline. David Western, on the Society's staff since 1973, monitored the ecology of Amboseli National Park in Kenya and worked out revenue sharing for the Masai people. He became the Society's director for conservation strategy and one of the principal thinkers and planners working on elephant and black rhino survival across Africa. In 1994, Western was appointed head of Kenya's Wildlife Services by President Daniel arap Moi.

The progression from field research to implementation has been repeated in many parts of the globe, so that by the mid-1990s the Society had become the primary agent for conservation in such crucial, and often extensive areas as Zaire's Ituri Forest, Congo's Nouabalé-Ndoki Park, Rwanda's Nyungwe Forest, Argentina's Patagonian coast, Peru's Manu National Park, Brazil's flooded forest at Mamirauá, Belize's barrier reef and Maya Mountains, Guatemala's Tikal National Park, Papua New Guinea's Crater Mountain Wildlife Management Area, the Chang Tang Wildlife Reserve on the Tibetan Plateau, and Sarawak's mangrove forests. The number of field projects conducted by the Society each year now exceeds 225, and the number of parks and reserves established with Society help is more than 110.

But again, numbers do not tell the story or solve problems. George Schaller realized early that neither understanding nor conservation can be achieved in the abstract. His projects and books reflect his awareness not only of the landscape but the human culture associated with it. Younger scientists, and the Society's international program as a whole, in fact, are particularly sensitive to the needs and aspirations of local communities. As new nations evolve and resources diminish, the process of saving enough nature to matter becomes more intricate.

Society field biologists are stationed around the globe. In addition to gathering crucial data and devising conservation strategies, they train local conservation biologists, try to meet the needs and aspirations of local people, work with government agencies, organize conservation groups and actions, explore the possibilities of ecotourism, and provide expert help in education, wildlife management, wildlife health, and even graphics and exhibition design.

What started out one hundred years ago as urgent, specialized pleading for the protection of wildlife has become a program that touches every aspect of modern life.

Above: David Western and
elephants in Amboseli
National Park, created in
1974 on the basis of his studies,
which began in 1967.

Left: William Conway (right)
at 14,800 feet in the Bolivian
Andes (1960). On Conway's
recommendation, the Laguna
Colorado Reserve was established here in 1961 to protect
the breeding area of the James
flamingo.

African lion in the Serengeti and lioness after the kill.

GEORGE B. SCHALLER

from "Introduction"

SERENGETI: A KINGDOM OF PREDATORS,
1975

*Extensive fieldwork in the Serengeti Plains
began in the 1950s, and in 1966 John Owen,
director of the Tanzania National Parks,
established the Serengeti Research Institute in
the center of the plains. One of several scientists
invited to work there, Schaller produced over
the next three years the first long-term study of
lions, with particular emphasis on the effects
of predation. Other studies followed, and the
5,600-square-mile area continues to support
a spectacular diversity of wildlife, despite
pressures from development, poaching, and
growing human populations.*

*Hunting in the Serengeti reached its peak
in the 1920s. Laws passed in 1937 and anti-
poaching campaigns reduced the killing but
could not help animals outside the parks.*

As a scientist I am by tradition expected to control my experience rather than yield to it. In this I failed yet am not displeased to have done so. I cherished my escape from the organized lunacy of life in the city to the elemental complexity of the wilderness. Yesterday, today, and tomorrow became one as I lived for the moment only, seeking a sense of unity with the earth, the animals. As weeks and months passed, I learned to recognize many of the lions and other predators. Ceasing to be mere animals, they became individuals about whose problems I worried and whose future I anticipated. They became part of my memories of an austere and seemingly harsh land in which man seems of no consequence until he imperceptibly becomes a part of it. This life of isolation, of spending hours alone each day with animals, was part reality, part illusion, and it suited me; it was neither a denial of life nor a retreat from those I loved, but a way of sustaining a sense of spiritual independence. Solitude provokes reflection, and the study became a quest for understanding, not just of the predators but also of myself, a personal *corrida*. . . .

The most pleasant way to approach the Serengeti is from the east, across the highlands, tracing the rim of Ngorongoro Crater, where wisps of cloud finger through the mountain forests, then dipping down into the grassy Malanja depression before suddenly topping a rise to see the plains far below, stretching boundlessly to the horizon. Gently rolling, they extend for some two thousand square miles. "And all this a sea of grass, grass, grass, grass, and grass. One looks around and sees only grass and sky," exulted Fritz Jaeger, who in 1907 was one of the first Europeans to visit the area. It is an exciting view, though alien in its immensity; the eyes roam, seeking a place to rest, but the plains seem without end except for the Gol Mountains in the north, subdued and featureless in the sun. The tortuous road drops down the escarpment and then heads west, at first flanked by an occasional acacia, then cut by the wooded depression of Olduvai Gorge, whose depths have revealed more of man's history than any other place on earth, before finally reaching the open plains. Trailing a ribbon of dust, one drives on without landmark, the horizon without depth and perspective, until at last Naabi Hill rises ahead, humped like a stranded whale. Here in the eastern plains the grass is short, but toward the west, where the soil is deeper and there is more rain, it reaches a height of three feet, measureless waves of stems which no plow has ever touched.

Jumbled piles of granite, the kopjes, jut from the plains like a string of islands, the boulders polished smooth by the wind and rain. These kopjes are worlds of their own. Fleshy-leafed aloes grow there and in moist clefts sometimes a *Gloriosa* lily, its crimson blossoms incongruous in this landscape of modest tones. I liked climbing in the kopjes, though always hoping that I would not disturb a lion or leopard in its shady retreat. Occasionally one finds some paintings, of shields and animals and little stick men, done with charcoal and ochre by the pastoral Masai, who had ruled this area for over one hundred years before it was made into a national park. The work is crude and recent, yet I took pleasure in finding this hidden art, rarely seen now except by the red-and-blue *Agama* lizards that scurry over the rock

faces. As one sits on a kopje, eyes squinting against the brilliant light, the plains distorted by quivering heat waves, the imagination conjures up visions, visions that inevitably dissolve into mere kopjes and zebra.

※

The first impression of an animal is often the one that remains most clearly in the mind. The day after I arrived at Seronera I found two lionesses at the edge of the plains, their tawny pelage so much a part of the golden *Themeda* grass in which they sat that to me any yellow sward is now somehow incomplete without a lion. Their eyes were fixed on a herd of Thomson's gazelle, their whole bodies straining toward it, as if willing it to approach. Moving in single file, the herd drew closer and the lionesses parted, one to the right, the other to the left, mere wisps of wind among the tall stalks as they snaked into position. Oblivious of danger, the gazelle continued along a well-worn trail until they were between the lionesses. A breeze stirred the midday lull and suddenly the gazelle scented lion. Leaping and twisting they scattered and raced away, still ignorant as to where the enemy lurked. One gazelle rushed toward a hidden lioness, and spotting the motionless form too late to change course it leaped high above the grass in a desperate attempt to escape. But with exquisite timing the lioness reached up and with gleaming agate claws plucked the animal out of the air. Incidents such as this help deflate one's sense of superiority, the feeling that man is somehow graced in all respects with greater power than other creatures. Every species has those attributes which best suit it for a certain type of existence, and looking at my own body so lacking in weapons, other than cunning, I can only marvel that man survived at all.

GEORGE B. SCHALLER

from "Lion"

SERENGETI: A KINGDOM OF PREDATORS,
1975

*Schaller's field assistant
radio-tracking lions
at sunset.*

A study is most interesting and satisfying when one deals with known individuals. As lions lack a distinctive coat pattern, such as the stripes of zebra and splotches of giraffe, I realized that there would be difficulties in recognizing many animals with certainty in the vastness of the park. I solved this problem in two ways. Selecting a limited area around Seronera, I concentrated on identifying every lion in it by such characters as torn and notched ears, scars, and other blemishes. Most lions lived permanently there and soon became acquaintances whom I knew at a glance. There was, for example, The Old One, whose worn canines, drawn look, and heavy tread showed that she was the local matriarch. One-ear and One-eye, both lionesses, often traveled together as if their deformities were a basis for their bond. And there was Flop-ear, the quintessential lioness, a big, bold, beautiful animal in the prime of life. Also using the area were three males with huge manes, an aristocratic trio who radiated an almost palpable power. Like the Three Musketeers they roamed together through their domain, but to name these sedate, shaggy beasts Athos, Porthos, and Aramis was not befitting and I called them prosaically Black Mane, Brown Mane and Limp.

To help plot the lions' movements, I placed ear tags on 156 of them. Driving close to a cat, I fired a syringe from a carbon dioxide-powered gun into its thigh. The muscle relaxant succinylcholine chloride is injected on impact and about five minutes later the lion rolls onto its side. First I clamped a colored and numbered metal tag into each ear, then sometimes took a blood sample for later disease studies, and finally withdrew into the car, watching the lion's recovery carefully. Usually it raised its head, fully alert, within twenty-five minutes, quite oblivious of the tags. In most instances the whole operation went so smoothly that other pride members either ignored me or watched the activity from as close as thirty feet. However, once a lioness died, to me such a traumatic experience that I nearly gave up this aspect of my work. Except for the sharp, sudden pain with the impact of the syringe, the lions suffered little discomfort. Yet I came to detest tagging and after the first few necessary months did little of it. In the beginning it did give me atavistic pleasure to squat by a lion and slide my palm over its sleek, slightly oily hide, to run my fingers through its tangled mane, but with time I developed such a feeling of tenderness for these beasts that I found it abhorrent to disturb them in any way. Tagged lions appeared occasionally near Seronera, where visitors saw them and objected to the adornments. Nobody seems repelled by large numerals painted on the hides of elephants or garish collars placed around the necks of wildebeest, but a tagged lion is a desecration. As Evelyn Ames noted: "Lions are not animals alone: they are symbols and totems and legend; they have impressed themselves so deeply on the human mind, if not its blood, it is as though the psyche were emblazoned with their crest." I had empathy with the protesters—tourists, park wardens, hunters—but I also needed the information that tagged lions would provide.

For example, without tagging, I would not have known male No. 57. I first met him in November 1966, at Musabi, a small plain in the western part of the park. He was about two and a half to three years old, a rather scruffy fellow with tufts of mane sticking untidily from his cheeks and a rakish ruff down his nape. Like almost all males of his age he had aban-

In 1962, the Society funded the purchase of the Lamai Wedge, a stretch of land near the Kenya border that is crucial to the traditional wildebeest migrations from the Serengeti to the Mara. For many years, these migrations were monitored by A. R. E. (Tony) Sinclair with support from the Society. Today, research zoologist Patricia Moehlman, while studying jackals in the Ngorongoro Conservation Area adjacent to the Serengeti, trains Tanzanian teams to monitor park ecology throughout the country.

doned his pride, maybe forced out by the adults or simply overcome by wanderlust, and he now roamed alone, a nomad with neither home nor companions. I saw him twice more around Musabi, but in March 1967, after the migratory herds had moved to the plains, he appeared there, fifty-five miles east of where I had tagged him. He was still on the plains in June, sometimes alone, at other times with lions he had met casually. Though not antisocial, he had a restless spirit and always left his newfound acquaintances. However, June 12 was a momentous day in his life. He had rested all day on a rise and at dusk set out purposefully on some mysterious errand. At 9:25 P.M. he met a male of his own age and they walked on together, and by some intangible process they cemented a friendship which lasted until death. They spent July to about December in the woodlands near Musabi and in January 1968 returned to the plains. I last saw them there in late May, now powerful, handsome males with full manes. Where they spent the dry season I have no idea. But I do know that on November 9, 1968, they were northeast of the park, outside of its boundaries. I know that a Land Rover or maybe a Toyota drove close to them, stopped, and a man with a rifle stepped out—assuming he obeyed the law. The males had no fear of cars and even a person on foot caused only uneasiness. Perhaps they stood watching, perhaps they lumbered off to continue their rest elsewhere. In any event, a bullet slammed into male No. 57. The outfitter of the hunt sent the ear tag to me. It was a generous gesture, yet I cupped the blood-encrusted silver tag in my palm with a terrible sadness. I would rather have retained my vision of male No. 57 wandering through his kingdom, the grassy plains, the hollow vastness of the sky. Now I see him nailed to a wall, staring glassy-eyed, his teeth bared in supplication.

More than one million wildebeest occupy the Serengeti Plains during the rainy season, from December to May. They return north for the rest of the year and are protected throughout their migration range.

Impala herds in the grasslands are composed of females and young.

Africa's Savannas

The vast plains of Kenya and Tanzania host unmatched congregations of wildlife— elephants, rhinos, lions, leopards, cheetahs, buffaloes, wildebeest, zebras, giraffes, hippos, various antelopes, and more. Wildlife parks and reserves have protected these living spectacles, at least in diminished form, but the need for study and vigilance is constant. Society scientists, most of them African, have been working in both countries since the early 1960s. The long-term emphasis is on monitoring ecological conditions and interactions between humans and wildlife in order to ensure the continued effectiveness of Tanzania's and Kenya's many protected regions, including Ngorongoro Conservation Area and Amboseli National Park.

Black rhino in Kenya's Nairobi National Park, with the city in the background. The park has been fenced to prevent poaching of the species, now reduced to fewer than twenty-five hundred animals.

Right: African elephants at sunset in Kenya's Amboseli National Park.

Below: Research Zoologist Patricia Moehlman (right) trains and works with ecological monitoring teams in Ngorongoro Conservation Area and other Tanzanian parks.

GEORGE B. SCHALLER

from "Among Gorillas"

THE YEAR OF THE GORILLA, 1964

George Schaller and his wife, Kay, studied mountain gorillas in the Virunga Volcanos of Zaire (then Congo) in 1959 and 1960, at altitudes of ten thousand feet and higher. Very little was known at the time about gorillas or, indeed, about any of the great apes. Schaller soon discovered that his subjects were not the raging beasts of myth, but gentle, group-oriented animals that fed primarily on plants.

As a champion of the species, Schaller was followed by Dian Fossey in the late 1960s and '70s and then by Amy Vedder and Bill Weber, who began the Mountain Gorilla Project (MGP) in Rwanda in 1979. Vedder and Weber's work on how mountain gorillas use the forest and how economics and human attitudes affect conservation, complemented by local education programs, led to greater protection for the gorillas and a popular ecotourism program before 1994's disastrous internal warfare. In Schaller's time, the population of this most endangered ape was estimated at four to five hundred. The number declined to about 250 in the late 1970s due to poaching, then rose to about 320 by 1990, as a direct result of the MGP.

Frequently my first intimation that the gorillas were near was the sudden swaying of a lobelia or a branch, jarred by a passing animal. Then there were two courses open to me: I could hide myself and watch the gorillas without their being aware of my presence, or I could remain in the open with the hope that, over the days and weeks, the animals would become accustomed to seeing me near them. The former method had a great advantage, since the behavior of the apes was not influenced in any way by my intrusion. But I soon found out that I often lost useful observations when I hid myself too well, for if I tried for a better view, the animals saw me and grew excited. I usually walked slowly and in full view toward the gorillas and climbed up on a stump or tree branch where I settled myself as comfortably as possible without paying obvious attention to the animals. By choosing a prominent observation post, I was not only able to see the gorillas in the undergrowth, but they could inspect me clearly and keep an eye on me.

Animals are better observers and far more accurate interpreters of gestures than man. I felt certain that if I moved around calmly and alone near the gorillas, obviously without dangerous intent toward them, they would soon realize that I was harmless. It is really not easy for man to shed all his arrogance and aggressiveness before an animal, to approach it in utter humility with the knowledge of being in many ways inferior. Casual actions are often sufficient to alert the gorillas and to make them uneasy. For example, I believe that even the possession of a firearm is sufficient to imbue one's behavior with a certain unconscious aggressiveness, a feeling of being superior, which an animal can detect. When meeting a gorilla face to face, I reasoned, an attack would be more likely if I carried a gun than if I simply showed my apprehension and uncertainty. Among some creatures—the dog, rhesus monkey, gorilla, and man—a direct unwavering stare is a form of threat. Even while watching gorillas from a distance I had to be careful not to look at them too long without averting my head, for they became uneasy under my steady scrutiny. Similarly they considered the unblinking stare of binoculars and cameras as a threat, and I had to use these instruments sparingly. As could be expected, gorillas were more annoyed and excited on seeing two persons than one. Kay had to remain home much of the time, and the park guard, who sometimes accompanied me, had to hide himself while I watched the apes. I decided not to follow the animals once they had moved from my sight, for pursuit could easily frighten them and increase the chance of attacks. In general, I put myself into the place of a gorilla and tried to imagine to what actions I would object if suddenly a strange and potentially dangerous creature approached me. In all the months I spent with the gorillas, none attacked me.

Establishing rapport with the gorillas was fairly easy, because their senses are comparable to those of man—not man of the city who is unable to react to the subtle stimuli of his surroundings amidst the incessant noise of the machine, but man attuned to the wilderness. As with man, sight is the most important sense in gorillas. The apes are very quick at spotting slight

movements, and often they watched my approach before I was even aware of their presence. Hearing, too, is well developed in gorillas, but they respond only to strange sounds, like the human voice, or sounds out of context. When a group fed noisily, my approach could be rather casual, but when they were resting all were alert to a stray branch snapping underfoot. The sense of smell seems to be relatively poor in gorillas: they rarely responded to my presence even when I was downwind and within fifty feet of the them. Twice, however, gorillas seemed to smell me when I sweated profusely—but, as Kay commented, it does not take an acute sense of smell to do that.

On several occasions resting animals became uneasy while I was watching them from a distance. I was upwind, completely silent, and they obviously had not seen me. Yet they seemed to sense that something was not quite right. Perhaps they responded to subliminal stimuli, too vague to be assimilated consciously; or perhaps some other sense warned them of possible danger. I have had similar experiences when wandering through the forest. Suddenly I had the feeling, in fact I knew, that gorillas were close by, yet I had neither seen, heard, nor smelled them. More often than not, I was correct. Most naturalists, I feel sure, have had similar encounters with animals. . . .

All apprehension of the gorillas had long since left me. Not once had their actions portrayed ferocity or even outright anger. The silverbacked males were somewhat annoyed, to be sure, and several animals were excit-

Above: Kay Schaller in a gorilla nest, one of more than three thousand studied by her husband in 1959. Constructed in trees or on the ground, of bamboo or other available branches, the nests are used for only one night.

Opposite: Male silverback mountain gorilla.

The Virunga Volcanoes
in Zaire, with a view
of Mt. Mikeno.

Female and infant
mountain gorilla.

ed, but all this was offset by their curiosity concerning me and their rapid acceptance of me. As long as I remained quiet, they felt so safe that they continued their daily routine even to the extent of taking their naps beside the tree in which I was sitting. Early in the study I had noted that the gorillas tend to have an extremely placid nature which is not easily aroused to excitement. They give the impression of being stoic and reserved, of being introverted. Their expression is usually one of repose, even in situations which to me would have been disturbing. All their emotions are in their eyes, which are a soft, dark brown. The eyes have a language of their own, being subtle and silent mirrors of the mind, revealing constantly changing patterns of emotion that in no other visible way affect the expression of the animal. I could see hesitation and uneasiness, curiosity and boldness and annoyance. Sometimes, when I met a gorilla face to face, the expression in its eyes more than anything else told me of his feelings and helped me decide my course of action.

The brief morning spell of sunshine had given way to dank clouds that descended to the level of the trees. For five hours I perched on a branch, chilled through and through, my fingers so stiff I was barely able to take notes. It began to rain heavily, and soon the rain turned to hail. The gorillas sat in a hunched position, letting the marble-sized stones bound off their backs. They looked thoroughly miserable with the water dripping off their brow ridges, and the long hairs on their arms were a sodden mass. I sat huddled next to the trunk of the tree, hoping for some protection from the canopy. My face was close to the bark, and I smelled the fungus-like odor of lichen and moldy moss. I could not leave the gorillas without disturbing them, and I had to wait until they moved away.

After the hail ceased and the rain was a mere drizzle, the gorillas spread out to forage. From behind a bush came a curious staccato sound, one which I had not heard before: a rapid series of loud ö—ö-ö-ö, with the first vowel forceful, emphatic, and separated from the others by a distinct pause. This sound was emitted over and over again, and after two or three minutes I became aware of the situation that elicited it. D. J. and a female were together. They were copulating. She rested on her knees, belly, and elbows, and D. J. was mounted behind, holding onto her hips. The male pushed, and since the slope was steep, the two animals moved downhill. They covered forty feet in fifteen minutes, with the female using her hands to part vegetation as they progressed. They stopped three times. D. J. was thrusting rapidly. His vocalizations grew harsher, and the female screamed piercingly. The male now clasped her by the armpits, and he was nearly covering her back. They came to rest against a tree trunk, and a hoarse, trembling sound, almost a roar, escaped from D.J.'s parted lips, interrupted by sharp intakes of breath. He sat back, the act completed. The female lay motionless for ten seconds, then walked slowly uphill, while the male remained, panting. In spite of these far from silent doings, none of the other members of the group paid the slightest attention. Even Big Daddy, the boss, who rested in full view of the copulators, was seemingly oblivious of the spectacle.

*Young male mountain gorilla
in the Virungas, Rwanda.*

In the forest of the Virungas, fog occurs almost daily.

Gorillas in the Midst

While small numbers of mountain gorillas (about six hundred) have been sustained in Zaire and Rwanda (at least until the recent upheavals there), the much larger populations of lowland gorillas (up to thirty thousand) have become increasingly threatened. Expansive tracts of equatorial African forest are still untouched, and therefore savable, but agriculture, logging, and other human encroachments are rapidly exposing wildlife there to danger. Society studies in Central African Republic, Congo Republic, and Gabon are particularly concerned with human impacts on lowland gorillas, and a census in Zaire has determined the vulnerability and population size of the Grauer's, or eastern lowland gorilla. Monitoring of the mountain gorillas in Zaire and Rwanda continues.

At Karisoke Research Center in northwest Rwanda, where she and Bill Weber began their mountain gorilla work in the late 1970s, Amy Vedder records the day's field notes.

GEORGE B. SCHALLER

from "Preface"

THE LAST PANDA, 1993

Like the mountain gorilla, the giant panda occupies a wet (though somewhat colder) mountain forest, and its numbers are few, perhaps only a thousand animals in the central Chinese provinces of Sichuan, Gansu, and Shaanxi. In order to protect the species, particularly from the periodic die-off of their bamboo food source, Schaller and his Chinese colleagues studied the feeding strategies, movement, activity patterns, population dynamics, and social behavior of the population in Wolong Natural Reserve from 1980 through 1984. Advising on the project, which was originally organized by the Chinese government and the World Wildlife Fund— International (now the World Wide Fund for Nature), were Society General Director William Conway on animal management and research facilities, veterinarians Emil Dolensek and Janet Stover on a breeding program, and nutritionist Ellen Dierenfeld on the panda's bamboo diet.

Schaller's book The Last Panda *(1993) details not only his earlier research but the poaching, inappropriate rent-a-panda programs, and bureaucratic bungling that jeopardized conservation. The book focused new attention, in both China and the United States, on the need for effective plans for the panda's survival.*

Staff from the Wolong Reserve transport the body of a female panda found by Schaller in a poacher's snare.

Having transcended its mountain home to become a citizen of the world, the panda is a symbolic creature that represents our efforts to protect the environment. Though dumpy and bearlike, it has been patterned with such creative flourish, such artistic perfection, that it almost seems to have evolved for this higher purpose. A round, rather flat face, large black eye patches, and a cuddly and clumsy appearance give the panda an innocent, childlike quality that evokes universal empathy, a desire to hug and protect. And it is rare. Survivors are somehow more poignant than casualties. Together, these and other traits have created a species in which legend and reality merge, a mythic creature in the act of life.

We are fortunate that the panda is still with us, that our evolutionary paths have crossed. Values should not, I suppose, be assigned to creatures to whom values are unknown, and who all have equal claim to our fascination and respect. Still, the panda would seem more of a loss than a primrose or piranha, for it epitomizes the stoic defiance of fate and stirs our emotions with pity and admiration. If we lose the panda, we will never look on its black-and-white face again, its evolution will stop, its unique genetic code destroyed; its name will soon have little more significance than that of thousands of other species listed in the dusty catalogues of the world's museums, *Ailuropoda melanoleuca*, meaning the "black-and-white panda-foot." As the obscurity of centuries separates the animal from us, we will be left with only mementos, a few massive bones, some faded hides. The pandas' lives will be forgotten, gone from our collective memories like the moa and mammoth. What a melancholy fate for so extraordinary an animal. All creatures, of course, are transitory, flourishing for a while, then fading away. However, pandas are survivors who were present several million years ago, before humankind became human, and they have outlived many other large mammals that vanished during the upheavals of the Ice Age. Their time as a species should not yet be over.

✺

Sounds downhill suddenly transform the forest—the snap of a breaking bamboo shoot, followed by the rustle and squeak of sheaths being torn away, and finally loud crunching as Zhen eats the tender center. Minutes pass to the sounds of her foraging. A panda's sense of smell is acute. Would she notice my presence and vanish unseen? But no, she angles noiselessly uphill. I detect a fleeting movement, then watch raptly as she emerges and sits behind a thin screen of bamboo. She leans sideways to hook in a bamboo shoot with the curved claws of a forepaw, and with the same motion breaks off the shoot near its base. Then, settling back and holding the shoot at a slant, she bites into the sheath and with mouth pulling sideways and forepaw jerking down while twisting, she tears away the sheath and drops it. She then takes a few quick bites, pushing the shoot into the corner of her mouth where it becomes rapidly shorter like a pencil in a voracious sharpener. Glancing around, she spies another shoot; peeling and chomping, she eats it too within a minute. A third shoot follows, her actions calm and deliberate in complete accord with her surroundings, yet at the same time fluid and rapid, as if she has little time.

As I watch her eat, I am impressed by her dexterity, forepaws and mouth working together with great precision and economy of motion. Evolution has provided the panda with special adaptations for subsisting on bamboo. There is a sixth finger, a prehensile elongated wrist bone, the radial sesamoid, that functions as a thumb, ideal for handling shoots and stems, even those of arrow bamboo a fraction of an inch thick. Stems are held as with forceps in a hairless groove connecting the pad of the first finger and the "pseudothumb." The panda's typical carnivorous dentition has been modified for crushing and grinding tough food; not only the molars but even some premolars are broad and flat. The skull is unusually wide and there is a bone crest on top of the braincase that provides a point of attachment for the powerful jaw muscles. The panda is a triumph of evolution. However, by becoming highly specialized on bamboo, it has reduced its options. Freed from choices, it may seem at first glance to be freer than most animals, yet evolution has robbed it of innovative vigor, imprisoned it with an ecological possessiveness that knows no reprieve: bamboo has fettered the species with its impassive power. Although I marvel at Zhen's evolutionary specializations, I am also touched by the tragic history of her species, her helplessness. Indifferent fates have mastered her.

Zhen raises her nose as if testing the air, apparently sensing my presence. With a rolling motion she rises and moves from behind the bamboo into a bower from which a path leads to my clearing. She steps forward with a combination of shyness and audacity. Her black legs dissolve into the shadows to create an illusion of a shining lantern gliding toward me. She advances to within thirty-five feet. There she stops, her head bobbing up and down as she snorts to herself in wary alertness, her apprehension and mine a bond of shared feeling. I look for some intimation of coming actions in her face, but it remains inert, showing neither passion nor docility. Here the panda does not invite familiarity but is imposing with the same durability as the fir trees and rugged peaks, complete in itself, final.

Not being a creature of self-expression, Zhen conveys none of her inner

GEORGE B. SCHALLER

from *"A Mountain of Treasure"*
THE LAST PANDA, 1993

Tang-Tang awakens from his rest in a pine tree in Tangjiahe Reserve, one of twelve giant panda reserves, mostly in Sichuan province.

feelings. I wonder what she will do now. Certainly she does something unexpected. After gazing intently in my direction, she retreats to the margin of the bamboo and there, slumped against the stems, gives agitated, bleating honks, a strangely vulnerable and timid sound from so large an animal. Hunched in repose, forepaws on rounded abdomen as if meditating, she has the aura of Buddha. Her honks grow softer as her head sags onto her chest. The slow rhythmic heaving of her body reveals that imperturbably she has fallen asleep.

Although Zhen has just eaten and is therefore programmed for a digestive trance, I hardly expect her to fall asleep in front of me. What intuition, what reason is there in that broad, hard skull? A panda has its version of the world and I have mine. What does the world look like to a panda? On meeting a gorilla or a tiger, I can sense the relationship that binds us by the emotions they express, for curiosity, friendliness, annoyance, apprehension, anger, fear are all revealed by face and body. In contrast, Zhen and I are together yet hopelessly separated by an immense space. Her feelings remain impenetrable, her behavior inscrutable. Intellectual insights enrich emotional experiences. But with Zhen I am in danger of coming away empty-handed from a mountain of treasure. To comprehend her, I would need to transform myself into a panda, unconscious of myself, concentrating on her actions and spirit for many years, until finally I might gain fresh insights. Yet I see Zhen and her kind so seldom that, although I can capture a little of the science of the animal, her being eludes me. I am not even certain how to begin. The panda is the answer. But what is the question?

Zhen soon awakens, and without hesitation or a glance in my direction she moves uphill, drawing the shadows around her so abruptly that her dissolution is as startling as her appearance. I remain sitting, unwilling to disturb her, wherever she is, and wishing to prolong these moments. Rain now whispers on the leaves and there is a sound as of distant surf in the tree tops. How long have I been in the clearing? Time has no single measure. Absorbed in Zhen, I am released from past and future until she breaks the spell of our meeting, leaving me with feelings stronger than any memory.

✻

GEORGE B. SCHALLER

from "Wei-Wei's World"
THE LAST PANDA, 1993

As an explorer in the ways of animals, I carefully observe what an individual does and write down everything to capture what I have seen. Later I take the unadorned facts and impersonal descriptions, neatly tabulate and graph them, and express the information logically, as if the work had progressed step by step to an inevitable conclusion. Truth and science are served. Lacking in such reports is the human factor, the joy of discovery, the pleasure of a new insight, the admission that research is sporadic and haphazard—and the fact that the information is not as objective as one would like to think. Statistics may help to describe the universe but not other beings; numbers cannot convey the quality of a creature, they cannot express love, anger, joy, and courage.

In addition, as Werner Heisenberg noted: "We have to remember that what we observe is not nature herself, but nature exposed to our method of questioning." A fact is not a fact until someone has posed the question, and slowly the world of an animal emerges from the questions raised and facts collected. But if someone else asks a different question, a different creature, a different reality, comes into existence. The animal is an illusion created out of the animal's interaction with an observer who decides what to measure and record and what to ignore. We constantly infer the unseen, we confuse ideas with facts. Furthermore, animals bound, prowl, slither, and flap through our subconscious in the form of myths about lions, bats, foxes, owls, snakes and doves, each culture with its own fantasies. Victor Hugo wrote, "Animals are nothing but the forms of our virtues and vices, wandering before our eyes, the visible phantoms of our souls." In such a way is science fashioned. Any biologist who observes a tiger, gorilla, panda, or other creature and says he or she has done so with total objectivity is ignorant, dishonest, or foolish.

Such thoughts were in my mind that winter because Hu Jinchu and I would leave Wolong in June for several months to write a report on our panda research. The task would be difficult. We had so far collected much valid and useful information. How would our two cultures, our two different systems of thought, treat this common subject? The Chinese biologists with whom I had talked and whose scientific papers I had read used methods, discussed results, and provided insights that seemed wholly Western in concept without even, as the Chinese would say, "eating a Western meal in the Chinese manner." It would be rewarding to find out what Chinese perspective Hu Jinchu had brought to the study of pandas.

The problem of penetrating the panda's mystery was made even clearer to me one foggy afternoon that found Hu Jinchu and me in an almost impenetrable bamboo thicket. Suddenly the fog grew intensely bright as if sundered by the sun, and in a shaft of strange light a panda was before us, leaning eerily calm against a fir, paws resting in his lap. At first I thought it was Wei, but he was uncollared. His expression was stern but with a touch of humor, and his eyes were vivid like a hawk's. I was somewhat astonished when he abruptly began a monologue that seemed to transcend ordinary language—though perhaps the magic of the occasion was only in my mind:

Honorable scientists: I want to compliment you on your efforts to study my kind. It takes dedication of the highest order to measure so many droppings. Day after day you follow my tracks with admirable persistence if not technique: I can hear and smell you from far away. Actually I'm not certain what you expect to gain from invading my privacy. You generate numbing statistics about the number of stems I eat in a day and the number of hours I sleep. Remember, time is not the same for all living things. This fir lives more slowly than you, and I more quickly. And as to counting stems, it merely shows that you have discovered some easy facts about me; most aspects of my life cannot be written in the language of mathematics. How can you understand me? We may seem to share certain moods, but you cannot comprehend mine. After all, it's not *your* perception of reality that matters. Look at each other. Your ways of thinking are vastly different, yet you belong to the same species.

You people are unbelievably conceited. Just because yours is the most prominent intelligence around, you also act as if it's the highest.

This field camp, nearly eight thousand feet up in the bamboo forest at Wuyipeng, housed Schaller, his wife, and his Chinese colleagues from December 1980 to June 1982.

There are many serious problems in your style of thinking; you must overcome your ideological prejudices and other unhealthy scientific tendencies. Some of you, for instance, hold that language is necessary before one can think, and that makes me and all others—except you—unthinking creatures. What frivolous nonsense! What arrogance! Your laboratory people first look to see what an animal can't do and then attempt to teach it that. Study what an animal can do best. No wonder someone even referred to me, a panda, as an interesting example of color over content. How can you measure my intelligence, my way of thinking, by your standards? At least you two merely try to observe, not judge. Keep in mind that we live in different worlds, each unimaginably different, I primarily in a world of odors, you of sight; I think mainly with smells, you with words. Ludwig Wittgenstein wrote, "If a lion could talk, we could not understand him." An intelligent remark for a human, and a foreign barbarian at that.

The panda shone with a blinding white light, and his body became dim and shapeless as smoke and dispersed. Just as casually it condensed again into a palpable yet transitory creature, form and emptiness coexisting, matter and space inseparable, energy and spirit integrated.

Another point. You study my diet, you study how many times I scent mark and mate and how far I travel. Remember, you cannot divide me into independent fragments of existence. At best you might perceive an approximation of a panda, not the reality of one. I am, like any other being, infinite in complexity, indivisible, a harmonious whole.

Let me make some suggestions for improving your work. Forget science now and then; silence the rational mind. Try to make my life real by using intuition, sensibility, and empathy. Never forget that all living things are part of the bamboo of life. All animals, even humans, are one great living being. You cannot describe a panda without also describing yourselves; separateness is an illusion. Send me your philosophers, poets, and children, for they will see me with a new vision. Even so, we shall always remain of two worlds. Humans can never know the truth about pandas. Therefore, enjoy the mystery— and help us endure.

With that emphatic ending, the panda pulled the fog around himself, the glow of light contracting to a spark that died.

But he left two droppings by the tree, and these I collected.

STONES OF SILENCE

The hills of Sind still wear a veil of heat as I venture from the hut. In midafternoon the landscape is bitter, a desiccated world in which nothing moves under a sun so hot the sky is almost white. Nearby the hostile wall of sun-blistered cliffs rises nearly a thousand feet above the plains. With the thermometer registering 105°F. I wearily shoulder my rucksack, pick up my spotting scope, and approach the cliffs over a stony flat and up a dry wash. Soon I reach the angular shade of Kira, a gray slab of wind-sculpted rock, and then follow the switchback trail which ascends a ravine. The defile is oppressively still. Every boulder radiates heat; the rocks underfoot clatter aside with a dry rattle, and even the meager stands of acacia trees that had found refuge here seem dehydrated. My sweat is the only available moisture. But as I approach the hard-edged crest, a breeze funnels down a cleft, and with renewed vigor I scramble up the last few feet to the top of the Karchat Hills.

There, partially hidden behind an outcrop, I stand looking over the convex plateau and the deeply eroded ravines that dissect it; I peruse the rugged scarps that fall to the plains below, searching each shadowy nook for evidence of life. But there is no sign of the Persian wild goat I have come to observe. I wait. As cliff shadows on the plains lengthen, the land seems less cruel, less abandoned, becoming almost gentle and tranquil in the mellow light. Hills, plateaus, and plains extend to the horizon, not crowded as in the northern mountains but with long vistas between each range. A black eagle skims past Kira. When no wild goats appear I leave this observation post, my feet treading upon a world of great antiquity which was once far different from the barren mountaintops of today. Among scattered fragments of limestone on the surface I find fossils: stems of crinoid lilies resembling pieces of wood, fanlike ribs of scallop shells imprinted on stone, small snail shells huddled among pebbles, delicate and perfect as if only momentarily at rest, and very rarely a sea urchin, gleaming like marble. As I collect a handful of treasures, squalls begin to buffet me, and soon a desert wind howls among the crags and defiles, stinging my face with sand. It will now blow throughout the night and into the following morning.

In the lee of some boulders I clear away the rock rubble, unroll a thin foam rubber pad and on it spread a sheet, my bed for the night. After eating an orange and several crackers, I tuck my binoculars and scope into a rucksack to protect them from drifting sand, then recline facing the first evening stars. I listen intently, but there is only the wind. From far away it ripples over the rocks and reverberates in the defiles, subdued yet insistent,

GEORGE B. SCHALLER

from "Mountains in the Desert"
STONES OF SILENCE, 1979

From October 1969 to May 1975 Schaller crisscrossed the high mountains of Central Asia—the Karakorams, Himalayas, and Hindu Kush—from Pakistan to India and Nepal, in pursuit of the first full-scale study of wild high-altitude sheep and goats in this area of the world. Along the way he also provided the first useful observations of snow leopards and thus initiated a continuing interest by the Society in saving this predator and its vast habitat. On Schaller's recommendation, the 1,400-square-mile Khunjerab National Park in the Karakoram Mountains of Pakistan was declared in 1975. Nine years later, the Chinese government declared the contiguous six-thousand-square-mile Taxkorgan National Reserve, thus creating an international sanctuary where Afghanistan, Pakistan, Russia, and China meet. Schaller resumed his high-altitude work in 1985 in the Tibetan Plateau, where his wildlife surveys led to the establishment of the 118,000-square-mile Chang Tang Reserve in 1993.

*Sand dunes near
Skardu stretching before
the Karakoram range
of northeastern Pakistan.*

then swells in volume as it races howling over all obstacles until it hurls itself so wildly toward me that I brace my body against its impact. Although partly protected by boulders, the wind still shakes me and lashes me with sand. For support my hands clutch the ground, but they find only limestone pebbles—and the fossils I had placed in a tidy mound by my side. I grip the fossils as the wind roars over me like waves of the sea, and for a moment I relive an ancient reality, floating among swaying stems of crinoids, water pressing me down, and sands from the ocean floor covering me slowly to form tomorrow's fossil. The earth's terrible power is palpably around me. Then silence until once again, far away, the wind begins another demented journey.

More than a hundred million years ago, during the early Cretaceous, that land which is now the Himalayan region was covered by the Tethys Sea, which separated Eurasia from the southern continent, Gondwanaland. At that time the Indian subcontinent was still attached to Gondwanaland, but then it broke away and began to drift northward. When the two land masses came into contact during the late Cretaceous, the earth saw the most spectacular period of mountain building in its history. India's northern edge buckled and slid beneath the Eurasian continent, thereby forming a huge depression which over the eons filled with sediments, the Indo-Gangetic Plain of today. Uplifts and horizontal thrusts slowly raised the floor of the Tethys Sea to create the Tibetan highlands. Restlessly the two land masses continued to grind against each other, crumpling and folding the rocks and sediments. The Himalaya rose in three major upheavals, during the Eocene, the mid-Miocene, and the late Pliocene and Pleistocene—and the mountains are still rising. Sediments of the Tethys Sea were folded not only into the great northern ranges, but also into peripheral ones, among them the Salt, Sulaiman, and Kirthar mountains in western Pakistan. The Karchat Hills on which I was lying had once been on the bottom of the Tethys Sea.

This creation of new mountain systems from the sea opened new habitats to the flora and fauna. Evolution proceeds most rapidly during periods of geological unrest, for at such times life is presented with new opportunities and necessities. The *Caprinae*, the subfamily to which sheep and goats belong, arose during the Miocene when mountains appeared and the Tethys Sea was in its final retreat. And today's sheep and goats made their appearance in the late Pliocence and Pleistocene when the earth once again buckled and climates cooled. Sheep and goats colonized many ranges of Eurasia together. They usually occupied simple habitats, such as deserts and terrain recently vacated by ice, where plant growth is sparse. It has become axiomatic in biology that when two related species of similar size inhabit the same area they tend to compete for the same resources and can persist together only if they are separated ecologically by habitat or food preferences or both. How then do sheep and goats divide their habitat? The goats—wild goat, markhor, ibex, depending on area—prefer cliffs and their immediate vicinity, whereas sheep occupy the plateaus above cliffs and the undulating terrain along their bases. American sheep are exceptions in that they usually are found on grassy slopes near cliffs, a habitat which in Eurasia is generally occupied by a goat. But true goats never reached North America to provide competition.

The first snow leopard Schaller saw during his mountain studies in Pakistan was this female in the Hindu Kush Range.

Below: Schaller's yak caravan approaches the 15,400-foot Darkot Pass through the Hindu Raj Range in Chitral, northern Pakistan.

At first glance sheep and goats would seem to be rather dissimilar animals. However, their bones are notoriously difficult to place into the correct genus, and the animals are genetically similar enough to be able to produce living hybrids on occasion. Differences are rather minor. For example, sheep have preorbital glands at the inside corner of the eyes, inguinal glands in the groin, and pedal glands between the hooves, in contrast to goats which have pedal glands only on the forefeet, if at all. Goats also have anal glands, possess beards and a potent body odor, and have flat, fairly long tails, bare beneath, whereas sheep have round, ratlike tails.

For several years I had been intrigued by the possible similarities and differences in the ecology and behavior of Eurasian sheep and goats, wondering, for instance, how life on cliffs affected goat society and how it differed from that of sheep. As one step in gaining such an understanding, I was now in the Karchat Hills to study wild goat. The Karchat Hills consist of a small massif, about thirteen miles long and four wide, at the southern end of the Kirthar Range bordering the western edge of the Indus Plain. To reach these hills from Karachi, one drives forty-five miles north toward Hyderabad, then turns onto a track to the substantial village of Thano Bula Khan. The place has a derelict look, burned into submission by the sun. Forlorn camels drift down sandy streets between mud-walled homes, and the inhabitants scuttle like desert rodents across alleys from one burrow to the next as if fearful of the brilliant light. From there a tenuous trail heads across wastelands for thirty-five miles, alternately crossing stony and sandy expanses. One tends to accept the desolate scene as inevitable, the product of a desperate aridity, for rainfall is only seven inches a year. But then one begins to better understand the landscape. Here and there stunted acacias have been cut and left to dry, to be picked up later by trucks and sold for firewood in Karachi. Some sandy flats are abandoned fields where an itinerant settler coaxed a crop or two before giving the soil to the winds. Herds of black-haired goats, thin, bony creatures, scour the terrain, leaving only thorny and ill-tasting plants in their wake. Had man not misused this land for thousands of years, I would be driving through woodland, with wild asses standing in the broad-crowned shade of acacias and cheetah stalking unsuspecting Indian gazelle through swords of golden grass. Perhaps down by the river a pride of lions would be resting after the night's hunt. The forests are gone now, the rivers dry except after a downpour, and the lion, cheetah, and asses are dead. Only a few gazelle remain. No wonder the land seems lonely as one drives toward the distant hills, trailing a funnel of red dust made incandescent by the sun.

Asia's Great Island Forests

*Hunting and massive logging operations threaten
the forests that cover the great islands of Borneo
and New Guinea, between Asia and Australia.
Efforts in Papua New Guinea have centered on
birds of paradise and other endemic bird species.
The Society has worked with local communities
for more than a decade, and in 1993 the one-
thousand-square-mile Crater Mountain Wildlife
Management Area was established. It is the first
instance of land being donated by local landowners purely for conservation purposes, in return
for permitting controlled traditional use.*

*In the 1980s, Elizabeth Bennett began to
work in Malaysian Borneo with the unique
populations of proboscis monkeys, which are
endangered particularly by the destruction of
Sabah's coastal mangrove forests. Now the
Society conducts a comprehensive program of
field research, conservation planning, and
training for local scientists throughout Sabah
and Sarawak.*

*Raggiana (above) and other bird of paradise species in Papua New Guinea
are central to traditional cultures and to the preservation of forests
now severely threatened by logging interests. Society staff initiated field
studies and negotiated the donation of land to the protected area by members
of twenty different clans.*

Proboscis monkey harems average nine animals but can number up to twenty, with a single adult male (above). Primarily tree dwellers, proboscis monkeys are great leapers and swimmers, talents they use in traveling more than a mile a day in search of food (right). Their wide ranging requires large areas of protection.

Logging in Borneo's riverine, peat swamp, and mangrove forests has drastically reduced habitat for proboscis monkeys.

PETER MATTHIESSEN

from "Pygmies and Pygmy Elephants:
The Congo Basin (1986)"

AFRICAN SILENCES, 1991

Since the late 1950s, Peter Matthiessen has written extensively about wildlife conservation, on several occasions based on his observation of Society field projects. In 1986, he joined David Western, then director of the Society's international conservation program, for a tour by light aircraft, truck, boat, and foot of Central African Republic, Gabon, and Zaire, where the Society was conducting a comprehensive census of forest elephants by Richard Barnes and others. Important work by James Powell in Cameroon, Michael Fay in Congo Republic, Lee White in Gabon, and Andrea Turkalo in Central African Republic has been crucial in protecting forest elephant populations.

At 2 A.M. in the new year, I am met in Nairobi by the savanna ecologist David Western, a husky, trim, and well-kept Kenyan citizen of forty-two. Dr. Western is the resource ecologist for the New York Zoological Society, best known for its Bronx Zoo and New York Aquarium; he is also pilot of the NYZS aircraft in which we shall embark the day after tomorrow on a survey of the rain forests of Central Africa, paying special attention to the numbers and distribution of the small forest elephant, which may be seriously threatened by the ivory trade. As Dr. Western—known since a small boy as Jonah—wrote me in a letter last September, "We still know remarkably little about either the forest elephant, which now accounts for sixty percent of the ivory leaving Africa, or the Congo Basin, an area including about twenty percent of the world's tropical equatorial forests. The forest elephant is something of an enigma, and reason enough for the entire trip."

The African elephant, *Loxodonta africana*, has been seriously imperiled by ivory hunters; recent analyses of market tusks show that the poaching gangs, having reduced the savanna or bush elephant, *Loxodonta africana africana*, to less than a half million animals, are increasingly concentrating on the much smaller forest race, *L. a. cyclotis*. Unlike *L. a. africana*, which is easy to census by light plane, *cyclotis* spends most of the daylight hours hidden in the forest, and estimates of its numbers have been mainly speculative. Proponents of the ivory trade maintain that the forest canopy hides very large numbers of small elephants, while ecologists fear that in this inhospitable habitat the numbers have always been low. It is generally agreed that an African elephant population of two million or more animals could probably sustain the present slaughter for the ivory trade, which until very recently, at least, has produced about seven hundred and fifty tons each year. However, computer analyses indicate that if fewer than a million elephants are left, as many authorities believe, then the species is already in a precipitous decline in which half the remaining animals will be lost in the next decade. The future of *Loxodonta* may depend, in short, on an accurate estimate of the numbers of the forest race, which would lay the foundation for a strong international conservation effort on behalf of the species as a whole.

"There will be a large gap in our understanding of the forest elephant until we understand the forest better," Western's letter said. "That is one of the purposes of this survey. The truth is, we know very little about forest ecology. Only in recent years, with the realization of how rapidly the rain forests, with their great abundance and variety of life, are disappearing, especially in South America and southeast Asia, have we come to realize that the forest is a very important biome that cannot be ignored by anyone committed to conservation and the future of the earth. Because of its inaccessibility and low human population, the Congo Basin is still largely intact, but there is no reason for confidence that it will stay that way.". . .

Flying east from Kisangani [northeastern Zaire], the Cessna follows the Bunia road, a rough red section of the trans-African track that winds across Africa from the Gulf of Guinea to the Kenya coast. This forest region still shows the effects of the anarchic period that followed Zaire's independence in 1960, when many people, villages, and gardens were destroyed by the successive waves of soldiers, rebels, and white South African and Rhodesian mercenaries that swept in and out of Kisangani. In the quarter-century since, with the region depopulated and communications broken down, the colonial airstrips and many of the side roads still indicated on the charts are little more than shadows in the trees, having been subsumed by the surrounding forest. Excepting the rivers, the trans-African itself, barely maintained, is the only landmark, a welcome thread of human presence in this dark green sea.

On all sides, to the shrouded green horizons, lies the unbroken Ituri Forest, in the region perceived by Henry Morton Stanley as the very heart of "darkest Africa." The Ituri extends north to the savannas and east to the foothills of the Central Highlands, with contiguous regions of wild forest to the south and west. In the nineteenth century, the region was a famous

David Western coordinated elephant studies and policies for the Society and the African Elephant and Rhino Specialist Group.

source of ivory, which was carried back to the coast at Zanzibar by the slave caravans of Tippu Tib, and by all accounts was a great redoubt of elephants throughout the decades of the Congo Free State and the Belgian Congo. Even today the Ituri remains largely intact, since it lies on the rim of the Congo Basin, above the waterfalls of smaller and less navigable rivers. In Western's opinion, any estimates we make of the Ituri's present population of forest elephants may be used as a fair gauge for the rest of Zaire's forests. In so much wilderness, in the absence of good information, it is tempting to imagine large companies of elephants passing unseen beneath these silent canopies, but past estimates are probably much too high. . . .

In the five-hour walk north from Epulu [in the Ituri Forest], Jonah reports, all they have seen are a few monkeys, high in the canopy. As an East African ecologist, Jonah is accustomed to large numbers of large mammals, readily studied; in the forest, as we have learned throughout this journey, large mammals are uncommon and elusive, and difficult to observe even when found. "I'm glad to have come to Central Africa, glad to have seen the rain forest," he says, "because it's one of the most neglected biomes, and one of the most important. But I could never work in forest. So much time is necessary to gather so little information!" . . .

In Central African Republic's Dzanga-Sangha Reserve, Andrea Turkalo has identified more than sixteen hundred forest elephants by individual markings in order to study their social dynamics.

More and more it seems apparent that unbroken rain forest is inhospitable habitat for large mammals. Except along the watercourses, or in clearings made by the fall of a giant tree, the available food is mostly in the canopy, far out of reach of okapi and gorilla as well as elephant. In the absence of elephants, which modify the forest by creating and perpetuating second growth, other animals are bound to be scarce as well. Jonah concludes that, while high human impact will impoverish the forest, moderate impact in the form of shifting cultivation—that is, slash and burn—creates a good deal of secondary forest that is accessible to animals, and that a patchwork of primary and secondary forest is the optimum condition for prosperity as well as diversity in animal populations. . . .

Increasingly Jonah is fascinated by the impact of man on the environment, which in his view is not always destructive to its wildlife and can, in fact, be very beneficial. In the sixties, he says, European and American biologists turned to the African savannas as the last great natural bastion of primeval life, unchanged since the Pleistocene; they held to the traditional view that this stability, providing time for evolution, was a condition for speciation and diversity, which accounted for the great variety of savanna life. Jonah concludes that, on the contrary, the savanna is a patchwork of different habitats, and is always changing, having been modified for thousands of years not only by fires and elephants but by man. . . .

In Dr. Western's view, man has always had a profound impact on savanna systems, ever since he burned off the first grassland to improve hunting. "Remember that savanna woodland between Garamba and Bangassou [northern Zaire]? Hundreds of miles of what looked like wonderful wildlife habitat, without any sign of human impact—where were the animals? I very much doubt if the complete absence of wildlife was entirely attributable to overhunting. When man and his fires disappeared, the wildlife declined, too. One can't say that man's activities are 'good' for wildlife, but neither are they always bad, and this is particularly apparent in the forest."

Tree burning restores minerals to the old soils for a few years, but it destroys the specialized fungi known as mycorrhizae that are critical to forest growth. Where large populations of primitive agriculturalists burn down the forests, as in the derived savannas seen in Gabon and western Zaire (and also throughout West Africa), the destruction must lead to flood, erosion, and degraded land on which only a few pest species can survive. (This is a necessary consequence, not of intense settlement but of poor land use; large populations have lived off certain Asian lands for thousands of years.)

But where humans are few, and the burning moderate, gorillas as well as elephants are drawn to second growth; abandoned clearings, which the elephants maintain, sustain many other birds and animals. Similarly, disruption and change through fires, floods, and landslides, the silting of deltas, the meanderings of rivers, even big trees crashing down and creating clearings—all these produce a patchwork of habitats that increases diversity of life, since it prevents dominance by a few species. This is why life in the open light of river margins, with thick growth accessible from the ground, is so much richer than in primary forests between rivers, which are almost empty.

Forest elephant numbers are very hard to estimate, not only because of the forest canopy but because of the variety of habitats—tall and low forests, disturbed and undisturbed areas, swamps, abandoned gardens—all of which affect elephant numbers. In 1989, after completing his studies in the field, Dr. Richard Barnes concluded that there might be about 400,000 animals in forested regions of West and Central Africa (a more recent estimate is 250,000), and that among all of these countries, Gabon was the most promising because of huge and uninhabited forest areas, large elephant populations (he estimates 74,000—1990) and small numbers of humans, low rate of deforestation, and an absence of those military weapons that have made poaching so devastating elsewhere. Gabon, Barnes feels, might well become the last great refuge of *Loxodonta africana*.

In 1986, on David Western's recommendation, Wildlife Conservation International (WCI) [the former name of the Society's international program] and the Leakey foundation returned Dr. Richard Carroll to southwest C.A.R., together with botanist Michael Fay. At the end of December 1990, their original idea of a forest wildlife reserve came into being with the creation of the Dzanga-Sangha Dense Forest Reserve and the contiguous Dzanga-Ndoki National Park, which together total 1,737 square miles of range of forest elephants, bongo, gorilla, and other species threatened by the destruction of this habitat. WCI also seeks to help establish contiguous forest reserves in the northern Congo Republic and in southeast Cameroon, which has the highest density of forest elephants—and probably elephants of any kind—now left in Africa. Since an estimated 40 percent of elephants are now in rain forests, and since the rain forest itself becomes more precious every day, this reserve is a stirring project that demands support from conservation groups around the world.

WCI's researches into forest elephant numbers, and the finding that these numbers were so low, had a direct effect on the campaigns of recent years to achieve full protection for the whole species, all the more so when it was realized that, small as it was, the forest population comprised nearly half of Africa's remaining elephants. . . .

In a single decade, the entire continental population was reduced from 1.3 million (1979) to 625,000, while the price of ivory doubled to one hundred dollars a pound. This made it worthwhile to kill juveniles as well as females, with three times the number of animals killed to produce the same quantity of ivory. And all too commonly the officials in the afflicted countries participated in the ivory trade, even though the income from illegal ivory was far less than the income from world tourism, which was now threatened. . . .

In October 1988, the United States Congress, under pressure from strong public sentiment as well as effective lobbying by conservation groups, passed the African Elephant Conservation Act, which stipulates that all ivory imported into the U.S. come from countries that adhere to the 102-nation Convention on International Trade in Endangered Species (CITES) ivory control system; Congress also established the "African Elephant Conservation Fund," to help finance the elephant's cause. Within a few months—May 1989—Tanzania, Kenya, and six other African countries

PETER MATTHIESSEN

from "Epilogue"
AFRICAN SILENCES, 1991

Forest elephants in Cameroon, difficult to track in their dense habitat, are being monitored by satellite in Africa and at the Bronx Zoo, where the device was tested on an Asian elephant.

The moratorium on trade in ivory was reaffirmed at a CITES meeting in 1992. The ban has continued to be effective and is scheduled for review approximately every two years.

called for an end to the ivory trade worldwide. To avoid last-minute slaughter by the poachers, the U.S. government immediately declared a ban on ivory imports, a move endorsed a few days later by the European Economic Community (EEC).

Only the countries of southern Africa, more distant from organized poaching, have enjoyed an increase in elephant population; Zimbabwe (where the people own the elephants, and villages share in safari fees and tourist income) must actually cull about one thousand animals each year. Similarly, Botswana and South Africa, which also make profit from a sustained yield of ivory, resist the ban, and so do Zambia, Namibia, and Malawi; these countries feel, not without justice, that they are being penalized for mismanagement and corruption farther north. Though sympathetic, Dr. David Western, addressing the world conference of CITES convened in Lausanne, Switzerland, in October 1989, withdrew his support of controlled sales in these southern countries in favor of a total ban. "The demand for ivory internationally is so overwhelming that the option of sustainability is declining," Western said. The CITES conference duly adopted the position of world conservation groups that a partial ban would almost certainly be ineffective. For the first time, CITES placed the elephant on the endangered list, which automatically put a halt to the legal trade. This worldwide ban—not incumbent on the southern countries, though destroying their markets—became effective as of January 18, 1990. Within the year, the ivory market had collapsed, and though sporadic poaching still continues, it is much diminished almost everywhere.

Like the volcanoes last year in its Virunga Range, where decades of accumulating faults and fractures finally ended in huge eruption, Zaire's political situation, after years of deterioration, exploded in September, plunging the country into a spiral of anarchy and decline that continues to the present. On September 23, unpaid soldiers rioted in Kinshasa. They were joined by the underpaid and hungry civilian masses and in just two days the capital (population 4 million) was entirely looted. The looting quickly spread to other cities and regions. The country remains insecure, the future uncertain.

Only the northeast, including the Epulu region, escaped the pillage. Spared, the project has become a haven for displaced Zairean ecologists fleeing the University of Kisangani and elsewhere. From the refuge of our forest vastness, the project maintains its momentum. The research projects flourish. Our continuing commitment to local staff and communities has actually strengthened our position. Ours and the other projects, Animals in Motion (AIM) and World Wide Fund for Nature (WWF), have emerged, with the Church, as the only viable institutions in the region. How and

TERESE HART AND
JOHN HART

*Field Report: "Ituri Forest Project—
July through December, 1991"*

The field research station at Epulu, established in 1985.

Despite difficult political conditions in Zaire, John and Terese Hart (right) work closely with the Mbuti people in Zaire's Ituri Forest (opposite).

Conservation work sometimes persists, even as nations crumble. Between 1985 and 1993, zoologist John Hart and forest ecologist Terese Hart saw the deterioration of Zaire's government, increasing social strife, the sacking of the universities, riots, the assassination of the French ambassador, and closing of the borders. Even so, they continued to accumulate data about the mysterious okapi, various species of duikers, and the Ituri Forest's ecology, involving local people in their work and gaining their support. In 1992, the 5,300-square-mile Okapi Wildlife Reserve was declared, creating an opportunity to launch further studies and get on with the real work of conservation.

whether this can be translated into long-term conservation gains for the forest remains to be seen.

At a national scale, the perspective is less optimistic. Among the consequences of the political unrest, no government decisions regarding park gazetting are being made. The Ituri will remain without official protection indefinitely. Other associated conditions also impinge seriously on conservation activities:

1. International funding bodies have cut off aid to Zaire.
2. Public educational institutions, including the university, are on strike.
3. Inflation of nearly 1000% in 1991 has reduced persons on fixed salaries to penury . . . this includes park guards.

In the immediate aftermath of the upheaval, the United States government announced that all its citizens should leave Zaire. Matt Etter, interim Project Director during our absence in New York, left Epulu for Nairobi for three weeks in October. John and Matt, with the directors of the AIM and WWF projects, made a short trip to Epulu in November. During their visit they found that construction of our USAID-funded research and training center and all field research, including radio telemetry, were proceeding on schedule. Our Zairean assistants had assumed responsibility during our absence with grace and competence. A meeting was held with project directors and the Institut Zarois de la Conservation de Nature (IZCN) conservator to establish project priorities and provide aid to the Epulu guards through the end of the year.

We spent September through December based at Wildlife Conservation Society headquarters in New York. This was a period for data analysis, writing, and organization. This year we were preoccupied with the effort to assure continued USAID funding for the research center. USAID ATLAS grants for graduate training for two Zairean University students associated with Epulu had been irrevocably withdrawn. However, USAID, in an extraordinary exception, did agree (as of this writing) to continue funding to assure completion of the research and training center construction. As far as we know, ours remains the only active USAID project in what was once a multimillion dollar program.

We have now returned to Epulu with our two youngest girls and are in full swing on what promises to be a very busy field research season (okapi, duikers, fruit phenology). We will return to New York for two months in May/June. We are making our Zaire plans on the short term, with an eye to continuing developments here.

The Harts conduct crucial research on the elusive
okapi (right), a member of the giraffe family, and
on the ecology of the forest, with help from assistants
like Dieudonné Batido (above), here analyzing
wildlife food plants.

ALAN RABINOWITZ

from "In the Realm of the Master Jaguar"

ANIMAL KINGDOM, MARCH/APRIL 1986

Pioneering work on the jaguar and its prey was conducted for the Society in the swampy Pantanal region of Brazil in the late 1970s by George Schaller and Howard Quigley. Because of its wide distribution, the jaguar, the largest predator in Central and South America, came to be understood as a key species in the effort to preserve Latin American rain forests. The work of Alan Rabinowitz in Belize is therefore pivotal and a precursor of the Society's Paseo Pantera ("Path of the Panther") program in Central America, which seeks to save an ecologically viable corridor the length of the isthmus corresponding to the extensive home of the puma, or cougar (see pages 217–21).

The morning sun was barely peeking through the trees when I climbed on top of the holding cage. It was covered with corrugated iron, yet as I crouched there, I sensed the anger of the jaguar pacing beneath me. Of six other jaguars captured over the last 18 months, none had been so restless. This was the first I had let fully recover from the tranquilizer before release. Though I expected he would run into the forest as soon as the cage door was opened, I felt a twinge of fear.

"Are you ready?" I hollered to Mike, another scientist, who had followed me in his truck to photograph the event. "It's going to happen quickly," I said, lifting the door up to my waist.

And so it did. The jaguar—a young, six-foot-long 90-pound male—lost no time in coming out of the cage. But 10 feet from the door he stopped and turned his head. And as I looked into his face, he swerved and came at me. Although caught off guard, I reacted instinctively and leapt into the rear of the pickup truck, parked three feet behind the cage. "Don't turn your back," I warned myself. As I moved, the jaguar also leapt, his eyes blazing and mouth agape like those of a predator closing in on its prey. I screamed, feeling for an instant what the weaker animal must feel before the kill.

But the jaguar had jumped too soon, seized perhaps by the overzealousness of youth or simply a flicker of indecision. As his head and forepaws landed on the edge of the truck bed, his hindquarters swung beneath it and hit the metal, knocking him onto his back. It seemed only a momentary reprieve; I had no time to get to the door of the truck and the cat's next jump would easily bring him within striking distance. Images of the crushed skulls I'd seen at jaguar kills flashed through my mind. But that next leap was never made. Instead the cat stood up, looked at me, then turned and walked slowly into the forest. As he disappeared from sight, my eyes locked on the spot where the forest had absorbed him. I was shaking uncontrollably. "What an animal," I thought. Even in the aftermath of abject terror, I couldn't help feeling admiration for the jaguar.

Sitting at my desk in New York City months later, that day in the forest of Belize seemed very far away. That jaguar had been the seventh and last I collared in my study of the species. He was the first male cattle-killing jaguar to be caught and moved into my study area to determine whether relocating problem individuals would work as an alternative to killing them. I had named him Kukulcán, for the king who ruled over the last great Mayan centers of culture. My jaguar project ended six months after his release, terminating two years of adventure and scientific research that produced new data on jaguar ecology.

I first learned about the Central American nation of Belize in October 1982, when Dr. George Schaller, director of Wildlife Conservation International (WCI) of the New York Zoological Society asked me to survey the country for jaguars and evaluate research potential there.

Two and a half months of intensive field work, networking the swamps and forests from daybreak to nightfall seven days a week, as well as living with Mayas, Creoles, and Black Caribs, uncovered a surprising fact. All the

Alan Rabinowitz in Belize.

evidence—jaguar tracks, feces, and kills, plus what the people had to say—showed that this little Caribbean country of 8,900 square miles and approximately 175,000 people was still a stronghold for *el tigre*, the largest land predator in Central and South America. . . .

The potential in Belize for research and conservation appeared tremendous, but the need to act was immediate. Encroachment into the forests from cattle ranching, logging, and slash-and-burn agriculture had escalated to a threatening level even in that sparsely populated nation. In addition, both the Belize government and the country's major conservation organization, the Belize Audubon Society, had already requested a study. Because of alleged jaguar attacks on livestock, ranchers were pressuring for reversal of a 1974 law that banned jaguar hunting. Some people speculated that because of the law there were now too many jaguars, but this seemed unlikely even to government officials. . . .

I chose a study area in southern Belize known as Cockscomb Basin. This rugged tropical rain forest of 154 square miles is enclosed by mountains, its only access being a six-mile-long narrow dirt road leading to a former timber camp taken over and inhabited by 60 Mayan Indians. From the camp, 20 miles of old logging trails ran out into the jungle. Although loggers had selectively cut large hardwoods in sizable areas of the basin during the past

Jaguars are shot as killers of live-stock throughout their range in Central and South America. By tracking jaguars he had radio-collared, Alan Rabinowitz proved that the problem does not exist when cattle are properly managed and the jaguar's habitat is adequately protected. His work led to the creation of the world's first jaguar reserve, in Belize's Cockscomb Basin. The reserve became a national park in 1986.

half century, the forest was still lush. Data from my earlier survey indicated an abundance of jaguars, their prey, and several other species—such as Baird's tapir, scarlet macaw, puma, ocelot, and margay—that are threatened elsewhere. Furthermore, the basin was abutted by numerous cattle ranches whose owners had complained about jaguar predation on livestock. The situation was ideal for the proposed project. . . .

During the first month, the Indians watched me constantly but did not approach. A stranger to their world, I thought it best to wait for them to make the first move. Finally, the children, unable to restrain their curiosity, made contact. I returned from the field one day to find five little girls waiting for me in my shack. Soon I was eating regularly in the Indians' thatched huts and giving them rides into town. Once they started talking to me and learning the details of my project, they made it clear that my desire to capture live jaguars, put something around their necks [radio collars], and release them back into the forest was both crazy and against the ways of nature. I was warned that there was a "master jaguar" who would be watching and—if I did anything wrong—might even choose to kill me.

I had been aware that the jaguar held a prominent place in the lives of the ancient Mayas. At most Mayan excavations, jaguar motifs depict an association with, among other things, the underworld. It surprised me, however, to learn that the modern Maya, who appear to retain little knowledge of their once distinguished culture, still fear and respect this animal to the great degree that they do. It was not the most reassuring way to start my project. . . .

Despite their fears, the Mayas were interested in the project and repeatedly asked how I could locate jaguars without seeing them. It was difficult to explain the technical aspects of radiotelemetry to them, so at first I just let them think I was a powerful human being. By the end of the project some Indians had a vague understanding of the concept and several learned to operate the equipment.

Although my general loneliness and all the mishaps often made me question whether the work was worth it, my friendships with the Mayas and the occasional encounters with jaguars touched a deep chord and drove me on.

I was beginning to get a picture of jaguar behavior while in the field, but it was not until I fully analyzed my records that I could see it clearly. The telemetry data, sightings, and pugmark locations, once put together as home ranges and movements, indicated that the cats were involved in a dynamic system.

During the first year of the project, the timber roads and log-hauling trails extending out from the camp were used by at least five adult male jaguars, two adult females, and one puma. In the second year, when two adult males died in the central study area, there was an immediate rearrangement of home ranges, and a new adult male jaguar, who was eventually captured and collared, moved into Cockscomb. No territory was left empty for very long. It was obvious that a balance between available resources and the numbers of jaguars (especially males) residing in the area was actively maintained.

Continuous tracking of five collared adult males for periods of up to 14 months indicated that each one regularly utilized at least 11 to 16 square miles and maintained overlapping ranges. I also collected limited data on three female jaguars. One was the young cattle-killer captured in northern Belize and collared and released in Cockscomb; she left the study area and established a range around a cattle pasture at the border of Cockscomb. Two additional females whose pugmarks I followed each traveled within the ranges of adjacent males. All three females used, at the least, about a third as much territory as did the males.

After a year of study, it was obvious to me that the jaguars were remaining within the confines of the forest and not leaving the area to kill livestock in adjoining ranches or villages. I carefully followed two of the collared jaguars whose ranges abutted cattle pastures at the border of the study area. Neither of them was ever known to cross into open pastures or even linger in the vicinity of livestock. Eventually, after the death of a collared male within the basin, both of these cats shifted their movements toward the interior . . . and farther from the livestock. This could have been in response to a greater food supply within the forest than along the edges of Cockscomb, where local people competed with them for food.

Much of the livestock problem seemed to rest with poor ranching practices. Cattle were often stolen by locals or ranch hands but the thefts were blamed on jaguars. In other instances, ranchers allowed livestock to range widely through wild forests inhabited by jaguars, who might naturally view the livestock as alternative prey items.

In cases where livestock was controlled but jaguars still came into villages and pastures to kill, other factors were at work. Post-mortem examinations of problem individuals showed that most of these animals had old shotgun injuries to the skull and body, which, while not killing them, had probably caused damage that contributed to abnormal behavior. Ironically, the policy of many ranchers to shoot all jaguars in their area *before* problems occur might be the causative agent in creating such deviants. . . .

The "jaguar problem," as I was to hear it called so often throughout Belize, should more appropriately be termed the "human encroachment problem." Large predators like jaguars once roamed the tropical forests unfettered by boundaries, but man is in a terrible hurry to take everything over. Roads, deforestation, and human settlement add up to the continual decline of wildlife. In Belize, the problem is not as advanced as elsewhere, one of the reasons a relatively thriving population of jaguars still exists.

I realized that it would be absurd to propose guidelines for jaguar management and conservation when there was no stable or long-term protection for these animals. We needed to get key areas protected—areas known to have viable jaguar populations—and then talk about management. Cockscomb, hosting approximately 25 to 30 jaguars, was ideal for such protection and had been chosen for study with this thought in mind. The basin is primarily shallow soil on granite bedrock, and it is also the source of three major waterways in Belize. To clear the forest could have serious negative consequences on the country's economy and general well-being.

In other areas of Central and South America, deforestation has already forced governments to spend large amounts of money to offset problems such as flooding, erosion and siltation, which had been controlled free of charge by the forests. Most countries have been slow to realize that the rain forest is a major asset to the economy only when properly managed or left

Rabinowitz subsequently spent four years, between 1986 and 1990, in Thailand, where he studied forest carnivores from civets to leopards and then undertook the nation's first status survey of declining Indochinese tiger populations. In a country where forest cover has been reduced from 57 percent in 1961 to less than 10 percent today, the hope is at least to eliminate hunting, poaching, and logging in the remaining sanctuaries.

In early 1994, Rabinowitz and George Schaller reestablished conservation connections in Myanmar (Burma), where the Society had last sponsored a field project in 1959–60. Looking for remnant populations of Sumatran rhinos, they surveyed the forests of Myanmar, which for political reasons had been closed to outsiders since the early 1960s; they then moved on to Laos, accomplishing the early stages of three-year wildlife surveys in both countries. Rabinowitz initiated the contact with Myanmar officials, and was asked, after some investigation of his relationship to the New York Zoological Society, if he worked for William Beebe, who had been in Burma in 1910. Rabinowitz replied that he did, but that Beebe was no longer among the living.

intact. Such forests thrive on exceedingly poor shallow soils and have evolved to capture and hold nearly all nutrients available, from the air as well as the ground. When all the trees are felled, decay is swift and nutrients or any fertilizer applied are rapidly leached away by heavy rains. That's when the problems arise—but by then it is too late.

From the end of my first year I lobbied the government to protect Cockscomb Basin, with little progress. In the last six months of my project, it came to my attention that private interests (timber and citrus companies) wanted Cockscomb for themselves. I decided to make one last push, for I knew that once I left, all hope of protecting the area would vanish.

In October 1984, Dr. Archie Carr III, assistant director of WCI, flew down to meet me in Belize. Jim Waight, president of the Belize Audubon Society, arranged a meeting with Hon. George Price, then Prime Minister, and members of his cabinet. We presented our case in concise economic terms but with all the fervor of condemned men pleading for a stay of execution. At the end of an hour, the Prime Minister and several of his cabinet were still undecided and would not adjourn the meeting. After two hours, the Prime Minister requested that the Minister of Natural Resources move ahead with protecting Cockscomb.

In November 1984, Cockscomb Basin was legally declared a forest reserve in which all hunting is forbidden. With this declaration, Cockscomb became the first area to be set aside specifically for jaguar protection and management. Although this legal statute allowed selective logging (usually of old, large-diameter trees) for the time being, any operation that resembled clearing of the forest was strictly prohibited. With hired men to watch the entrance road and a restriction on firearms, the entire area could be controlled. . . .

We have won a major battle. But we have still to fight the war. In the face of ever-increasing pressure from outside interests seeking short-term economic gains and flashing dollars in front of governments, Cockscomb still stands in jeopardy. Even if it remains intact, Cockscomb is only the beginning, for it alone cannot guarantee the survival of the jaguar. There are more battles to engage in and many more areas that need immediate protection.

What is the rationale for putting so much time, money, and energy into such endeavors? There are many reasons, but one stands out: The jaguar, caught up in a destiny over which it has no control, has a right to survive.

Paseo Pantera
(Path of the Panther)

Since its formation more than three million years ago, the Central American isthmus has been a bridge of accelerated biological diversity between North and South America. The cat called mountain lion, puma, or cougar, which ranges from Alaska in the north to Tierra del Fuego in the south, symbolizes the importance of this biotic corridor. Paseo Pantera—signifying the "avenue of great cats," and much else besides—is the name given to the Society's program there by Regional Coordinator Archie Carr III. This integrated project involves seven nations, from Belize to Panama, and hopes to save enough of the rain forest and coastal ecosystems in parks, buffer zones, and connecting corridors to sustain the dynamic interaction of life between North and South America.

Male puma in Belize.

The Hol Chan Marine Reserve was created in 1987, based on field studies by the Society's Jacque Carter. Working with the Belizean government, Janet Gibson has devised a conservation plan for the country's entire 150-mile barrier reef, the longest in the Western Hemisphere.

Carolyn and Bruce Miller head the Maya Mountain Project in Belize, where they are working to link critical habitat areas in the rain forest.

Tracking ocellated turkeys at the ancient Maya city of Tikal is part of the effort to save both cultural and biological treasures in Guatemala and the contiguous forests of Belize and Mexico.

Keel-billed toucan in Belize.

Below: Male puma in Belize.

Young green turtles saved after a storm and later released in the Caribbean. They hatched at Tortuguero, Costa Rica, one of the four main nesting areas of this most common of the sea turtles, all of which are endangered.

The Paseo Pantera team helped the Honduras forestry service devise a protection plan for the rain forest and coastal lands of the Miskito people.

ROGER S. PAYNE

from "The Songs of Whales"
PROJECT INTERSPEAK, 1979

Roger and Katharine Payne's work for the Society on humpback whales in Bermuda and right whales in the southern Atlantic—particularly their interpretation of whale songs—has been crucial in the battle to save the great mammals. The songs themselves, widely celebrated in popular and classical music during the 1970s, stirred the public outcry against the slaughter of whales. On the recommendation of the Society, whale ocean reserves were established in Golfo San José, Argentina (1974), and the Maui County Islands, Hawaii (1977). Increased development and mismanaged ecotourism now pose new threats, particularly in Golfo San José.

The species of whales divide conveniently into two major groupings: the toothed whales and the baleen whales. Most toothed whales, like porpoises and dolphins, live in social groups and, with few exceptions, are a lot smaller than baleen whales. Because only a few species have been kept in captivity, and then for only brief periods, there is very little known about them; they must be studied in the wild. That, to me, is one of the great charms of whales—they are by and large inaccessible. We must go to them, and when we stand before them we find that we are beneath their notice. The baleen whale species include the largest animal that has ever lived on earth—the blue whale, which is some two to three times the weight of the largest dinosaur.

The blue whale is simply the largest species in a group of five species which have very similar body form. These are (in order of descending size) the Blue, Fin, Sei, Brydes, and Minke whales. We do not have recordings for all these species, but where we do we find sounds included that are very low and very loud. The blue whale makes what are probably the loudest sounds produced by any animal. This is a recent discovery, but before the vocalizations of blue whales were known the sounds of fin whales had received considerable attention. Though they produce a variety of sounds, one common utterance of fin whales is a monotonously repeated series of low moans centered on 20 Hz (20 cycles per second), a frequency which is too low for most adult humans to hear. Each sound is a relatively pure tone lasting about one second. The moans are rhythmically repeated, singly or in couplets, at any one of several fixed time intervals, which are usually faster than once every 25 seconds. After about 15 minutes of making its tones, there is a silence of 2 or 3 minutes (suggesting that the whale is now breathing at the surface) followed by another period of moaning, another rest, and so on for hours at a time. When I first heard these loud, low sounds I was very impressed. I calculated the distance to which they might travel in deep water before they were overwhelmed by the background noise. The result was so surprising I didn't believe it myself and got help from Doug Webb of the Woods Hole Oceanographic Institution . . . By our calculations, whale sounds could currently travel a few tens or hundreds of miles before being lost in the background noise level of the ocean. . . .

I first realized, with Scott McVay, then of Princeton, that humpback whales sing songs, by listening to some tapes made by Frank Watlington of the Columbia Geophysical Field Station in Bermuda. They posed an interesting problem; for within the single structural format we found two distinctly different sets of songs. All the songs recorded in 1961 fell into one song type, and all those from 1963 and 1964 into another. Were there different populations of whales, each with its own dialect, in Bermuda in these different years?

This has been one of the main questions behind a series of expeditions to record humpback whales in the Bermuda area over the years from 1967 to the present. We work out of a small sailboat, since it is quiet and allows us to hear through hydrophones hung over the side even when moving slowly.

Roger Payne observing a southern right whale, which he studied from 1970 to 1975 in Argentina's Golfo San José.

Humpback whale breaching.

By combining our recordings with those of others, my wife Katharine has made a fascinating discovery. We now have a sample of Bermuda humpback whale songs from late April of each of 17 years between 1957 and the present. From analysis of this sample she has learned that humpback whales are doing something quite unique with their songs—they are changing them, progressively, with time. The changes are often radical, usually making every year's song surprisingly different from that of the year before. After about four years the songs sound completely new. All the whales in an area at one time sing the same song as each other, and all keep up to date with the current version of the song. Humpback whales are thus both imitators and irrepressible composers—perhaps the only ones in the animal kingdom except man. . . .

Humpback whale.

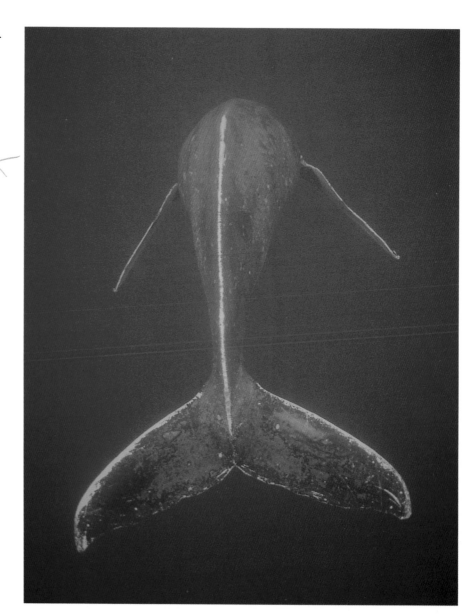

We are now studying humpback whales in Hawaiian waters as well as near Bermuda. We find that songs recorded from both populations in the same year are very different even though they follow the same rules of form. This isn't surprising since these two populations live in different oceans and have probably been isolated for many generations. Our results suggest that humpback whales inherit their laws for composing songs and improvise within these laws, memorizing changes sung by nearby singers.

The existence of dialects in different areas, and the constant progressive changing of the song in each area, leave no doubt that the humpback whale songs are transmitted by learning. Through this we know that the whales are capable of hearing all the frequencies in their songs and of memorizing long and complex patterns. By studying how the whales alter their song— how they introduce new material and drop out the old—we have started to learn what the composition process consists of. By studying how the whales maintain a consensus as to what shall be the song at a given time, we are learning about one way in which they coordinate the life of the herd. The changes in humpback whale songs thus provide a window through which we can begin to see some basic ways in which whales must think.

What Is a Field Biologist?

How do you define a field biologist? Presumably he or she is not merely a person who views a trip to the wilderness as a refreshing interval, a touch of scientific ecotourism. One test of authenticity might be the length of time this biologist lives afield: someone who suffers from culture shock not when settling into a project, but on returning home. Feral biologist, as an article once called me, is a more apt description than field biologist.

However, random thoughts on field biology may be useful if for no reason other than to dispel the notion fostered by television that we biologists usually lead romantic and adventurous lives. Even seemingly easy projects such as studying lethargic lions and amiable apes require long days and nights without sleep, tracking animals through dank or thorny vegetation. Some species are solitary, shy, nocturnal, and reluctant to be observed. Searing heat or arctic cold are the field biologist's frequent companions. Tropical diseases are an occupational hazard and political upheavals are annoying distractions. Cut off from urban amenities, a perpetual emigrant isolated in alien cultures, affected by an unsettled family life, a field biologist must work for years toward an elusive goal that local coworkers are often reluctant to embrace, and perhaps unable to comprehend. A spouse must share these hardships as well as endure long separations. And it's not always easy to tolerate another's obsession.

Most research is mundane, a tedious and repetitive process of recording facts. Patience becomes a more valuable commodity than intellect. One must be resigned to waiting; waiting for the animal to appear, for the rain or the snow to stop, for the porters to arrive. Then there is the pressure to do well; for whatever the problems that confront you, you want to justify the financial support others have given for your project, and you are in a competition—with yourself, as well as with all previously established standards of excellence. Adventures are rare, and at any rate, usually result from bad luck, poor planning or carelessness. Indeed, a field biologist's greatest danger lies not in encounters with fierce creatures and treacherous terrain, but in being seduced by the comforts of civilization.

The naturalist William Beebe noted, "After we have tried to be sandpipers and ants, silversides and mackerel, we may attain to the honor of such knowledge as our prejudiced, but humbled minds will permit." But these days anxiety and guilt about the fate of the animals we are studying cast shadows on our research. Curiosity is tinged with sympathy, a premonition that we are witness to the last days of Eden.

As a boy, I collected birds' eggs, kept a mini-zoo of salamanders, snakes, opossums, and other creatures, and I liked to roam the countryside. Later, during my undergraduate years at the University of Alaska—which I chose partly for its wilderness setting—I discovered that I could extend boyhood activities into a legitimate adult pastime. Curiosity about the natural world is inherent, I suspect, in a field biologist. I am not referring to the abstract intellectual curiosity of a laboratory biologist who uses animals as tools to elucidate some concept, but to an emotional involvement that treasures animals for themselves, enriching us by a sense of kinship. To me fieldwork is not a career but forms the core of my existence.

GEORGE B. SCHALLER

from "Field of Dreams"

Wildlife Conservation,
September/October 1992

A project has its genesis in a scientific question that is worth answering, a valid goal that is worth fulfilling. Good research also demands a passion to understand, emotional commitment, and an urge to probe beyond the limits of knowledge. In the 1950s, when I began fieldwork, a one-year study of a species was generally considered ample. Now a study ideally involves at least the normal life span of an animal, perhaps fifteen years for lions and fifty years for elephants. Yet, no matter how deeply I immerse myself in another species, after three years or so my mind grows restless and seeks new goals, striving to break new ground. I can rationalize this by saying that other creatures perceive the world in ways so unimaginably different from us that I can record only the most basic facts about them. But I may simply have a short attention span. Although my research reports are limited, I find it deeply satisfying to provide a species, for the first time, with a new reality, a written history, especially if I also am able to convey the joy of discovery, the pleasure of a new insight.

I look for aesthetic experiences with animals, as well as intellectual involvement. Some of the species I have studied—mountain gorilla, tiger, giant panda—have such a transcendent beauty that it becomes an almost sensual pleasure to be near them. Through photographs and words an objective vision fuses with subjective feeling. While photographs are often little more than sentimental evocations, idealized scenes that appeal to a sense of beauty and arouse compassion, at their best they create a harmony that encompasses both viewer and subject, forging a bond between us and the snow leopard or the butterfly in ways that words alone cannot achieve. Pen and camera are potent weapons against oblivion, helping species to survive—or serving as memorials.

Another idiosyncrasy determines what and where I study: I like to explore the physical as well as the intellectual realm. The more rare and remote a species, the greater the challenge to become the chronicler of its life. I view myself basically as a nineteenth-century wanderer with a scientific bent on an intangible and elusive search. There is an atavistic pleasure in crossing the Tibetan plateau, our camel caravan lonely and lost between earth and sky, or trailing a string of porters through the mysterious silence of a rainforest. At times I have been labeled misanthropic because I usually avoid the conviviality of a scientific team on such ventures. Aside from my wife Kay and my sons, I prefer my own kind in small doses. Author Peter Fleming noted some years ago that "the trouble about journeys nowadays is that they are easy to make but difficult to justify." Conservation now offers ample justification.

I began to study animals out of curiosity. But anyone who observes the exponential destruction of wilderness must become an advocate for conservation. To preserve a remnant of beauty becomes an ideal, and this ideal possesses one until it is transformed into a faith. . . . Over the years I have evolved from biologist to conservation biologist: Research enhances my role as an ecological missionary. The goal is to balance knowledge and action.

Conservation problems are social and economic, not scientific, yet biologists have traditionally been expected to solve them. Research is easy; conservation most decidedly is not. Since conservation cannot be imposed from above, it must ultimately be based on local interests, skills, and tradi-

George Schaller in the Gobi Desert, Mongolia.

tions. A field biologist must work with local people and institutions to find innovative solutions. The establishment of a nature reserve often creates hostility, for deprived of their land, local people are no longer able to collect fuel, hunt, and graze livestock. Yet the traditional lives of indigenous people must be considered. Unfortunately, appeals to moral enlightenment seldom lead to progress; one cannot discuss the philosophy of conservation with a man cutting the last tree for fuel. Principles must always be juggled with practicalities. Seldom clear-cut, environmental issues often involve moral ambiguity. Instead of being just a biologist, something for which I was trained, I must also be an educator, diplomat, fund-raiser, politician, anthropologist. . . . No wonder that I seek solitude where physical obstacles are minor compared to political ones.

Environmental destruction will never cease, not even in a truly moral world. Sustainable development, the Holy Grail of today's conservation movement, will not save that which many treasure most: pieces of wilderness undeveloped, unaffected by greed, where we can experience the calm rhythm of life and recapture a feeling of belonging to the natural world. Wilderness is a state of mind; and, though it is part of our past, it is doubtful that future generations will even miss it. They may grow apart from the wild. But they should be given the option of glimpsing the splendor that once was. We all strive for a private sense of merit; in addition, I now aspire to an ideal beyond science in that my goal is to help fragments of wilderness endure.

THE FUTURE OF THE WILD

After World War II, though doubts were appearing in the writings of Fairfield Osborn and others, the broad assumption was that the earth could continue to absorb punishment from human industry and/or that solutions to shortage and degradation would always be invented or found. Today, it is apparent that we have very little leeway. There are as many intricacies in finding answers as there are in defining problems, and pressures come from all directions—ecological, biological, political, socioeconomic, and philosophical. As American conservationist John Muir observed about a century ago, "When we try to pick out anything by itself, we find it hitched to everything in the universe."

Today, even the most optimistic conservationists sense nature being overwhelmed by economic development, overpopulation, political corruption, resource waste, and environmental ruin, by lack of knowledge and caring. George Schaller has said, "The destruction will never end. Never." In this chapter, William Conway, Annette Berkovits, and John Robinson express serious doubts about conservation surviving human prerogatives, the effectiveness of education, and the cooptation of conservation by development, respectively.

Yet all four, and many others working around the globe, represent an extraordinary resolve to overcome these obstacles, to explore and activate every possible mechanism of survival. The fact, as Conway noted in 1992, that there were five hundred million cars in the world, where there had been just fifty-three million forty years earlier, makes the situation seem ludicrous. All the more reason to insist, finally, on conservation as the overriding issue of our time.

In an age of complexity, specialization, and fragmentation, organic unity—Fairfield Osborn's circle—is an essential concept. Using the earth's resources as needed or desired, then patching things up with protective regulations and reserves once seemed a workable if not entirely reasonable course. No longer. The pressures are too great and too many. Every action for the environment has consequences that must be understood if the totality is to survive. It is not possible to rationalize this process completely, nor to entirely control how the environment is affected, but the balance must at least be shifted so that preserving life and its cycles becomes paramount.

Under Osborn, the Society began both to diversify and consolidate its conservation mission. Integration and expansion quickened under William Conway, who became Bronx Zoo director in 1961 and general director of the Society in 1966. Vital to the new approach was the growing international program, in which Conway was both a moving force and a participant, effecting significant changes in Argentina and elsewhere.

Other crucial activities were becoming part of the overall conservation process as well. While helping to establish the Institute for Research in Animal Behavior in 1966, Conway began to redefine the role of the zoo and aquarium as partners in conservation. He saw the importance of long-term breeding programs for endangered and other wildlife and said so in 1966

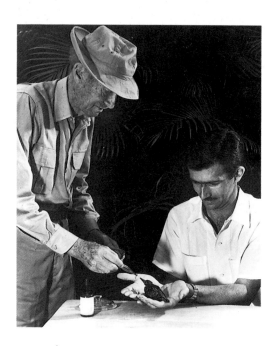

William Beebe with William Conway at Simla, Trinidad, in 1959.

before the American Association of Zoological Parks and Aquariums (AAZPA), of which he was president. Such programs would not only make zoos and aquariums more self-sustaining in terms of their animal collections, but they would shift the focus from simply exhibiting species to sustaining life that is rapidly vanishing in nature. Species that had no other

Left: The World of Birds introduced new techniques of open display and controlled lighting in an imaginative design by Morris Ketchum, Jr., and Associates. From the early plans of 1961 to the opening in 1972, funding was provided by Lila Acheson Wallace. The New York Times called it "surefire drama and painless education."

Renovation of the 1899 Aquatic Bird House as a series of natural habitats was the first major project planned by William Conway (second from right) at the Bronx Zoo. The new building opened in 1964.

chance might be saved, and eventually, with enough care for and restoration of habitats, they might be returned to their original homes.

Without delay, Conway also attacked some severe conservation problems on the home front. He spoke out against the importation of endangered species and their products and published several powerful articles on the subject. A special investigation of the American alligator skin trade and a special conference convened by Curator of Reptiles Wayne King led to laws banning such trade in every state. Conway's and King's testimony also aided passage of the Mason-Smith Act in New York State, preventing the sale of many fur- and hide-bearing animals, and then contributed to the broadening of the federal Endangered Species Conservation Act.

Meanwhile, the emphasis on breeding had immediate results at the zoo and aquarium, and in 1974 the Society, led by trustee Frank Y. Larkin, created a special endangered species and study facility in a climate warmer than New York's—the Wildlife Survival Center on St. Catherines Island, Georgia, supported in large part by the Edward John Noble Foundation. It was at about this time that the zoo community, led by Conway and others in the AAZPA (now the American Zoo and Aquarium Association, the AZA), began to form a network to coordinate breeding programs. Conway was, in fact, the father of the Species Survival Plans, or "SSPs," which were established in 1982 to create such a network. By 1994, there were seventy-two SSPs, ranging from Asian elephants to white-naped cranes, and the Society participated in forty of them, eight coordinated by Society staff.

As breeding programs evolved, so did the need to understand social and reproductive behavior in captive animals, which can be complicated and

Mrs. Brooke Astor funded Wild Asia, the zoo's monorail tour around thirty-eight acres of Asian habitats, and starred at the opening in 1977.

Working with giant pandas in China (1981) and on other projects abroad, veterinarian Dr. Emil Dolensek made field medicine an important part of international conservation.

mystifying. Conway encouraged the unraveling of these mysteries by hiring a new generation of curators and staff, led by three young scientists who arrived at the zoo between 1967 and 1970. All three were made curators in 1975: James Doherty of mammals, Donald Bruning of birds, and John Behler of amphibians and reptiles. Doherty became general curator in 1979. Christine Sheppard and Fred Koontz joined them in the late 1980s as curators of birds and mammals, respectively. Their accumulated body of knowledge has led to remarkable breeding successes, many of them firsts. Hundreds of endangered species—including snow leopards, lowland gorillas, beluga whales, Malayan tapirs, Siberian tigers, gaurs, Grevy's zebras, barasingha deer, several species of crane, guam rails, Bali mynahs, Malayan peacock pheasants, several curassows, red and lesser birds of paradise, Chinese alligators, broad-nosed caimans, and radiated tortoises—have produced offspring in long-term programs.

Expertise in the larger realm of animal management, to which Lee Crandall had contributed so much, also grew in subtlety and scope under his successors. How much space do various species need, and how do they use their space? How can characteristics of behavior in the wild be retained in captive animals? What can be applied that will help us understand the needs of animals in nature? Zoo studies provided close-up knowledge of individual animals difficult or impossible to obtain in nature—not only facts about basic physiology but insights into behavior, longevity, sexual maturity, gestation and incubation duration, developmental stages, and so forth. Virtually all genetic and many behavioral studies have had to be done on captive animals. Gradually, zoo and field studies have begun to reinforce each other, helping to determine conservation strategies.

And so it is with wildlife health as well. When Dr. Emil Dolensek became the Society's chief veterinarian in 1969, the orientation turned perceptibly to the preservation of species, though the care of individual animals had never achieved a higher level. Preventive measures were stressed—examinations and tests, proper diets and healthy conditions, thorough pathology and accurate record-keeping. The correct handling of animals was emphasized, a training program for young veterinarians was set up, and experts in human medicine were consulted with increasing effectiveness. Dolensek was a pioneer in establishing the dietary importance of vitamin E and in bringing veterinary help to studies in the field. When Dolensek died in 1990, Dr. Robert A. Cook continued to expand every aspect of the program, with Dr. Ellen Dierenfeld establishing a comprehensive compendium of nutritional information based on studies in the wild and in the zoo and Dr. William Karesh forging new links with fieldwork in the Society's unique Field Veterinary Program, which provides clinical expertise to conservation projects around the world.

Conservation consciousness and globalization also changed the tenets of zoo and aquarium wildlife exhibition. The world's first zoo exhibition and graphic arts department was established at the Bronx Zoo in 1963. For the sake of a fidelity to nature that would both educate the public and provide for the animals' well-being, the Society continued to re-create natural environments and establish a rational, global overview of the natural realm. Osborn had started the process with African Plains and zoogeographic zones. Conway continued, with a grand progression of projects. Beginning with the remodeled Aquatic Birds House in 1964, each of the succeeding facilities—World of Darkness (1969), World of Birds (1972), Wild Asia (1977), JungleWorld (1985), Baboon Reserve (1990), and many others—expanded the visitor's experience and the possibilities of education, animal management, and breeding. The aquarium, under George Ruggieri and Lou Garibaldi, came up with Discovery Cove (1990) and Sea Cliffs (1993). New techniques emerged of fashioning artificial rocks, trees, and vines and using indigenous live plants to replicate habitats, from deep rain forest to rocky coast.

These more dramatic environments created new opportunities for education at the zoo and aquarium. By the early 1980s, such programs were reaching most of the school districts in metropolitan New York. By the early nineties, on-site classrooms and observation posts were established within several habitat facilities, and Bronx Zoo wildlife and conservation curricula, for every grade from kindergarten through high school, were being used in forty-three states. The Society's redesign and takeover of three smaller city zoos—now called the Central Park, Prospect Park, and Queens wildlife centers—also provided a means of bringing the conservation message to more people through education and direct contact with animals and their habitats.

Current approaches to field science, animal management, education, wildlife health, and even exhibition design, appear more controlled and studied, more defined by scientific parameters, than ever before. But their practitioners remain, in a world of obdurate problems, passionate in their commitment, recognizing themselves as fundamental activists in a much larger effort to save wildlife and wild places. In 1993, reflecting this commitment, the New York Zoological Society became the Wildlife Conservation Society.

The Society began labeling endangered species and in the 1970s created a yearly cemetery for extinct species at the Bronx Zoo.

WILLIAM CONWAY

*from "The Conservation Park: A New Zoo
Synthesis for a Changed World"
Address at "The Role of Zoos and Aquariums
in Biological Conservation: Past, Present,
and Future," AAZPA Annual Conference*

SEPTEMBER 17, 1992

*Conway's vision of the modern zoo as a
"new kind of institution" was spawned in
his early years at the Society. He has written
and spoken frequently about zoos as centers
of education for urban people who are no
longer in contact with nature and about the
obligations of zoos to propagate endangered
species and expand the body of behavioral
and biological knowledge. Since the mid-1960s,
he has sharpened his definition of the zoo's role
in a world experiencing environmental crisis.
His full-blown concept of the conservation
park as a home base for worldwide action
emerged in this 1992 speech.*

All over the world, nature and wildlife are being destroyed at an ever faster rate. Zoological parks and aquariums have seemed destined to become no more than living museums of natural history—until recently. However, a new synthesis of zoo programming and expertise is developing. It is possible that the future of zoos is to become "conservation parks" actively contributing to nature's survival—not quiescent museums.

There are at least 1,100 zoos and aquariums in the world with a combined annual attendance of about 800 million; a global activity significant both to wildlife and society. But, for the vast majority of human beings, the survival of the wildlife they do not eat is irrelevant. It is doomed to become more so. Saving competitive, possibly dangerous, creatures must seem an insupportable luxury to the growing ranks of poverty-stricken peoples. Supportive North American and western European wildlife attitudes are as much a modern anomaly as their economies. And the main problem is human population growth.

There are 97 million more of us every year—3 every second, about 2.5 billion pounds every twelve months; a proliferation fueling exponential change. In forty years, motor vehicles have increased from 53 million to 500 million. The next few decades can be depended upon to bring national disputes over food, fuel, and water, even if there are new crops and systems that produce more food.

There will be disruptive migrations of poorer peoples, even if there are gradual declines in population growth. New diseases will appear, even if new cures for old ones also appear. Crowding and poverty will stoke tribal warfare, as they have from Afghanistan to Yugoslavia. Thus, society's chances of caring for Earth's surface in ecosystems, rather than fragments, are remote. And the advances we make in feeding our burgeoning crowd will subtract from what is left for the rest of life on Earth.

Moreover, nearly 90 percent of human population growth is taking place where the most abundant and fascinating wildlife dwells, in less developed tropical countries. Yet, there are hopeful signs: China, Thailand, Cuba, and Singapore have cut their fertility rates by 50 percent and another fifteen countries have reduced theirs by 40 to 48 percent.

However, accelerated climate change is probably inevitable and its effects upon wild animal communities confined to ever-shrinking fragments of habitat in a swelling sea of humanity will be catastrophic, no matter what its impacts are upon humans. Although much marine life is threatened, terrestrial wildlife is almost infinitely more endangered.

Thus, the foreseeable future of the zoo and the wildlife it stands for can be likened to that of a library whose books are decaying and authors dying; a museum whose paintings, artists, and even history are expiring. As species biomass declines, the rare creatures left behind are made obsolete, not only economically but also ecologically, for they can no longer fulfill their roles in nature. The reasons for preserving or restoring them dwindle to the intellectual ones of curiosity, ethics, and esthetics—inducements likely to win strongest support in a world free from want.

Our apocalyptic perception of the terrestrial extinction crisis is partly drawn from the observation that tropical forest invertebrates are extraordinarily numerous, localized, and diverse. Now, there may be more than 30 million species, but deforestation is proceeding at the rate of 16.8 million hectares each year. Thus we stand to lose hundreds of thousands, perhaps millions, of forms not yet even known. What seems worse is that we shall also lose thousands of larger creatures we do know—members of the family.

Extinction forecasts for vertebrates are less dramatic, for there were few to begin with, but their survival also depends upon available habitat. About 47,500 vertebrate species remain alive. Twenty-four thousand five hundred of these are sharks and fishes, and twenty-three thousand are mammals, birds, reptiles, and amphibians—of which perhaps 12 percent have some representatives in zoos and aquariums. At the least, 25 percent of the tetrapods and 10 percent or more of the fishes are threatened with extinction during the next hundred years.

But we tend to forget that extinction is first the loss of populations—a demographic demise, only secondly a taxonomic one. Thus the number of vertebrate species lost in the continental U.S. during the last four hundred years is small. What is gone forever are the numbers: the vast herds of bison, the great flocks of shorebirds, the countless concentrations of turtles and toads, waterfowl and wolves. Their replacements are 99 million cattle, 54 million pigs, 11 million sheep, 356 million chickens (which produce about 5.5 billion broilers each year), 260 million turkeys, and nearly 250 million people, with a combined biomass of roughly 111 billion pounds. (I have not tallied the horses, dogs and cats, introduced rats, pigeons, starlings, sparrows, and the like.)

But who would have thought that a market for bear gall bladders would attract poachers in America as easily as in the "third world," thereby threatening black bear populations? Who would have guessed that fishing fleets of "civilized" people would be so barbarous as to crisscross the oceans with nets thirty miles long, indiscriminately killing hundreds of thousands of seabirds, cetaceans, and pinnipeds, and far greater numbers of fishes, marketable or not? As wildlife populations become ever smaller, many will become extinct by anthropogenic accident; sort of an, "Excuse me, I didn't mean to jar your coffee" kind of extinction.

Nevertheless, some less developed countries decry the "green imperialism" of Northern and Western nations who would temper the use of undeveloped lands, waters and wildlife. Will it be "politically correct" to save wildlife in our changing world?. . .

In 1947, Florida's Everglades National Park was established "to protect the finest assemblage of large wading birds on the continent," and hunting and encroachment were halted. By 1989, the populations of these birds had declined by 90 percent. Refuge management by benevolent neglect does not save wildlife communities when their ecosystems are too small or are modified by activities outside their borders. Besides, nature reserves, as currently managed, alter over time, becoming less suitable for many original denizens. In 1987, a study of seven of the largest national parks in western North America found that populations of twenty-seven species of mammals had gone extinct in one or more of these sacrosanct reserves. Such tragedies are being replicated around the world.

We tie refuge wildlife in place, suppressing its migrations and colonizations with our surrounding development. It is not clear what will survive outside these protected vestiges other than species which are already successful in altered landscapes and the commensals which follow man from place to place worldwide. But it is clear that only 3.7 percent of the planet's land area is in its 5,300 more or less "protected areas" and that only about a thousand of these are in nations with relatively supportive budgets.

If any of the specialized big mammals, birds, and reptiles are to be retained in the shrinking crevices between human populations, or the great places—whether North American old-growth forests or Serengeti savanna, whether Chile's Salar de Tara or Kenya's Lake Nakuru, or the great wildlife kingdoms in Zaire's Ituri or Peru's Manu—it will have to be on the basis of a much more supportive kind of conservation. Such areas will inevitably become anthro-dependent megazoos. The future of these megazoos, as well as of zoos and aquariums, will depend upon public perceptions.

Public attitudes toward wildlife in the United States are deeply confused. We are touched with sadness at the plight of vanishing species but more readily brought to tears by the individual difficulties of E.T., Bambi, or Black Beauty. And we are just as readily concerned with Star Wars wookies as with Australian wallabies, with Ninja Turtles as with giant tortoises. We are moved to indignation by the animal researcher's scalpel but thrilled with admiration for great predators rending the loins of anguished wildebeests.

It is a challenging educational paradox that so many human beings agonize over humane treatment of specific animals but ignore the millions daily brutalized by the destruction of their environments. Few perceive the difference between the well-being of a creature and the survival of a species. . . .

As we enhance zoo education, we must not allow technology, wonderful

Since the Everglades National Park opened in 1947, ninety percent of the big wading birds, such as tricolored herons, have vanished from the area.

Acid rain, here reflecting smokestacks belching sulfur-laden smoke, is particularly hard on the lakes and forests of the northeastern United States and adjacent Canada. Gray wolves (below) have been largely exterminated from this region.

tool that it is, to distance our visitors and students from the reality of the life that inspires our goals and purposes. The reported final comment of a child talking about the Atlanta Zoo's plans to enhance its education program with computerized-video offerings was not about animals. It was, "Can I use the computers?" Marshall McLuhan noted, "The medium is the message," while Max Frisch observed, "Technology is a way of organizing the universe so that man does not have to experience it."

Among the most serious threats to wild creatures is that they will be ignored; condemned by humanity to the same closets of irrelevance and curiosity as silent movies and corset stays. In our increasingly unnatural world, live zoo animals and their simulated habitats provide profound and moving experiences. They live *with us*, daily creating news and arousing interest. They do not permit us to ignore the fact that their kind exists. But even more competitive entertainment is in store.

Recreational experiments in "virtual reality" claim true experiential transport for their participants. A British group plans a video and virtual reality "zoo." Can Aldous Huxley's "feelies" be far away?

No doubt our future visitors will find it an easy choice when the time comes that they must decide between visiting an exquisitely interpreted rain forest of live plants and animals—or taking a simple interlude in the back seat of an auto with Marilyn Monroe or Clark Gable.

That much of our task is educational is self-evident, so it is especially troubling that, among industrialized nations, U.S. students are among the lowest scorers in science comprehension. American zoos and aquariums deal increasingly with intellectually impoverished people who have little understanding of how their biosphere's life systems evolved and work. A 1991 Gallup poll found that 47 percent of respondents believe humans were created by God during the last ten thousand years, pretty much in their present form.

Given the world extinction crisis, the future of zoos and aquariums will be determined by their ability to effect a new synthesis of their assets and to become proactive "conservation parks." They have too much to do to subside into "Ye Olde" Williamsburg-like museums representing idealized habitats of yesteryear; Potemkin villages filled with wonderful creatures that no longer survive beyond zoo fences.

Teaching about a living nature that demands saving is a compelling mission. Teaching about a world that no longer exists is much less so. Zoos *must* focus their central efforts upon the preservation of nature.

In fact, zoos have arrived at a level of proficiency which could, theoretically, enable them to breed thousands of species in *ex-situ* programs. Realistically, the economics of sustaining large numbers of diverse creatures in captivity over long periods of time, even with advanced reproduction technology, restrict propagation programs to a fraction of their potential—and always will. Although revisions of priorities may provide new space and resources, major governmental support is still not available to propagate wildlife, and such programs probably cannot be vastly expanded by private efforts.

For many species losing their homes in nature, some sort of habitat restoration may eventually occur. For many more, it will not. But zoo propagation can probably aid the survival of 15 percent or more of all the terrestrial vertebrates likely to become extinct in the next century—perhaps 40 percent of larger species—and that is eminently worth doing.

While aiming propagation programs at short-term rescues, such as those for the Arabian oryx, the American bison, golden lion tamarin, or the peregrine falcon, zoos must also commit to the long-term nurturing of painstakingly chosen species which have no reasonable hope in nature and whose passing would be generally recognized as an unacceptable loss to our planet's heritage. There is no doubt that such efforts will be at the core of the zoo's future public service. . . .

But *ex-situ* propagation can only avert *species* extinction. It cannot save animal *populations* in nature, except for a few *in extremis* through genetic and demographic reinforcement. It cannot save habitat. It provides no substitute for the loss of those wondrously rich and populous wildlife communities now dying with the tall trees of the great rain forests; for the disappearance of the awesome colonies of seashore pinnipeds and seabirds, the great herds of migrating ungulates in their thousands—for all those grand wildlife spectacles that so move our hearts and inspire our souls. Once you have seen half a million wildebeest on the move in the Serengeti, half a million penguins on the shores of Punta Tombo, a remnant dispersed in a few collections is simply not an adequate fulfillment of the responsibilities of society's one institution most especially devoted to wildlife.

The next major step for zoos and aquariums is to focus programs directly upon the survival of their collection's creatures in their native habitats, whether those be local or overseas. Taking that step distinguishes the "conservation park" of tomorrow from the zoo of yesterday. It is a high step, and the footing is slippery.

The two toughest questions are: Can zoos and aquariums afford to dedicate a significant portion of their resources, unique skills, enormous public presence, and worldwide interconnections to helping to save nature more directly? And, can they afford not to?

Teaching people in Sheboygan about coral reefs and rain forests is not enough to save habitats in Belize or the Congo. Although most zoos were created as local cultural resources, like art museums and libraries, unlike these institutions they are indissolubly attached to their living exhibits. Few libraries or museums find it necessary to sustain writers or artists, but no zoos will survive unless they sustain wildlife.

The conservation park backs up local wildlife preservationists with science and training. It helps with wildlife monitoring, disease control, and public education. It acts as ombudsman for the local protectors of wildlife areas. It supports these efforts by making double use of recreational dollars—making payment for a trip to the zoo also an act of conservation. . . .

Future zoos and aquariums in our changing world will be caretakers of life in an ongoing extinction crisis. Whatever we professionals choose to call our institutions: "zoo," "living museum," "aquarium," we must make them evolve into "conservation parks"—environmental resource, education, and rescue centers. We must collaborate with other institutions and other conservationists to effect an interconnected, mutually reinforcing *global* conservation park.

If zoos do not act to help save nature now, much wildlife will be lost that might have been saved. The zoo's moment will have passed. Its relevance will disappear.

About 420 miles of oil pipeline in Alaska was elevated to allow caribou migrations, but it has frightened nursing females. A new pipeline planned for the Arctic National Wildlife Refuge would damage the calving grounds of the famous Porcupine herd of caribou.

Mountain goats, introduced to Washington's Olympic National Park in the 1920s, have disturbed the area's delicate ecology, while clear-cutting has reduced old-growth forests there and throughout the northwest to mere remnants.

*Grevy's zebras, one of more than 225 endangered species
at Society facilities, breed successfully at the Bronx Zoo and
St. Catherines Wildlife Survival Center.*

The Society's Conservation Parks

Discovery Cove, opened in 1989 at the Aquarium for Wildlife Conservation, teaches about marine environments and adaptations in a series of living classroom exhibits and alcoves.

If zoos and aquariums represent the human need to observe and understand nature, they also have become essential tools in the effort to restore nature, a purpose that was enthusiastically advocated by the Society's founders. Still, the transformation of zoos and aquariums into conservation parks did not really start until the 1960s, when much of its practical ideology was provided by William Conway. The changing mission of the Society's facilities has become clear in the ensuing thirty years. Today, about fifteen hundred zoo babies are born or hatched each year, many of them representing endangered species. Most of the zoos' and aquarium's animals live in carefully replicated landscapes, made possible by rapidly developing exhibition technology. Some 135 conservation studies are conducted by curatorial and veterinary staff at the zoos and aquarium each year, along with 225 studies by field scientists overseas. And environmental education programs reach hundreds of thousands of students and teachers through courses in New York and curricular programs across the country.

Left: Siberian tigers, like this one in Wild Asia, are now more common in zoos than in the wild. They and the other animals on this page thrive at the Bronx Zoo today.

Center: At the head of Astor Court, the 1908 Elephant House is now the Keith W. Johnson Zoo Center, with habitats for elephants, rhinos, and tapirs.

Below: Indian elephants are seen by captive viewers in the Khao Yai Reserve area of Thailand in Wild Asia.

Opposite above: With dense vegetation and elaborately replicated cliffs, streambeds, giant trees, and intricate vines, JungleWorld was created to dramatize the disappearance of Asian forest habitats, including those of the Indian gharial.

Opposite below: Dramatic confrontations and other typical behavior are played out by two troops of gelada baboons in the Ethiopian highlands of the Baboon Reserve, opened in 1990.

Below right and right: Angulated tortoises court and a newborn slender-horned gazelle is examined by John Iaderosa at the St. Catherines Wildlife Survival Center in Georgia, where severely endangered species are bred and free-ranging groups are studied for possible reintroduction.

Below: Snow leopards at the zoo have produced more than seventy-five cubs since the mid-1960s, contributing to breeding programs for the species in fourteen other zoos.

Left: On August 8, 1988, Mayor Edward I. Koch officially dedicated the new Central Park Wildlife Center, one of three city zoos to be remodeled and operated by the Society.

Harbor seals (next page) and walruses (below), as well as fur seals, sea otters, black-footed penguins, and many associated species, occupy the rocky habitats of the aquarium's Sea Cliffs, opened in 1993.

A *beluga whale is born at the aquarium on July 6, 1993, and becomes the first to be successfully raised in captivity.*

Left: The Prospect Park Wildlife Center, reopened in 1993, is a children's educational zoo, with close-up views of such species as the Hamadryas baboon from Ethiopia, Somalia, and Saudi Arabia.

Right: Buildings on Central Park South provide a backdrop for Japanese snow monkeys in the center's Temperate Zone.

Below: Roosevelt elk are among the mostly North American species at the Queens Wildlife Center, which reopened in 1992 under Society management.

A N N E T T E R . B E R K O V I T S

*from "Zoos: Urban Centers for Conservation
Education"*
*Paper presented at the Royal Ontario Museum
Rainforest Conference*

OCTOBER 1990

*Under Annette Berkovits, vice-president for
education, the Bronx Zoo has pioneered the
use of zoos and parks, beyond the classroom,
as educational resources. At the zoo itself,
the program has grown to include a broad
roster of courses on wildlife biology, ecology,
and conservation, many taught at sites
within animal habitats. Full curriculums,
from "Pablo Python Looks at Animals" for
the early grades to "Wildlife Inquiry through
Zoo Education" for high school students,
and intensive teacher training seminars are
leading a revival of science education in
the United States and reaching teachers and
students in several other countries.*

We have established that exciting exhibitions can influence the learning of conservation-minded attitudes in zoos. We also know that more than 100 million people visit zoos in North America each year—more than all sports events combined! We should, as a result, have battalions of citizenry prepared to launch endangered species rescue efforts.

Why then do the predictions on the state of the environment, and the rain forest in particular, sound grimmer each year? Why do environmental educators pursue what sometimes seems like a lost cause—getting urban people to care about distant places and changing their life-styles? How many acres of rain forest have been saved as a result of rain-forest education programs or new exhibitions in the last decade? In the last year?

A pessimist might say that the answer to the last two questions is alarmingly close to zero. An optimist will no doubt point to new initiatives on behalf of cleaning up the environment, recycling, and swelling the ranks of contributors to conservation causes.

Mark Twain once said that one of the most satisfying jobs in the world is chopping wood. The results of one's effort are immediately visible. Education, on the other hand, is the most discouraging of professions because its practitioners must wait years to see the results. But while we wait we also need to focus on what we can do *now* to increase the impact and effectiveness of our programs. It may well be that the odds are stacked against our success, but if institutions such as zoos, aquariums, arboretums, and museums join forces and pool expertise in educating their vast audiences, rain forests may stand a slightly better chance of survival. . . .

Will there be remnants of rain forest to nurture and protect by the time our educated urban public has reached the right critical mass? In other words, how can knowledge of rain-forest ecology help people, and more to the point, how can such instruction advance the cause of rain-forest conservation? . . .

When we teach about the rain forest and other threatened habitats, we expand the public's world view, making people more responsible citizens of their own countries and citizens of the world. As technology and multinational corporate economics propel us toward more international interdependence, understanding across national boundaries will become a precondition of peace and a stable world economy.

Rain-forest programs enrich the school curriculum. This is as true in the science curriculum as in the humanities. Study of the ecology of major world biomes should be an integral element of learning for any educated person. Yet, all too often this is left out of the curriculum. . . .

When we teach about the rain forest, we help people deal with the future. Despite much talk about futuristic society, not much is done to prepare the public, and especially our young people, to cope with the complex changes that are predicted for the twenty-first century. Changes in climate, patterns of fuel use, consumption of resources, world demographics, and the international economy, can all be anticipated and addressed within an in-depth rain-forest inquiry. . . .

It is far less clear how such education can benefit the rain forest itself, especially over the short run. Education takes time. It is a process of sowing seeds for the future. But the problems facing the rain forest are so acute. They demand immediate action. There simply is not much time left in which to act, in which to take advantage of the creative initiatives that today's students might invent tomorrow.

At the present rates of deforestation there will be no rain forest left in forty to fifty years. Even if we were wildly successful in the next several years and managed to properly educate today's children about the value and plight of the rain forest, we would have to wait ten to twenty years before realizing the benefits of that education in tangible results. . . .

Students measure ambient conditions in a class that involves observing animals from a classroom built into the forest habitat in JungleWorld.

Shall we give up, then? Clearly, our instincts say no, even while our rational minds cause us to feel frustrated. We must muster every ounce of optimism. We must continue with more programs, newer programs, more creative and effective programs that will have a lasting impact. But, we must not get lulled into a sense of complacency. We must look for other solutions, for new frontiers, new audiences. . . .

If rain-forest education is beneficial, why not think of the classroom in much broader terms? . . . Teachers can carry our message into the classroom. But there are others who can have a more immediate impact. There are the parents of the children who visit our institutions. They are the consumers of rain-forest products; they are also voters. They have the power of the purse and the power of the vote. And what about businessmen and investors in rain-forest ventures—the purveyors of rain-forest products from parrots to mahogany, from inexpensive beef to periwinkle extract? What about local legislators, bankers, and politicians? How many zoos or museums have taken on the task of educating these key people in any substantive way? Much remains to be done. We need to create educational approaches that will work with these groups, or even attract them in the first place.

Aquarium class on the beach at Coney Island.

We need to think of incentives that will bring these untraditional audiences to our "classrooms," whether they be located in school buildings, zoos, government offices, or museums. We have to come up with tantalizing programs to reach the hearts, as well as the minds; the pocketbooks, as

Teachers in Belize learn about the use of "Wildlife Inquiry through Zoo Education" (W.I.Z.E.), a Bronx Zoo curriculum for grades 6–12. Schools in forty-three states and several nations, including China, have adopted Society education programs.

Prairie dog "pop-ups" are part of the environmental Children's Zoo, which has been emulated around the world since its inauguration in 1981.

well as the souls. Our institutions have to make education a priority equal to that of research or propagation. Education should not be only a fashionable buzzword, on the chopping block with every fiscal crisis. Conservation education is the key mission of institutions with living collections and it should become equally important to museums whose only living species is *Homo sapiens*.

FALLACY OF THE WOOL WEARER

I received a letter recently from someone who was disturbed that several women who attended one of the New York Zoological Society's conservation meetings had worn fur coats—specifically mink. My correspondent noted that anyone who wanted to keep warm could do so with woolens, without depriving any minks of their lives. In me, she found a sympathetic ear, though one a bit battered and cauliflowered from the fur debates.

I am one of the people who led anti-fur and -hide battles back in the 1960s. My articles and testimony on behalf of the NYZS at legislative hearings helped protect crocodilians and spotted cats and made me many friends—and some acquaintances of the other kind. My concern, however, was particular to endangered species. That was, and still is, an important distinction.

Human use of other species is so indiscriminate that singling out for condemnation people who wear furs of domestic or non-endangered species is almost like scolding traffic lights for purse-snatching. I do not mean to imply that wearing domestic fur coats is an irrelevant issue. It is not. But focusing attention on the use of such furs, especially, as evil and inhumane, diverts us from more serious conservation issues, seductively comforting us

WILLIAM CONWAY

from "Down with Mary's Little Lamb!"

WILDLIFE CONSERVATION,
JANUARY/FEBRUARY 1992

William Conway always comes down on the side of nature and its processes. But he also has recognized that the "advances" of civilization create a balancing act (of which zoos are one expression) between people and nature, and that issues concerning how much we are taking from nature must be addressed, based on facts.

Land use by wool-bearing sheep, here at Ophir Pass in Oregon, destroys more wildlife than fur-animal farming.

William Hornaday took on the fur trade's destruction of wild animals in the March 1921 Zoological Society Bulletin, *opening with this photograph of a $55,000 chinchilla wrap.*

Crocodilian expert Peter Brazaitis of the Central Park Wildlife Center has helped curb the trade in reptile skins through his work with the U.S. Fish and Wildlife Service and other groups.

with righteousness along the way. If we stop there, we are either sadly ill-informed or dishonest.

What shall we say to people who attend our conservation meetings who eat meat, poultry, or fish? Or wear leather shoes and belts? Or have more than two children? How can we possibly allow dog- and cat-owners to attend? The number of domestic and wild animals used in pet food is downright enormous. Furthermore, studies show that suburban cats are powerfully destructive of local wildlife populations: Some individuals kill as many as 400 small birds and mammals each year—and not at all humanely. In addition, canine and feline pets now produce more than 15 million surplus dogs and cats annually, which themselves must be killed—about 1,000 a week in New York City alone.

Then, of course, there are our acquaintances in the construction business, who by building shopping malls and other structures, wipe out wildlife habitats at the rate of more than a million acres a year—not only killing everything that lived on the sites but destroying any chance of wildlife recovery . . . forever.

And what about the people in the petroleum industry and its subsidiaries whose businesses resulted in more than 10,000 oil spills in the U.S. alone last year and caused the needless death of uncounted thousands of birds and fishes? Or the people in the chemical industry who produce biocides, particularly biocides for agriculture? Of all human endeavors, agriculture is the most broadly and permanently devastating to wildlife, causing the poisoning and starvation of millions of animals and the loss of their age-old homes on hundreds of millions of acres. And don't forget those people who cut down entire forests each week to bring you the Sunday paper—and this magazine.

Although it may be satisfying to vilify the readily identifiable fur-wearer, that really is too easy. There is no comparison between the magnitude of wildlife slaughtered or the cruelty caused by any of the industries that I have mentioned (or by many more) and that caused by the domestic fur industry—if only because the fur industry is, and probably will always be, so small. We must not allow ignorance to hide from us the responsibility we have to understand and address the more significant conservation problems.

All chinchilla coats (I saw one at the meeting my correspondent mentioned) are made from the skins of rodents that have been selectively bred for that purpose for generations—just as chickens are bred for the table. The same is true, I believe, for almost all mink coats. In contrast, hardly any reptiles are bred for the skin trade, which depends almost entirely on skins flayed from wild crocodilians, lizards, turtles, and snakes. (When did you last hear a protest about snake belts or wallets?) Moreover, exceedingly few of these reptiles are being harvested "on a sustained-yield basis," as the lumbermen like to put it—the underlying principle of sustained yield being that development may use resources but only at the rate they are replenished by natural processes. (Regrettably, the timber industry is not doing this with trees in most places.) The trade in reptile skins endangers many of the species it exploits—and that is the critical point we must all address. Extinction is the ultimate cruelty.

In 1968–69, as the skin wars warmed, my research turned up the fact that

U.S. importers had brought in 3,168 cheetah, 23,347 jaguar, 17,490 leopard, 99,002 otter, and 262,030 ocelot skins. None of these species was (or is) being bred for the skin trade; none was (or is) harvested on a sustained-yield basis. All were being killed in what little is left of the wild. Some of the big cats were clearly headed for extinction. Most of that trade has since been stopped. But we must keep in mind that cheetah coats have quite a different implication for wildlife conservation than coats made from domestic furs.

And so to Mary's little lamb. The oft-repeated recommendation that one should wear wool instead of fur is a sore point with me, for I have been trying to promote conservation in Latin American "sheep country" for the past 30 years.

Woolens are produced at the cost of hundreds of millions of wild creatures and also of millions of domestic sheep. Many thousands of square miles of wild lands have been and are being annexed and degraded by the ravaging woolly hordes placed upon them by sheep-raisers. (There are more than a billion sheep around the world—more than 11 million on U.S. lands, 162 million in Australia, and 29 million in Argentina.) Sheep farming, more than most agriculture, has resulted in widespread predator control programs and in the destruction of harmless grass-eating competitors such as rheas and guanacos in Argentina and emus and kangaroos in Australia. In the U.S., more than 400,000 coyotes were trapped, shot, and poisoned in 1988 alone, mostly to protect sheep; about 20 million have suffered the same fates since 1900. In Australia, it's dingos that are being eradicated. Sheep also crop grass close to the ground and, in arid lands, are the main agents of erosion and habitat loss—the root cause for the decline of many birds and mammals.

But what is it, I have often wondered, that makes sheep-killing more humane in the eyes of "green" thinkers than mink-killing? People don't seem to realize that those billion sheep are not allowed to graze blissfully to ripe old age with only an occasional shearing to worry about. The fact is they are kept until they reach their peak of productivity and then are slaughtered, just like pigs, cattle, chickens—and mink.

Sooner or later, all animals must die, but humanity's use of domestically bred or non-endangered individuals is one thing, and its elimination of whole species and permanent destruction of habitat, quite another.

Well, what should you wear? Must you move to a warm climate, where you can go about in cottons? I suspect that a bit of research would prove cotton to be one of the agricultural crops most damaging to wildlife and natural habitats and that the production of manmade fabrics is a major, if secondary, source of environmental destruction and pollution.

So, begin by consuming less. Keep the old sweater (or mink) another year. Do whatever you can to induce people to keep their own numbers down, because that will reduce the sheep-caused damage and ease most of the other environmental problems. Think deeply before you cop out as a conservationist by simply addressing the shallow end of conservation complications or those that leave you and yours guiltless. Instead, seek perspective—with humility. Explore alternatives and above all, act to help save the few fragments of nature we have left . . . and, give some thought to how we could get rid of a few more of Mary's little lambs in favor of wonderful wild creatures.

A *newly hatched Magellanic penguin*
is measured by Pablo Yorio and
Dee Boersma (above), whose project
has achieved increased recognition
and protection for the colony of
250,000 at Punta Tombo since
1981. Magellanics feed in the waters
off Punta Tombo (left) during
their nesting season between October
and February.

Opposite above: Patagonian sea
lions at Punta Pirámides, Península
Valdés, one of several impressive
but vulnerable Patagonian marine
wildlife colonies.

Opposite below: Claudio Campagna
attempts to mark a female elephant
seal. Working to prevent their
exploitation, he has studied and
monitored wildlife populations
along the entire length of the coast.

On Patagonia's Shores

The fifteen-hundred-mile Patagonian coast of Argentina boasts some of the last great wildlife spectacles in the world, including tumultuous aggregations of Magellanic penguins at Punta Tombo, elephant seals and sea lions at Península Valdés, and seabirds at Punta León. The Society has been involved in conservation along the coast since 1960, when William Conway, with Trustee Robert G. Goelet, conducted a wildlife survey throughout Argentina. Later trips helped stimulate the establishment of six coastal reserves, and since then numerous long-range Society studies have been conducted there. In 1993, the Society and its Argentine colleagues began a three-year project, sponsored by the United Nations Development Programme, to develop a Coastal Zone Management Plan for Patagonia, where oil spills at sea, commercial interests in wildlife harvesting, chemical runoffs, and overfishing have been serious threats.

JOHN G. ROBINSON

*from "The Limits to Caring: Sustainable Living
and the Loss of Biodiversity"*

CONSERVATION BIOLOGY, MARCH 1993

*As its vice-president for conservation, John
Robinson heads the Society's international field
program. Here he severely criticizes* Caring
for the Earth: A Strategy for Sustainable
Living *for its emphasis on "traditional
development at the expense of the conservation
of natural resources and diversity." Robinson's
argument is an important one. Because* Caring
for the Earth *was produced (in October 1991)
by three of the world's most respected conservation organizations—the World Conservation
Union (IUCN), the United Nations Environmental Programme (UNEP), and the World
Wide Fund for Nature (WWF)—it has
considerable clout and currency as a model
and guide, particularly in the Third World.
At stake are major decisions being made
by developing nations, with guidance from
developed nations and large amounts of
money from the World Bank, the European
Community, the U.S. Agency for International
Development, the United Nations Development
Programme, and other multinational organizations, about the future of living environments. Understanding the effects of human
encroachment is part of conservation, a field
that boasts powerful scientific and moral
authority, but infinitesimal financial support,
compared to other interested parties, such as
national and multinational corporations.*

Caring for the Earth, within its specified limits of interest and within its own definitions, is an admirable document and sets out basic tenets of living that we all must follow if we are to survive on this planet. Its failure is that it does not acknowledge that the goals of development are different from the goals of conservation, and it offers no general principles by which we might resolve conflicts and balance contradictory demands. *Caring for the Earth* does not recognize that while improving the quality of human life, we will inevitably decrease the diversity of life. If we do not acknowledge the contradictions, we will smugly preside over the demise of biological diversity while waving the banner of conservation.

The goal of national development in the 1950s and 1960s was to increase the Gross National Product (GNP) of countries, especially in the South. The mechanism was technological progress. The result was supposed to be an increase in the consumption of natural resources and their use by people, an increase in national export and import of goods, and an increase in the human standard of living. The problem was that by the 1970s it was clear that the process was not working in much of the world. Consumption of natural resources was up, but the disparity between and the economic dependence of the South on the North had increased. In many countries, per capita incomes were down, deforestation, overgrazing, and overcultivation were up. Environmental degradation in the countries of the South was becoming increasingly evident, and the economic costs of this were becoming appreciated. The loss of wildlands and the disappearance of species were provoking alarm.

Popular concerns with the consequences of national development crystallized in the publication *The Limits to Growth* (The Club of Rome, 1972), which examined the long-term trends in world population, resource use, food production, and industrialization. In the same year, the United Nations Conference on the Human Environment was held in Stockholm, and led to the establishment of the U.N. Environmental Program (UNEP). These initiatives were followed by the *World Conservation Strategy* in 1980.

The *World Conservation Strategy* retained the traditional concept of development, which it defined as activities that "satisfy human needs and improve the quality of human life." Its innovation was that it acknowledged that alone this approach was not sufficient. The *World Conservation Strategy* advocated the approach of *sustainable* development, which incorporated social and ecological considerations for *long-term* as well as short-term advantages. Conservation was then linked to development, by defining it as activities that "yield the greatest sustainable development to present generations while maintaining its potential to meet the needs and aspirations of future generations.". . .

In the 1987 report of the World Commission on Environment and Development (otherwise known as the Brundtland Commission), there was a significant redefinition of sustainable development, which was defined as development that "seeks to meet the needs and aspirations of the present without compromising the ability to meet those of the future." This definition is virtually identical to the *World Conservation Strategy*'s definition of "conservation." This definitional shift followed from the Commission's focus on the failure of development and from the environmental consequences of that failure. The Brundtland Commission focused on the environmental problems associated with development—not on the conservation of the natural environment. The concern is with "the impact of ecological stress—degradation of soils, water regimes, atmosphere, and forests—*upon our economic prospects*" (my italics). The commission was able to appropriate the language of conservation in its definition of sustainable development because it adopted an exclusively utilitarian approach—not considering the need to conserve any life that was not explicitly useful to human beings.

In *Caring for the Earth*, the goal is to build a sustainable society. This requires sustainable development, which is defined as "improving the quality of human life while living within the carrying capacity of supporting ecosystems." Whatever its intent, this definition emphasizes traditional development at the expense of the conservation of natural resources and biodiversity. . . .

This definition of sustainable development requires that it take place "within the carrying capacity of supporting ecosystems." However, carrying capacity is not an ecosystem characteristic, but is defined for the population of a given species. In the case of *Caring for the Earth*, the species of interest is the human being. The carrying capacity of earth for humans depends on a complex interaction of environmental potential, lifestyle aspirations, technologies, and sociopolitical and economic organization. Yet as a general rule, human beings are more able to use ecosystems at young successional stages, which tend to be more productive. Accordingly, a general characteristic of human development is that we tend to maximize productivity by creating and maintaining ecosystems at such stages. This requires energy input, in forms such as irrigation, insecticides, fertilizers, mechanical alterations of the environment, etc. In contrast, undisturbed ecosystems, not subject to such inputs, become mature, and tend to be less productive, but more biologically diverse. In other words, the goal of maximizing the carrying capacity of human beings will encourage intensive agriculture at the expense of natural systems, pine plantations in place of hickory-oak forests, and maize fields instead of tropical savannas. . . .

Caring for the Earth formally limits sustainable use to sustainable development. To keep within the carrying capacity of an ecosystem requires that resources be used sustainably. Sustainable use requires that resources are used "at rates within their capacity for renewal.". . .

To understand sustainable use, one needs to consider three interdependent questions. What will be the impact of human use on the *environment* or the *biological resource*? This considers the ecological sustainability of human activities. What are the *needs* and *aspirations* of resource users? This is a consideration of economic sustainability. Finally, what are the rights of different user groups to the resource? This is a social and political consideration.

Ecologically sustainable activities are defined as those that do not degrade the natural resource. Consider the sustainable harvest of a species. The only requirement for ecological sustainability is that harvest from the

The results of slash-and-burn agriculture in Amazonian Peru (above) and road clearing in Madagascar (left). Tropical rain forests worldwide lose an area the size of Florida each year.

Opposite above: Penan tribesmen in Sarawak (Malaysian Borneo) unsuccessfully resisted logging concessions in their deep forest homeland.

Opposite below: Bison meet cattle at the border of the National Bison Range in Montana, the native species supplanted by the commercial domestic species.

population must not exceed the potential yield. Yield is total production subtracting natural mortality. There are therefore many population levels at which any species can be sustainably harvested. Very small populations, for instance, will have a very small potential yield, but as long as harvest does not exceed that yield, it will be sustainable. There is a population level at which yield is maximized . . . and managing populations to this level is the goal of many resource managers. . . .

Species therefore can be exploited sustainably, but requiring sustainability does not prescribe the intensity of exploitation. One must also specify a minimum population level that is acceptable, and this presumably is defined by the requirements of population viability and by the importance of the species as part of its biological community. Any use of a species however is likely to encourage the overall loss of biological diversity.

Ecologically sustainable activities at the level of the biological community are defined as those that do not degrade the capacity of that community to sustain human beings. One must recognize however, that any use of a biological community will ultimately involve a loss of biological diversity. While one can naively imagine human beings in the modern world living as part of a natural community, taking, as envisioned in *Caring for the Earth*, "no more from nature than nature can replenish," humans will always encourage desirable species and remove competitor species, and all human groups have the capacity to change their environments radically. . . .

Economically sustainable activities are defined as those that meet the economic needs and aspirations of the human users. The level of use of a species or a biological community, however, also varies with the identity of the human users. Different human users require different levels of use to meet their economic needs. Accordingly, any plan of sustainable resource use needs to specify the human consumers. Who will use the natural resources? Is it the indigenous groups, local communities, local landowners, regions, an entire nation, or foreign countries? The decision to allocate rights to the resource is usually based on social, political, and perhaps ethical criteria. And it is a decision to empower specified social groups or classes. Socioeconomically sustainable activities therefore are those that meet the economic needs and aspirations of those users who have been allocated rights to those resources. . . .

Most discussions of sustainable use assume that it is in the interests of all social groups that resource use be sustainable. This is frequently not the case. For instance, the decision, at the national level, to create rubber "extractive reserves" in western Brazil—areas managed by local communities and reserved for specific resource extraction—is commonly trumpeted as a successful approach to sustainable resource use. But the applicability of this approach depends on the political power of the rubber tapper's union, the interests of local cattle ranchers, the market demand for their products, and the ability of local communities to get their products to the market, to name a few considerations. The international political and economic structures will also have an impact on the long-term viability of such extractive endeavors. Until these influences are understood, it is unclear whether a resource use will be socioeconomically sustainable. In isolation, a local community might be able to meet their socioeconomic needs, but when national or international politics or markets are considered, they might be unable to do so.

Ecologically sustainable socioeconomic activities are those that are both ecologically and socioeconomically sustainable. Both types of sustainability must be considered because each alone does not specify an intensity of use. In the case of ecological sustainability, one must also define an acceptable loss of biodiversity or environmental degradation. For socioeconomic sustainability, one must also define the consumer group that is the beneficiary of the resource use and consider the interaction with other human interest groups. *Sustainable use only occurs when the rights of different user groups are specified, when human needs are met, and when the losses in biodiversity and environmental degradation are acceptable.* . . .

With many types of resource extraction under many different socioeconomic conditions, sustainable use will be impossible. This conclusion contrasts with *Caring for the Earth*, which believes as an article of faith that sustainable use is always possible. The failure to use resources sustainably is viewed by *Caring for the Earth* as being a consequence of poor planning, inefficient bureaucracies, inappropriate institutions, and the unthinking waste of human and financial resources. Once people are enlightened, and with appropriate intellectual input, then any resource can be used sustainably. *Caring for the Earth* promotes a utopian vision in which belief in sustainable use promotes sustainable use. Unfortunately, there are real contradictions underlying the frequent failure to use resources sustainably. . . .

Caring for the Earth presents us with a simplistic vision of development and conservation. Critical concepts, such as human "quality of life" and "carrying capacity" are loosely used. There is confusion between the concept of sustainability and that of ecological equilibria. There is a failure to distinguish ecological from socioeconomic sustainability, and the necessary relationship between these two types of sustainability—a relationship that defines sustainable use—is never explored. *Caring for the Earth* places no limits on the loss of biodiversity that is acceptable, neither does it acknowledge that different human consumers have different interests and needs. The result is that the process of socioeconomic development is never examined critically, and sustainable development appears to be easily attainable. While positive thinking is praiseworthy, there must also be a reality check.

Caring for the Earth is also limited in its vision, focusing as it does almost exclusively on human beings. It is concerned with improving the quality of life of people. This is a worthy goal, but it is not the same goal as conserving the full spectrum of biological diversity. Because of this anthropocentric orientation, *Caring for the Earth* emphasizes sustainable use of natural resources as the only approach to conserving natural systems. Sustainable use is a powerful approach to conservation but is not the only one. Many special and biological communities will be lost unless they are protected and managed with the express goal of their conservation. Sustainable use is very appropriate in certain circumstances, but it is not appropriate in all. It will almost always lower biological diversity, whether one considers individual species or entire biological communities, and if sustainable use is our only goal, our world will be the poorer for it.

Caiman are hunted and sold illegally in Brazil's flooded forest.

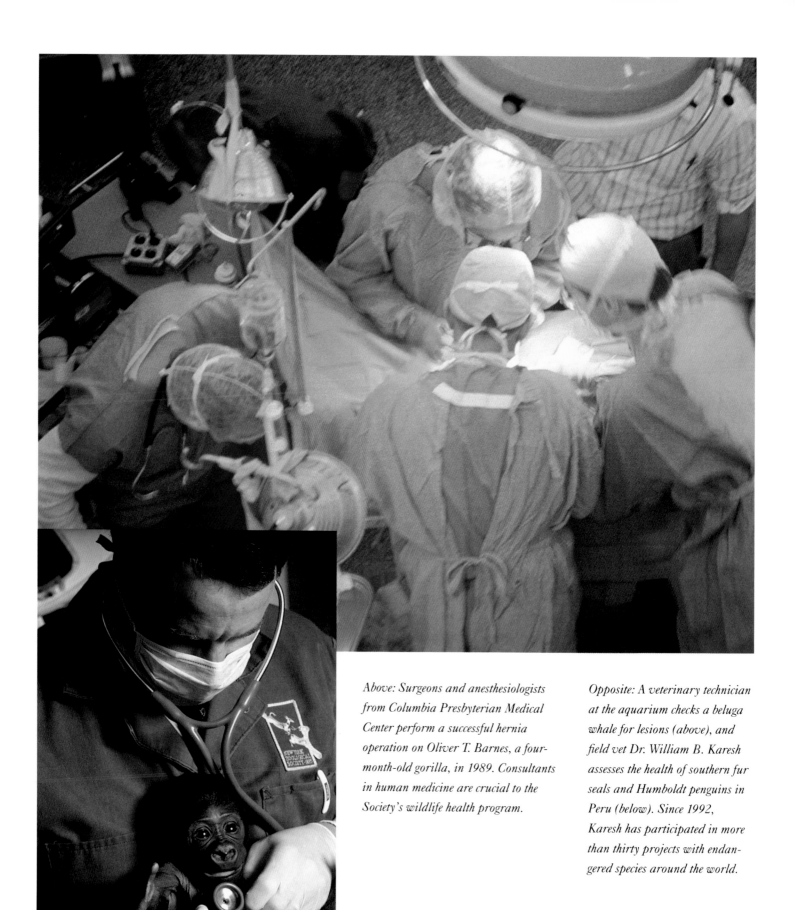

Above: Surgeons and anesthesiologists from Columbia Presbyterian Medical Center perform a successful hernia operation on Oliver T. Barnes, a four-month-old gorilla, in 1989. Consultants in human medicine are crucial to the Society's wildlife health program.

Opposite: A veterinary technician at the aquarium checks a beluga whale for lesions (above), and field vet Dr. William B. Karesh assesses the health of southern fur seals and Humboldt penguins in Peru (below). Since 1992, Karesh has participated in more than thirty projects with endangered species around the world.

Left: A baby male lowland gorilla, born July 11, 1993, is examined by Director of Wildlife Health Sciences Dr. Robert A. Cook.

Wildlife Health: Saving Lives and Species

The Bronx Zoo, in 1902, was the first zoo to hire a full-time veterinarian (Dr. William Reid Blair, who later became the zoo's director) and the first, in 1916, to build a fully equipped animal hospital. Today, the zoo's modern Wildlife Health Center features surgery and radiology suites that can accommodate an elephant or a hummingbird, specialized, climate-controlled care areas for a variety of species, and laboratories for clinical, nutrition, pathology, biotelemetry, and reproductive services and studies. This teaching and research hospital is headquarters for the care of nearly ten thousand animals at the Society's New York and Georgia facilities. But its responsibilities extend to wildlife around the world through the Department of Field Veterinary Studies, and to the survival of species as well as individual animals.

ROGER CARAS

*from "William Conway: Zoo Director,
Conservationist, Wildlife Ambassador"*

INTERVIEW IN *GEO*, AUGUST 1982

*Naturalist Roger Caras, a prolific writer and
broadcast correspondent on animals, wildlife,
and the environment, became president
of The American Society for the Prevention
of Cruelty to Animals in 1991. His 1982
interview with William Conway focuses
on the consequences of losing wildlife species.*

GEO: Does man need to domesticate new species? We are, after all, painted into a relatively small corner, given the diversity of the planet's resources.

Conway: We have domesticated virtually nothing in several thousand years. I think that people working with animals are far behind those working with plants. Think where we would be today if we didn't have all these wild varieties of corn to resort to every time a new corn blight hits us. One of these days we could run into a problem with domestic animals. It is remarkable how few forms of domestic animals we have and how little research is going on in this area. So I strongly believe in the preservation of biological diversity, if only for the purpose of finding out which kinds of creatures may be useful to man.

GEO: Haven't there been enormous strides in reproductive physiology and engineering?

Conway: Yes. . . . One of the great problems we are concerned about in domestic animals as well as in wild animals is the loss of genetic diversity. If it is possible to store fertilized ova and sperm indefinitely, and increase the sophistication of our technology in this area, the problems of inbreeding will be a thing of the past. But there is not going to be a technological "fix" to the extinction of species. One of the reasons there won't be is, who will care? Who is going to re-create the woolly caterpillar? Who is going to re-create some rare frog? Who is going to re-create the black rhino? For what purpose? I am afraid that reproductive technology is not a substitute for maintaining live populations. The real problem is not to preserve the species—it is to preserve a living animal and plant community. How do you do that? You can't take a whole national park and put it into a test tube. And you can't freeze it all. If you recognize that your parks may have to get a lot smaller, you have to figure out how to get over the "island" effect. When animals are kept in small populations—in zoos or on farms, in parks or on islands— extinction begins to occur at an accelerated rate. We need to design preserves better, and we need to develop a technology to support them. Maybe some technology can help in sustaining these very small populations, which will otherwise inbreed and become extinct. Maybe we can transfer an embryo that has been stored for fifty years into a population and suddenly bring the full genetic complement of opportunities back to that species.

GEO: What if you unfreeze an egg fifty years later and there is nothing left of its original ecosystem? Isn't that like dumping *Tyrannosaurus rex* into the middle of Central Park? There would be nothing there it originally interacted with.

Conway: I would still argue that for quite some time we should do everything we can to prevent the extinction of species. . . .

If that means hanging on to a few species that have lost their ecosystems, that may still be worth doing for a while, because there may come a time when we can re-create those systems. We are constantly moving the earth and changing it. This means that a lot of habitats we are creating could be suitable for something that they weren't suitable for originally. . . .

I think we are inevitably heading toward highly managed parks and refuges. I believe we will see parks and refuges that are basically managed for a single species but in which other species, smaller forms, will live. I see the zoological garden becoming an integral part of a system that will have to be called upon to reinforce these small populations and parks. You know, the biggest park in Nepal is the Chitwan National Park, and it can carry fewer than fifty tigers. Perhaps it can carry only thirty. There is no way that any other tiger population can connect with that group. They are separated by agricultural lands that tigers do not cross. That type of population is too small to survive genetically. It isn't going to make it.

GEO: I suppose if there is a real crisis, there is no step that is not legitimate.

Conway: I think that's true. There is an interesting situation right now. We have just learned that the Chinese want to get some more Siberian tigers for their zoos and intend to go out and trap them. We have a surplus of Siberian tigers in this country. We will be writing to Chinese officials, asking how many tigers they want. We're going to make it unnecessary for them to take more animals from nature.

GEO: Can people and wild predatory animals coexist in close proximity?

Conway: Large predators are a special problem. For a guy who has a goat and a cow and three daughters and loses any one of them to a tiger, it is pretty hard to live with tigers. Solving the large-predator problem is something that needs to be addressed very carefully. Is there room? Are there techniques? If these species are to be preserved, there are some interesting problems that have to be solved that we haven't even approached philosophically. If someone were to say tomorrow that a species has the secret to Hodgkin's disease within its blood—as, to some extent, some species of South American rodent do—you could be sure that species would be safe.

GEO: Do we have to find that pragmatic a use for a species in order to stave off extinction?

Conway: We may well have to. If we are preserving a wildlife community that is part of an ecosystem, we can offer pragmatic reasons to save the animal that may make a difference. But I am very concerned about two kinds of arguments. One argument says that because we don't know what wonderful things a species may hold for us, we must save it. I don't think that argument means very much to the farmer who lives next door to a troublesome lion or tiger. The other argument that I find discouraging is the one that says mankind must do this and must do that as though somebody were in charge. There is nobody in charge. Mankind isn't going to do anything. Individuals are going to do something; an association is going to do something; a corporation is going to do something; a religious sect is going to do something. The sociopolitical management of the saving of a species might best be undertaken as a religious project, but we can't promote that as a regular thing in other countries, and that's why we end up bringing black rhinos to the United States. We have remarkable confidence that rhinos will be safer in Texas than they are in Zambia.

GEO: Is it going to be possible to convince relatively unsophisticated people that there is any point at all in making sacrifices for wildlife? How are you going to talk a Nepali into losing a yak to a snow leopard? Is conservation something for the rich of the West?

Above: Lion-tailed macaques have been reduced to about four thousand in the Western Ghats of India. An unconfined breeding troop at the Society's Wildlife Survival Center may one day help to reintroduce the species in its native habitat.

Left: Sumatran rhinos are practically gone in Sumatra and Borneo. Rhino populations have declined 85 percent since 1970, leaving all five species in Africa and Asia close to extinction.

Black rhinos still roam Ngorongoro Crater in Tanzania. Their numbers throughout East Africa have been reduced more than 95 percent since 1970, mostly from poaching for horn.

Conway: Some of the best conservationists I have met, some of the shrewdest, are not Caucasian. . . . It is certainly true that much of the world sees conservation as a luxury only the rich can afford. Many people see education as a luxury only the rich can afford. If endangered species are left in the hands of the people who live around them, I would judge that the future of those species is very precarious. But we always have to assume that nations will be interested in the greater good and that people can be convinced, at least some of them, to withhold satisfaction today to protect the rights of future generations. If we didn't do that, we wouldn't have any art museums, we wouldn't have any parks, and our educational establishment would be much smaller than it is today. The highest and most admired efforts of humankind simply would not exist. So, while in my pessimistic moments—which are few—I believe that we are going to lose a tremendous amount of wildlife, I still believe that we are going to save a great deal, that we are not going to lose a lot of species. If I had to postulate a percentage, I would say that we could lose as much as twenty percent of today's species by the end of the century—between fifteen and twenty percent. There are going to be quite a few species that hang on with very small numbers for a while.

GEO: You mentioned large predators as probably causing the greatest problems because they directly infringe on man's livestock. What about indemnification for losses suffered? Wouldn't that work?

Conway: The idea of indemnification is fine. There are techniques that are being used in some countries, but as a rule, there is usually a breakdown in delivery. Very few nations operate efficiently, as we discover every time one of our food or aid programs tries to help somebody. They can't get the food where the people are starving, or they can't get the equipment where the farmer needs a tractor. So, again, our approach will have to be eclectic. Perhaps an indemnification program can work. That's essentially what they have in Kenya, where the wildlife comes out and eats the farmers' grass. Okay, that program works there. In other places, there is a tourism program through which the local people get income. And in still another place, it may be that a moral philosophy or religion is sufficient and will protect wildlife for a long time. In other places, there may be a scientific concern within a government or perhaps an idea of the potential of a wildlife area so that it will be preserved for ethical reasons. I don't think that any one system can possibly work in every place. But there are some things that are encouraging. Let's look at a country that is very much in the news—Argentina. Recently there was a threat by a Japanese-Argentine company to harvest penguins down around the town of Camarones. The company wanted to convert the penguins into meat paste and gloves. That was stopped by local people who wanted to protect those penguins.

GEO: Yet those are the people who were supposed to get jobs killing and processing the penguins.

Conway: Why do they want to preserve those penguins? What is it that made those people in Patagonia parade through the streets near the governor's residence with signs protesting the killing of the penguins, while our neighbors to the north for whom we have the warmest feelings, the Canadians, are up there beating the bejesus out of a bunch of poor, defenseless, soulful-looking little harp seals? Now, there is a lesson there. What can we learn from them? I'll bet there are a lot of techniques out there just waiting to be discovered that will help us save wild animals in the future. Conservation biology has only been considered a science for about five years. Before that, to be a conservationist was not very respectable in the world of science, and there are darned few people who go through a university science program today with the idea of being a conservation biologist. They want to be an animal behaviorist or a geologist or an ornithologist or a systematist or what have you. But that is changing, and conservation biology is suddenly becoming a whole new discipline in itself. We need to build a conservation profession. . . .

GEO: What about the direct man-animal relationship? How important do you think it is?

Conway: Maybe the opportunity for human beings to watch other animals will be shown to have all kinds of wonderful effects. We certainly know that there are aesthetic effects, emotional effects. In zoological gardens, we find that when handicapped children are brought in contact with wild or domestic animals, their reactions and interest levels increase enormously. To see a blind child attempt to form an idea of a living creature by touching a tame camel or a bull—any wild animal, whether it be a snake, a frog or a rabbit—or to see a child who is disturbed or brain damaged have that opportunity, is one of the more rewarding parts of this business. It helps reinforce the idea that there is a bond between human beings and other creatures. On Sunday, I was walking around the zoo. We had a very large crowd—thirty-five thousand people—and I was really astonished by the amount of time people were spending watching animals. I make it a habit to measure the amount of time people spend looking at exhibits. With living creatures like our herd of bison, you could sit there with your watch and wait and wait and wait. People just stand and look, and it's very interesting to observe the expressions on their faces.

GEO: What are the most exciting things happening in conservation today?

Conway: One of the things that excites me is to see the young people you run into in other countries. I was in Africa last year talking to some of the young African biologists there. They're approaching the same problems that we had fifty or sixty years ago, but they have the technology of 1982, which we didn't have. Unfortunately, the disastrous area is Southeast Asia. The thing that worries me is what we are going to do to save the most spectacular species there. It all has to be done in the next thirty years, or it's going to be too late.

GEO: Can you give a brief catalog of what you mean when you say "spectacular"? What is at stake there in the next thirty years?

Conway: We are going to lose, as breeding populations, virtually all rhinos except the white rhino. There is a possibility that the Indian rhino will hang on. We have five species of rhino, but unless we do something extraordinary, we are going to lose three of them.... Hornbills are the most spectacular forest birds in the world. They nest in great hollow trees in primary forests, most of them in Southeast Asia. The present predictions are that there will be virtually none of these big hornbills left in twenty years. Most of the big macaws are in serious trouble. The cockatoos in Australasia, wherever land is being developed, are all in trouble. The major loss in the

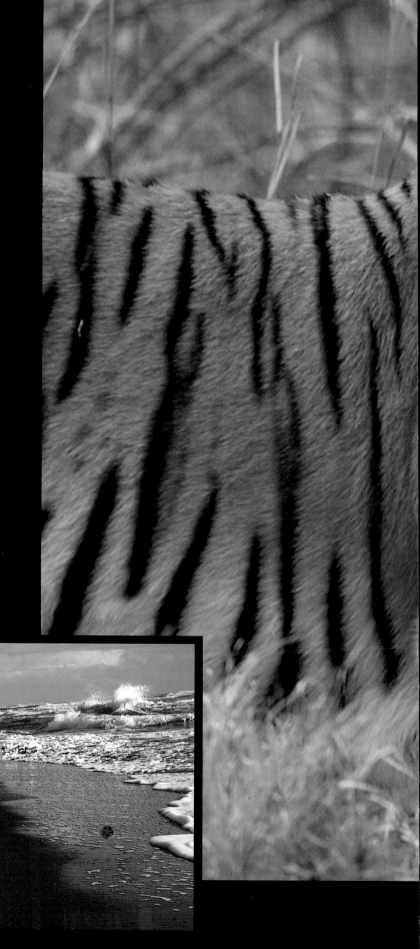

Three of the eight tiger subspecies are already extinct; the remaining five, including the Bengal (right), are nearly so. The Society is leading a global campaign to save the species.

A green turtle returns to the sea after laying its eggs on the beach at Tortuguero, Costa Rica. All four species of sea turtle, which spend most of their time in the ocean, are endangered.

parrot family is going to be in the island forms, particularly birds like the marvelous shining parakeets of Fiji. They are among the most spectacularly colored birds there are, with feathers that almost glow. They are going to be pushed into extinction. I don't expect that we will lose any of the whales, curiously enough—too big an area. Of course, there are a number of seals that are just on the edge now. Nobody knows about the Mediterranean monk seal; those are going to be gone in all probability. The great wild cattle, the kouprey, the gaur, the banteng, the anoa—all of these animals are going to be lost, or nearly so.

GEO: What will North America lose?

Conway: If North America has any sense, it is not going to lose any spectacular creatures. The condor, of course, is on the edge. The seaside sparrows are essentially gone; there are five males left in captivity in Florida. Aside from that, there really isn't too much else that I would expect to lose. I am worried about the manatee. The pelicans are coming back very nicely on the Atlantic coast. They are still in trouble in the Pacific. The ospreys are coming back. The red wolf is essentially gone; it is being held primarily in zoos. The black-footed ferret is looking a little better. We hope to provide a grant that will help continue a study on the ferret.

GEO: I guess in some cases we are going to have to bite the bullet.

Conway: Yes, we are going to see tragedies. We know of no species in historical times that has become extinct from natural causes. As far as we know, every species that has become extinct has become so either directly or indirectly because of man. That is a remarkable thing. People say extinction is a natural process. That is true. It's a natural process, but not on our time scale. It is of damned little interest to a creature that has only been on the earth in its present form for less than three hundred thousand years, namely you and me. I think of the St. Kilda wren, a flightless wren native to an island in the Outer Hebrides. The whole species was killed off by the lighthouse keeper's cat. One cat killed and ate them all.

Amazonia:
Heart of Hope

Former architect Eduardo Nycander von Massenbach, head of the Society's Tambopata macaw project, builds new nests for the birds to aid in their breeding and inspects the young twice a week, one hundred feet above the ground.

The fate of the wild is most famously associated with the plight of the Amazonian rain forest, the image of thousands of dense green acres burning or falling to the ax every day. It is an image of ambitious industrial and agricultural schemes gone awry, of greed, of migrating armies of the poor, of murdered indigenous peoples, and of wildlife forced to extinction. But resistance to this waste is widespread. The Society conducts major conservation projects in the forests of the Río Blanco and Río Negro in Bolivia, the Río Nichare and Henri Pittier National Park in Venezuela, Manu National Park and the Tambopata Reserve in Peru, and the flooded forest of Mamirauá in Brazil. Charles Munn's work with macaws and with local people in Peru has helped create and strengthen reserves for the world's most diverse populations of parrots. Márcio Ayres heads a team of scientists and community leaders in the 5,167-square-mile reserve he worked to create at Lake Mamirauá in northern Brazil, where an extraordinary cycle of life occurs in waters of the Amazon that rise as much as forty feet each year.

More than a thousand macaws and parrots may gather at the 130-foot-high Tambopata cliffs to eat the clay that will neutralize the toxins in their diet of hard seeds. They arrive and fly away in groups. The remoteness and protection enjoyed by the reserve have so far saved the birds from habitat destruction and the pet trade.

The varzea, or flooded forests, of the northern Amazon may be the most biologically diverse region on earth, home to white uakaris (above), howler monkeys, sloths, and many species of reptiles, birds, and fish.

During flood season, the red fruit of the munguba tree (left) opens to feed tambaquí and other fishes, which then disperse the seeds, part of the complex cycle of life being studied and protected by the Mamirauá project. The project may save the carnivorous arapaima (below) and other popular food fish from extinction.

Many people in the varzea *live in floating houses that rise with the water.*

Research biologist Márcio Ayres (below right), here observing uakaris, has created a multifaceted project at the Lake Mamirauá Ecological Station that includes field studies, field training for conservationists, and educating and gaining the support of local community leaders.

As William Hornaday and William Beebe began their careers with the newly formed New York Zoological Society in the 1890s, small flocks of Carolina parakeets and passenger pigeons still flew in Eastern forests. The Eskimo curlew whistled musically from beaches and mud flats, and the ivory-billed woodpecker drummed in Southern forests, but the bison was being hunted to extinction. Public interest in native wildlife conservation was unawakened, and the idea of concerning oneself with the fate of wild creatures in foreign lands had not yet been born. The development of a "science" of conservation biology was many decades in the future.

All four species of birds have now been lost, the bison has been saved, and public concern for conservation has been aroused by strong voices and new scientific revelations. The organization that became the Wildlife Conservation Society played a major role in shaping the early conservation movement and plays an even larger one in international conservation today. But it all began with a zoo.

As can be seen in this volume, despite disparities of time and background, a curious continuity links the words of those who have worked with the Society during its first century. This may reflect no more than an inherent similarity in people attracted to nature and wild animals, but it may also identify the Society's almost proprietary commitment to the perpetuation of wildlife. Perhaps this special covenant, and the Society's uniqueness as a conservation organization, has something to do with the actual experience of running zoos and an aquarium, which involves a day-to-day responsibility for thousands of animals of hundreds of species. It also involves the education and entertainment of zoo and aquarium visitors, more than three hundred million since 1899 and now more than four million each year.

Every informed person who loves nature and wildlife looks toward the future with apprehension. Only the ignorant imagine that a majority of the natural communities of 1995 can be sustained, or those of 1895 restored. We will have to understand, care for, and protect wildlife if much is to survive until 2095. Most predators, fragile specialists, and large animals that compete with humans for food will survive in limited reserves with zoo-derived technologies. Outside such reserves, only fauna compatible with human agriculture, industry, and habitation are likely to be tolerated—for example, the American robin, white-tailed deer, and European starling in the eastern United States, and the glossy starling, impala, and various kinds of pigeons in East Africa. The loss of the diverse and spectacular wildlife of East Africa will be far more dramatic than the parallel loss that has already taken place in the eastern U.S.

At the least, it is essential that we develop the science and information necessary to sustain wildlife reserves where biodiversity can survive away from human settlement. The animal gardens we call zoos or conservation parks will become ever more significant in caring for particularly precarious species. The Wildlife Conservation Society is unique in developing knowledge and sustaining action on both fronts, through the work of its field scientists, veterinarians, educators, wildlife curators, and other conservationists.

There is still time to save vast numbers of magnificent wild creatures, to preserve beautiful and wondrous wild places now headed toward oblivion. But this can happen only if people are educated to care and if more imaginative and inspired wildlife conservationists are chosen and nurtured; if more energy is devoted to the development of a new human role model—the conservation hero. The Wildlife Conservation Society's long history has shown that such heroes exist, and that conservation is achieved primarily by individuals, and only secondarily by organizations.

William Conway

A gathering of animals at a water hole in Amboseli National Park, Kenya.